A MAN OF PRINCIPLE

The autobiography of a railway man who refused to
let politics overrule common sense - and paid the price

RAY BARDEN

Copyright © 2021 by Ray Barden

All rights reserved.

ISBN: 978-0-6482842-7-7

No part of this book may be reproduced in any form or by any electronic or mechanical means, including information storage and retrieval systems, without written permission from the author, except for the use of brief quotations in a book review.

Images reproduced with the kind permission of the Keeper of Public Records – Public Records Office Victoria (PROV). Reproduction is on the clear understanding that copyright remains with the State of Victoria.

Contents

Foreword — vii
Acknowledgments — xi
Introduction — xiii

1. The Early Days — 1
2. School Days — 7
3. My Working Life Commences — 22
4. Life In Railways — 33
5. North Port — 48
6. Married Life — 57
7. Life as a Relieving Stationmaster — 60
8. Train Control — 71
9. Traffic Inspector — 85
10. Into Middle Management — 92
11. The Crute Days — 114
12. Passenger Operations Division — 133
13. New Head of Branch — 137
14. Overseas Study Tour — 142
15. The Freight Branch Created — 153
16. Housing and Family Changes — 158
17. Management Problems — 162
18. Main Line Enquiry Boards — 170
19. Rationalisation Attempts — 178
20. Operations Branch — 181
21. New Branch - New Policy — 189
22. Restrictive Work Practices — 197

The Reaction	209
ARU to Justice McKenzie	212
23. Unsolicited Publicity	217
24. Politically Inspired Industrial Action	222
25. New Deal Passenger Services	228
26. Relief From The Grind	234
27. Shunter Invasion	241
28. Rationalisation of Depots	245
29. Interbranch Problems	256
30. Barnawartha Collision	262
31. New State Government	266
32. The New South Wales (NSW) Express Passenger Train (XPT)	276
33. Vale VicRail	281
34. Record Wheat Season	301
35. Freight Gates	305
36. Area Controllers, Main Western Zone	313
Liberal Party News	347
37. Compulsory Transfer	350
38. The End	357
39. New Life	359
40. Consultancy Work	361
41. Life on the Hobby Farm	364
42. Possible Re-employment	369
43. The Fast Rail Project	371
44. Current Projects	375
45. Travel and Overseas Holidays	377
46. Community Work	379
47. My Brother Max	381
48. Finale	384
49. Holiday photos	387
50. Glossary	392

Foreword
DAVID WATSON

It is fortunate indeed that Ray Barden's daughter prompted him to "get started" on the task of compiling his memoirs, for in doing so he has produced this superb social history.

Having joined the Victorian Railways in 1952, Ray progressed through a number of positions before his 1980 appointment to that of the Chief Operations Manager of the restructured organisation which by then had been rebranded as VicRail. However, this work is far from being just another compilation of a railway employee's anecdotes. What follows is in every way a detailed personal record of a lived experience of the past and as such meets one of the accepted definitions of Social History. Beginning with Ray's upbringing in the small Victorian country town of Nyora during the Depression years, the author shares with the reader his recollections of childhood and working as a teen-aged farm labourer, of family life and a high-profile railway career culminating in retirement under difficult circumstances and of post-retirement community work and other activities.

Few of those growing up today will experience the privations of the life-style described of a 1930s family living in a two-roomed cottage without plumbing or electricity in tiny

Foreword

Nyora which, although a busy railway junction, was nevertheless remote in the sense of it being some distance from the nearest sizeable town. Similarly, to leave school at thirteen and work as a live-in labourer on a dairy farm is far from anyone's experience these days. It is little wonder that several years of farm labouring at various places including far-off Mildura caused a seventeen-year-old youth to seek pastures new which led to a railway career spanning nearly 34 years.

The Victorian Railways of the 1950s was stuck in a sort of time-warp. The war years had taken their toll and a lack of capital funding precluded any significant modernisation so that nothing much changed. By the mid-seventies the railway, bedevilled by over-manning and outmoded work practices, was struggling to regain or even maintain relevance and it became clear that radical changes were necessary for survival. Major organisational restructuring began and in 1980 the lad from Nyora, having progressed through many coal-face operating positions to middle and senior management as well as having undertaken an overseas study tour, was selected to head a newly created Operations Branch.

A large part of Ray's memoirs deals with what followed as sections of the highly unionised work-force, anxious to maintain the status quo, vigorously resisted implementation of the changes that were essential to the achievement of desperately needed operating efficiencies and cost savings. Unfortunately, management of a deteriorating situation was hampered by the prevailing political climate and by managers recruited at a senior level without knowledge of the industry and experience of its industrial volatility.

As well as being a fascinating exposé of what was, what is and what might have been, this book has many frank observations and gives at times quite personal glimpses of the author and his family. To read it is to understand the feelings of a man who undoubtedly possesses the fortitude and resilience needed to survive extreme adversity and frustration. The poignancy of his statement –

Foreword

"*.... it may well have been a different story with a happier ending.*" will not be unnoticed.

Whether interested in past life-styles, railways, industrial relations, management, personalities, politics, relationships or human emotions, the reader of *A Man Of Principle* will not be disappointed.

David Watson
    October 2021

Acknowledgments

The Powelett Train Arriving at Nyora Station. Powelett was the name of the Wonthaggi area. The 'State Mine' at Wonthaggi was the source of black coal for the Victorian Railways both for steam locomotives and the Newport Powerhouse. Image courtesy State Library Victoria.

The writing of my life story has been achieved in a very simple way - just by sitting down and recalling people, locations, events, challenges, highlights, happy times and the not-so-happy times.

Acknowledgments

I did not have to do any research as it was all in my head. However, there were many times when I needed help, advice, opinions, re-assurances or just a yarn about different matters.

I therefore acknowledge the important part played by the following people each of whom, with two exceptions, worked for me at different times of my railway career in middle and senior management. I am deeply indebted to them and proud to call them my friends – Adrian Ponton who managed this project for me from start to finish, Phil A'Vard and Hughie Gaynor who came up with the title for this book, David Watson with whom I worked on and off over many years kindly wrote the foreword and Tony Palermo, David Ward and Hughie Gaynor who did the final proof reading. Thankfully they detected a number of niggling errors before going to print.

I am grateful to the typists who had to decipher my difficult hand-writing and the railway jargon-Joanne my daughter, Gillian, Sue and then David for the last few pages and the tidy-up.

As the manuscript moved towards becoming a book, additional assistance and resources were needed to finish the task. Thank you to Bob Wilson for providing some additional photos, Pauline Hook for agreeing for her late husband's cartoons to be reproduced, Steve Malpass for developing the early iteration and Ebony McKenna for taking on the painstaking task of transforming the words into a book. Additionally, I acknowledge the Public Records Office Victoria for permission to use some of the images in this book.

Last but not least, I express my sincere gratitude for the patience and support of my family, particularly my wife Carmel who survived being married to a workaholic which all too frequently made her a "railway widow" for long periods.

Should I have missed anyone I apologise profusely and thank them gratefully. It certainly was not intended.

Raymond Thomas Barden

Introduction

Portrait of Ray Barden by Claire Barden

I have long had a notion to write my memoirs but have had doubts as to whether I had the ability to make them interesting enough to warrant the effort involved, and to do justice to the part of history of the extremely exciting era of change that has spanned my lifetime. I hope my writing will at least be of interest to my grandchildren and their descendants.

Although I had numerous jobs beforehand, I worked for

Introduction

thirty-four years in the railway service and was fortunate enough to have travelled to all corners of Victoria, coming into contact with, and giving service to, people and communities from all walks of life. For several years, I was required to travel interstate on a regular basis on railway business and in 1975, did a study tour of railways in Europe, England and North America, embracing nine different countries.

Such a railway career would not have been possible without the full cooperation and encouragement of my wife Carmel, who was often at home alone for relatively long periods, raising our four children without the day to day support of a father and husband. She did a marvellous job and I hereby acknowledge the great debt I owe her and my children, all of whom I love and admire very much, and am very proud of. Indeed, it was Joanne, my eldest daughter who prompted me to finally get started on this project.

1

The Early Days

I WAS BORN on the 26th March 1935 at Nyora in South Gippsland, the second child of Thomas and Alice Barden (Cosgrove). My sister Gloria was nearly two years old at that time. There were subsequently another four children, two boys and two girls, born into the family.

Nyora was a very small town comprising of two churches, Methodist and Church of England, a community hall, a store and post office, a state school, butcher shop, bakery, hotel and Railway station. Nyora was really a railway town as it was the junction where the Wonthaggi line branched off the main South Eastern line to Korumburra, Leongatha and Yarram.

The State Mine (black coal) was located at Wonthaggi and provided most of the fuel for the fleet of steam locomotives operating throughout Victoria. Rail staff at Nyora totalled about thirty, including drivers, firemen, guards, shunters, station staff, refreshment room staff, track maintenance staff and a train examiner. One side of the main street was all railway houses, about twelve in all. The township was completely surrounded by scrub although there were some outlying dairy farms, and it was said that it rained nine months of the year and dripped off the trees for the other three.

My first recollection is of the two-roomed cottage we lived in on the fringe of the township about one kilometre from the post office. There was no electricity or telephone and no plumbing in the house. The primitive conditions must have been a real challenge for Mum. Dish washing was done in a tin dish. Face and hand washing was done in an enamel dish and as there was no bath, bathing was done in a large tub. Water was brought in from a rainwater tank at the side of the cottage and heated on a wood stove. Clothing was washed in a tub or boiled up in an outside copper. Firewood was not a problem as it could be collected from the bushland at the back of the home, or from the sides of the roads. Clothes ironing, I guess would not have been required very often, but I clearly remember Mum heating flat irons on the top of the wood stove.

Times were really tough as the great depression was still taking its toll throughout the country. Many families were in a similar situation. Before Dad joined the Army after the outbreak of World War 2, he did not have a regular job. I recall him getting casual work from time to time with the Country Roads Board, and also with the Railways, shovelling coal for the steam engines at the coal stage and shovelling the ashes from the ash pits. Other casual work he undertook included clearing of scrub and forking loose grass hay at harvest time. He was a hard-working labourer and would in fact do almost anything to support his family.

Dad was an excellent shot with his rifle or shot gun and in between casual jobs he fed us all by shooting game. We practically lived on rabbits and Mum was an expert on cooking them. We would have them baked, braised, stewed or done in white sauce. Sometimes she would mince up the meat and make fritters or rabbit paste to spread on bread. For a change, we would sometimes have kangaroo steak and kangaroo tail soup was another of Mum's dishes. Dad often shot wild duck, quail, bronze wing pigeons and snipe, all for the table. Occasionally he would go deer shooting and it was a real treat to eat venison.

Dad, Sonk the Fox Hound, my sister Gloria and
me with the carcass of a hog deer dad had shot

Dad had two fox hounds called 'Sonk' and 'Goofy.' They were very handy when kangaroo shooting or deer shooting, but he seemed to mainly whistle up the foxes. A very small but regular source of income was from the sale of rabbit and fox skins. Hats were in fashion for men at the time and this created a market for rabbit skins. Women wore fox skins over their shoulders and some had fox skin jackets or coats. Dad was also a competent fisherman and often caught black fish and eels from the local streams which gave us a change of menu. His only form of transport was his Malvern Star bicycle which he rode everywhere with his gun or fishing gear, and a sugar bag was always slung over his shoulders to bring home the catch or skins.

My brother Max was born in September 1937. Life for my parents must have become extremely difficult in such cramped and primitive conditions, and in 1939 we shifted to a house which had been built earlier in the century by people called Cornish. It was a large house on about fifty acres, much of which was uncleared scrub. The house had a passage running from the front door with seven rooms, but the front two either side of the passage were locked up and not available to us. From time to time a Mr Frazer would come up from Melbourne for a weekend and make use of these rooms. He had apparently inherited the property when the Cornishs died.

The house seemed to be enormous. Not only did the lounge room have an open fireplace, but also the bedrooms. Electricity was not connected. There was a pantry off the kitchen and part of the back verandah had been closed in and housed a tin bath and a set of troughs. There was a rose garden in front of the house and an orchard at the side. There was also an area that Dad made into a vegetable garden. Pine trees lined the driveway from the road to the house and at the top of it was a tin shed which was locked the whole time we lived there. I recall peeping through the small window on one side and seeing an old car. I have no idea what make it was. We rented this house for about two years, but the car was never taken out during this time.

Some distance from the back of the house was a large shed with two cow bails, a little dairy containing a separator, and a feed section. Mum and dad hand milked about six cows, separated most of the milk, and sent the cream to the Poowong

Butter Factory. This would have provided a very small but important regular income. We were about three kilometres out of town. I really loved this house and property. There were so many interesting things to do like walking in the bush, picking wild flowers, climbing the fruit trees in the orchard, gathering wood and pine cones for the fire and most of all waving to the drivers of the steam trains. Both the Korumburra and Wonthaggi rail lines ran parallel to each other past our house and the rail tracks formed our southern boundary. There was never a shortage of trains both passenger and goods in each direction. The coal trains often had two steam engines at the head. I guess this is where my lifelong love of Railways began.

The song about Davey Crockett, the American folk legend, says he "killed himself a bear when he was only three." I cannot match that, but I distinctly recall playing with Dad's rabbit traps and finding one that obviously had a weaker spring than the others. Although I would have been no more than five years old, I was actually able to set this one and often caught a rabbit for the table. At that early age, I was also able to skin rabbits and peg out the skin to dry as Dad had shown me.

Dad had joined the Militia and from time to time was away from home attending training camps in the Seymour area. In 1940 he joined the A.I.F. and soon after he had his final leave before sailing to the Middle East. He was in the 2/8th Infantry Battalion. I clearly remember his colour patch which was oblong in shape, coloured red and white with grey edging. Because of the colour, his battalion was known as "Blood and Bandages." We kids were quite excited when we later learned he had sailed on the Queen Mary, the second biggest passenger liner in the world, which had been converted into a troop ship.

In the early war years, many young men enlisted in the services, and at Nyora a farewell function was always organised in the community hall for all locals when they were on their final leave. These functions were always well attended, children included, and took the form of speeches, presentations and supper. Dad was presented with a wallet from the R.S.L. and a certificate from the Shire Council which was headed "For King and Country." It was very impressive – to me at least. At the conclusion, those in attendance would encircle the serviceman and his family, join hands and sing the Auld Lang Syne. Till this day, whenever I hear this song sung or played, I immediately think of the old timber hall at Nyora, which was sadly destroyed by fire in the 1960s.

2

School Days

Pupils of Nyora State School 1940 Teachers – Miss D Brennan and Mr J Gardiner, Ray Barden 4th from right, front row sitting. Gloria Barden 4th from the left second row also sitting

I STARTED SCHOOL IN 1940. The road to our house was little better than a bush track, but I loved walking to school through the bush and over the railway crossing. In the summer, we would see blue tongue lizards, an occasional snake and sometimes an echidna. There were many varieties of birds. In winter, I would have fun jumping the many puddles or breaking the ice on them after a frost. The roadside could be quite spectacular with heath, coloured red, pink and white, and cobwebs glistening in the sunlight. In spring, there were many wild flowers including blue and greenhood orchids. Kids starting school now days would not experience such joys as most of them are driven. The only downside was that I did not have a raincoat or overcoat. On wet days, Mum would make me wear a "hand me down" coat of my sister's which embarrassed me greatly. I would always take it off before I got to the school gate, even if it was raining, as I thought it was less obvious carried over my arm.

Most kids walked to school, some of them much greater distances than us. A few rode bicycles and four of them rode ponies. None of them were driven to school. Indeed, it was very rare to see a car go past the school. The exception was on Monday, Wednesday and Friday when the local baker delivered bread to the small hamlets of Woodleigh and Kernot. The ponies were of course popular and kids would feed bread from their sandwiches to them through the pony paddock fence at lunch time. One pony owner, Ken Dunlop, would sometimes let me ride his pony after school as our road branched off his road a short distance from the school. The kids rode bareback, the only piece of equipment being a bridle. The ponies were not shod.

I remember the 1939 Black Friday bushfires. As far as I know our house was not under direct threat but the smoke in the area was quite thick. Mum must have been a lot more concerned than she appeared to be, but luck was on our side and there were no dramas. Once Dad went to the army, it must have become quite difficult for Mum living in relative isolation with three young kids. In 1941 we shifted again. This time into the township, into a small timber miner's cottage type house situated at the far western end of the main street. There were four small rooms and a bathroom/laundry. There was a rainwater tank at the back door but no plumbing into the house. Cooking and heating was provided from the wood stove in the kitchen. For the first time, we had electricity, but it was almost a year later that Mum bought a wireless. It was probably the biggest event in the life of us kids up to that time, as not only did we have electric lighting instead of kerosene lamps and candles, but we could now listen to our very own radio.

Again, we lived quite close to the railway opposite the Melbourne end of the marshalling yard. The coal stage, loco shed, water tower, turntable and ash pits were nearby. I had a good friend called Stan Cornwall, one of a family of nine who lived just around the corner from us. He was a couple of years older than me. In the summer months, on hot days, we would often climb the ladder on the side of the water tower for a swim. Stan had Khaki Campbell ducks and sometimes we would take a couple of them to the top for a swim also. Other times, we would find the turntable unlocked and spin it around. The railway yards were a great playground to us. Looking back, it is a wonder we did not injure ourselves, perhaps seriously, but I cannot ever recall being told to leave. We could not be seen from the station office and of course at weekends, it would only be manned at limited times. Even in the school holiday periods it seemed that very little shunting activity took place in the middle of the day, rather it was in the evenings and right throughout the night. Railway wagons all had buffers on them in those days and I could be in bed and hear the impact as trains were being assembled.

Although on a much smaller scale, railway facilities at Nyora, because of operating requirements there, were similar to those at much bigger depots and stations. In addition to those which I have already mentioned in the loco area, there were two more water towers, one each end of the single faced passenger platform, refreshment rooms on the platform, a goods shed, stock yards, a wagon weigh bridge, a spare standby carriage which the Station Master could arrange to place on passenger trains should overcrowding occur and a "hospital" road where the train examiner could do repairs on wagons. There were also two track maintenance gang sheds, one for the Korumburra line section and one for the Wonthaggi line section.

The station was a hive of activity each morning and evening with the arrival of the passenger trains in each direction. The hotel closed at 6.00pm and television had not yet arrived. On summer evenings locals would sometimes walk to the station to meet the trains and watch the proceedings. I suspect some of them sneaked into the refreshment rooms to have a beer undercover of the travellers partaking of refreshments. Tea, coffee, beer, spirits, fruit, meat pies, sandwiches and cake were some of the refreshments available. In the mornings in particular, there was an extremely interesting and I believe, unique railway operation performed in order for the passenger trains in each direction to cross one another on the single line and separate trains from Yarram and Wonthaggi to combine as one, thus saving locomotive power, man power and improving track capacity for the remainder of the journey from Nyora to Melbourne. Conversely, the train ex Melbourne which had an extra brake van in the middle had to be divided at Nyora. The front section went to Leongatha and the rear section to Wonthaggi.

The train, ex Wonthaggi, would arrive first, discharge the passengers, attach a fresh engine to the rear and detach the front engine. The train would then be hauled back to the Wonthaggi branch line clear of the main line. The train from Yarram would then arrive at the platform and the Wonthaggi train would be pushed back onto it, coupled up, and passengers would re-join after having partaken of refreshments. The combined train was then pushed back over the road crossing, then moved forward to number two track. By this time, the combined train from Melbourne would arrive at the platform. The front section would be detached and depart for Korumburra. At the same time the combined train for Melbourne would depart from the number two track. Meanwhile, Wonthaggi passengers would be partaking of refreshments. A freshly serviced engine would then be attached and the journey resumed.

My brother David was born in 1941. Our house stood on a couple of acres of land and at about this time, Mum bought a Jersey heifer which we called 'Tiny'. She calved soon after and I had to learn very quickly how to milk a cow. It became my lot to milk the cow and feed the calf whenever it was not convenient for Mum to do so. We used to separate the spare milk, which meant that there was always an abundance of beautiful cream for the table. That was the good part, the bad part was that we had to make our own butter. I shall never forget how I hated this task. We did not have a churn, just a wooden spoon. After the evening meal, a couple of times a week we would sit at the kitchen table stirring a basin of cream for what seemed "endless hours". Eventually, the butter milk would come away and we kids would drink it as the taste was delightful. We would then work some salt into the butter and finally wash it by pouring cold water over it. We would then work the butter in the water two or three times. The freshly made butter was beautiful but as there were no preservatives in it apart from the salt, it did not keep for long. The deterioration was probably hastened by the fact that we did not own a refrigerator. Meat and other perishables were stored briefly in a fly proof safe. Later, when food rationing was introduced, Mum became very popular with some families around the town as she didn't use her ration tickets for butter which were in great demand. On top of that, some housewives would buy the homemade butter from her to use in baking.

Although I was still quite young, with Dad being away at the war, many jobs were thrust upon me that otherwise would not have been the case. Mum used to buy firewood from

Gordon Casey who was a horse breaker and trainer, and also had a bullock team. He would bring a wagon load of wood, which comprised of long lengths of saplings, often very black because of fires having passed through, and I would have to cut them up with a blunt old axe. They were stringy bark saplings and therefore relatively easy to cut and did not require much splitting. I acquired a bit of skill with an axe as a result, and still love to go out into the bush and gather our own firewood, although these days I have a chain saw. In winter months, when a lot more wood was burnt, I would supplement the fuel supply by going to the railway coal stage and nicking a large lump of coal which I would carry home and break up. This lasted longer in the stove than the stringy bark wood, had more heat and smelled like a steam engine. A daily task of course was to ensure there was a supply of kindling to light the fire the next morning. As a result of having to complete these tasks, I had to be home from school each afternoon strictly on time and was in big trouble with Mum if I dawdled home or stayed back to play cricket or football.

In the last few years everyone, even in the city, has become very conscious of water use, but this was drummed into us at a very early age. We really had the same problem as exists today. There was plenty of rainfall at Nyora but we did not catch and store enough of it and it went to waste. We had one tank for the household and a well for the animals.

I used to have a rope on a bucket to bail water out of the well for the cows and chooks and to put on the garden. I can remember Mum tapping the rungs on the tank in the summer months to determine what water was in it.

The water tower in the loco area which I have previously mentioned had a shower under it which was screened off for privacy purposes with corrugated iron walls. When the supply of water at home was low, my younger brother and I would go to this railway shower instead of having a bath at home.

Bullock wagon with my three cousins from the city, my two younger brothers (only the top of my head visible) on board.

The cold water was always invigorating. The railway of course had plenty of water, gravity fed from their own reservoir situated in the hills about three kilometres from town.

The number of children attending the Nyora State School was usually around the fifty mark. It did fluctuate a bit depending on the size of the railway families at any given time. Railway staff usually had to transfer when they took a promotion and of course others transferred for family reasons such as education, job opportunities, or simply because they didn't like the place and couldn't settle down.

In those days, the school catered for students up to grade eight (Merit Certificate). There were two teachers, the Head Teacher, Mr Gardiner who took grades four to eight inclusive in the big room; and a female teacher who taught the lower grades. My first teacher was Miss Brennan, whom I liked very much. She got me off to a good start and by the standards of that school, over time I became a fairly capable student. I can't say that I really liked school as I was always glad when classes finished for the day, and when weekends or school holidays were coming up.

Comparing the education system of today, which my grandchildren enjoy with that of my era, I believe that I was very fortunate to have been at school then rather than now. Looking back, the teachers I encountered at Nyora were in the profession because they had a vocation; they wanted to teach and it seemed that they would not rest until they had got through to each and every student. I have no doubt that there are still a fair percentage of teachers of that calibre in the system but there is also ample evidence that many present-day teachers do not have such a calling and treat their situation simply as a job or as a stepping stone to some other calling. They are therefore not as effective.

I acknowledge that the world has changed enormously over this period and many of the methods and disciplines in vogue in my time are not now considered acceptable, or perhaps are no longer practical. Not only is corporal punishment outlawed both at home and at school, but it appears that detention and the writing of lines are also out, or at least rarely used.

These methods of discipline were frequently utilised in my day on students who committed misdemeanours or were not performing to their capacity. Furthermore, if you got the strap or some other form of discipline, you did not tell your parents because of the real possibility that they would further discipline you in support of the teacher.

Other teaching methods which I derived great benefit from was the practice of stamping the work you handed in, rating it fair, good, very good or excellent. This was a great incentive to me to do my best, as was the practice to post up the marks each student obtained at the twice-yearly examinations. I don't think there was ever more than about eight kids in my grade and I always finished in the top two which encouraged me to strive to maintain my top position or to achieve it in the next examination. I believe that had I finished at the bottom of the class I would have been just as motivated to improve my performance and lift my grades at the next examination. I believe that being competitive is just as important in your academic life as it is in your sporting life. My favourite subjects were geography, history and nature study, but I coped quite well with arithmetic, grammar, spelling, reading and poetry.

I think the system of having a school reader for each grade which was in force for many years was a good one, and as a result, to this day I am still a great fan of A.B. (Banjo) Paterson and can recite some of his work.

School Report, Grade IV, 1943

DAD WAS DISCHARGED from the army in 1945 and this made quite a difference to my life. I no longer had to cut wood or milk the cow on a regular basis. Soon after his discharge Dad got a full-time job as a track repairer with the railways. It was of course a lowly paid job and Dad supplemented his income by doing casual work and shooting rabbits and foxes for their skins. He bought a second hand .22 Browning semi-automatic rifle and taught me how to safely handle it and shoot. Seventy odd years later I still have that rifle and often shoot rabbits and occasionally a fox on our property at Gisborne. I was by then trapping rabbits on a regular basis. I had a number of regular customers who would buy from me at one shilling (ten cents) a pair. I also used to collect bottles. I got sixpence (five cents) a dozen for beer bottles and three pence each for lemonade bottles. I saved up and bought myself a bicycle. Another of my favourite pastimes was catching eels in the Bass River and for a while I had a ferret. Space was at a premium in our small house. The front verandah was closed in each end but open at the front. Mum bought a canvas blind and installed it on one side of the front verandah putting a single bed behind it for me to sleep there.

During the war years, my Aunty Mary and my three cousins, Maureen, Valerie and Janice would now and again come up on the train and stay with us. I'm not quite sure how we all fitted in the small house, but we did. They were fun times as us country kids showed the city girls aspects of the country life. Alternatively, my brother and I would go to Auntie Mary's for a holiday. She lived in Abbotsford and Nana Barden lived just a couple of streets away. We would always have a great time with trips to the beach on the bus and Saturday afternoons at the pictures. Although several blocks away I can recall the noise of the crowd emanating from the football ground when the Collingwood team played at home. The famous Lou Richards lived in the same street as my aunt and I would often see him going to training or the match. As a result of this, I became a very keen Collingwood supporter throughout my life.

My Dad had grown up in tough times and had to work hard from a very early age on the small farm his family had at Exford near Melton. His philosophy was that if boys were to make good in a tough world as adults, they needed to be disciplined and be conditioned to hard times when quite young, so equipping them to handle the hard knocks which were bound to come their way later. Being the eldest boy and having become fairly self-sufficient over the war years while Dad was away, his attitude was not a real problem for me, but looking back, my younger brothers had it pretty tough.

Conversely, my older sister was the apple of my Dad's eye and was given all the encouragement possible to become a 'lady'. In March 1946 my younger sister Kathleen was born. I clearly remember how happy dad was to have another daughter and as time went on, he absolutely adored her.

My older sister Gloria had a close friend at school called Margaret. At about this time, Margaret announced that she would be leaving Nyora School at the end of the year. The following year she would be a boarder at the Notre Dame Convent in Warragul. Gloria immediately expressed a wish that she go with her. This matter became the subject of endless discussions in our household over the next few months. It was obvious that we could not afford the fees and other costs involved, but it seemed that Mum and Dad were just as keen as Gloria for her to have such an education. They finally decided that if Dad could get additional casual work to supplement his income further, and Mum could obtain casual work at the Railway Refreshment Rooms, and all the rest of the family "tightened their belts", she would be able to board at Warragul. This meant that things would be even tighter in our household over the next few years.

At about this time a school bus commenced doing two daily round trips. Korumburra to Bena, Loch, Nyora, Poowong, Korumburra. This enabled students from these towns to attend the High School at Korumburra. There is no doubt that I should have gone there in 1946, but I was not particularly keen to change schools, and didn't realise the implications of not doing so at that time. My parents thought that it might be better for me to stay at Nyora as the hours I would be away from home each day would be much longer if I went to Korumburra. In the winter months it would be dark soon after I got home and I would not be available to perform chores as required. This turned out to be a big mistake. I got my Merit Certificate at the end of 1947 at twelve years of age and belatedly started at the Korumburra High School in 1948.

However, a big shock was in store for me. I was informed on the first day that even though I had obtained excellent results at Nyora the previous year, I would have to repeat year eight (form two) at the High School as I had missed two years of algebra, geometry, French and science. Since I was quite young it would do me no harm. I objected strongly to this proposal and asked that I be allowed to do Form three on the basis that if my performance was unsatisfactory I could repeat it the following year. I was really upset and embarrassed as there were two or three older kids in Form three whose performance at Nyora over the years had been inferior to mine. The motivation I had to do well previously completely disappeared and I became disinterested and lazy – near enough was good enough. The whole year was wasted as I made up my mind that since I could leave school at fourteen, in those days it was the school leaving age, I would in fact leave at the end of this year as I would turn fourteen at the end of March the following year.

During this last year at school I continued to trap rabbits at weekends to make a bit of pocket money, and I also got a part time job at the new milk bar that opened in the town. I worked for a couple of hours each week night instead of studying as I should have been doing. Pictures were then being screened in the hall each Friday night and I was the lolly boy selling ice creams and confectionery at interval. The hotel closed at 6pm in those days, but in the football season, although the bar doors were closed, people moved into the commercial room and the billiard room and they continued serving drinks. They were able to do this as there was no policeman in the town. The milk bar was quite close to the hotel and I would take tray loads of hot pies in over a period of a couple of hours. Some nights I could sell them quicker than the pie heater could heat them up. Nyora Hotel did not provide meals at the time. Notwithstanding my lack of interest and failure to study during the repeat year of 1948, I did pass and could have gone into Form three the next year. Regrettably, my mind was made up and I did not return to school.

Each country town has its characters and Nyora was no exception. Bill Major, known far and wide as "Bottley" because of his build, was one of the engine drivers on the railways. He was a bachelor and lived at Mrs MacIndo's boarding house in the main street, between the general store and the bakery. When not at work he spent his time either sitting on the front verandah of the boarding house reading newspapers, or at the hotel. He would have been one of the hotels best customers. For some years he had always spoken to me when I passed the boarding house going to or from school. He knew I was keen on railways and one day he said to me that if I wanted to have a ride on a steam engine, I should be up at the station a bit before 5am on the Saturday morning. I fronted up in good time and when the paper train arrived and the Melbourne crew got off, I climbed up onto the engine with the Nyora driver and fireman. I considered myself quite privileged and was thrilled to bits. We went through to Korumburra and Leongatha and on to Stony Creek where we waited for the arrival of the Melbourne bound Yarram passenger train, then changed over with the Yarram crew. Approaching Korumburra, I was told to squat down in the corner of the cab and remain there until we departed, 'in case there was a boss around'. This trip was a terrific experience and I was invited to repeat it two or three more times during that year.

Another character at Nyora was Bill Bellingham, who was a train guard and lived with his family in a railway house opposite the bakery. He was quite tall and slightly stooped, with a shock of almost white hair. Because of his build, he was mostly known as 'Bamboo', although at the pub, he was often called the 'Quivering Hairpin', his rather loud voice had a quiver in it, particularly when he got a bit excited while telling stories. Bill supplemented his income by shovelling coal at the coal stage and also clearing ashes out of the pits. He too was a regular customer at the pub. He was renowned for his story telling and could hold an audience spellbound for long periods, even though they knew he was either grossly exaggerating or telling downright lies. He would be asked to tell his stories over and over again. Bill was really quite a solid citizen as at various times he was the secretary of the school committee and secretary of the hall committee. He was secretary of the Nyora sub branch of the Australian Railways Union and must have been involved with the Australian Labor Party. I remember at one election, he paid me and my brother five shillings to stand at the hall all day and hand out how to vote cards. Many years later when I was working in the railways in Melbourne an Inspector asked me if I knew Bill. I answered in the affirmative. He then related to me how in his younger days he had been sent to Nyora to relieve Guard Bellingham who was off injured with a bad back. He was shocked and surprised a day or two later when shunting in the yard to see Bill shovelling ashes out of the ash pit. Still many years later after he had transferred to Spencer Street and just before he retired, I walked out of my office in Head Office and bumped into Bill in the corridor. I asked him how he was and he answered in his inimitable fashion in his loud quivering voice, "I just brought the *Southern Aurora* into Spencer Street and went to clear a dog out of the van box when the "bastard" bit me. I'm going to the Railway Medical Officer to get a tetanus shot and see if the wound needs stitching." Alas, I never saw or spoke to Bill again, but I firmly believe that he was the greatest character I ever met on or off the railways.

Before he was transferred to Nyora, Bill was stationed at Orbost. One of his often-repeated stories was about dingos along the banks of the Snowy River. They used to go spotlight shooting and were very successful, as you would see a pair of eyes in the beam. He claimed that as the numbers reduced the remaining dingos got very cunning. They would hunt in pairs and when the spotlight went on them, each would close the inside eye and when you fired you missed, as the shot went between them. He had a raft of other tall stories from Orbost about the height of maize grown on the river flats, the size of beans and pumpkins grown and claimed they used to cut the big pumpkins in half, hollow each half out and then use them as a boat to cross the river. My favourite story Bill told concerned the quality of railway watches issued to train guards. He claimed he was out rabbit shooting one day when he lost his watch climbing a fence. Notwithstanding that these were mechanical watches which had to be wound daily, he stated that when climbing the fence over a year later, he found his watch lying on an ant hill. It was still going and on the correct time. He asserted that "little ants crawling over and over the winder each day actually wound the watch up!" Then with a flourish he would pull his watch out of his vest pocket and say, "and here is the very bloody watch."

3

My Working Life Commences

MY FIRST JOB was on a dairy farm at Kernot about ten miles (16kms) from Nyora. I was required to live-in and the farmer's wife provided meals and did my clothes washing for me. The share farmer owned the herd but not the property or equipment. He ran the farm and shared the income with the absentee landlord. I worked seven days each week, but every second Sunday I could go home on my bicycle after the morning milking. I could have the afternoon off milking, eat the evening meal with my family, and return so as to be available for the next morning milking. With the aid of machines, we milked eighty cows night and morning. The procedure was to get the cow into the bail, wash her udder, keeping an eye on the glass for the flow of milk from the cow in the adjoining bail, and when the flow reduced, take the cups off her and place them on the freshly bailed and washed cow. You were then required to 'strip' by hand, milking the remainder of the milk from the previous cow. When this was done, she was released from the bail and a fresh cow was brought in. You really had to be on your toes the whole time to maintain the regular movement of cows into and out of the shed. Hygiene was a high priority and some cows would foul the bail necessitating a clean-up before the next one was admitted. This meant you had to move even quicker to avoid delays to the milking of the herd.

When milking was completed the shed had to be hosed and swept out, and all equipment washed and made good for the afternoon milking. We would then go up to the house for a cooked breakfast. After breakfast there was plenty of other work to be done in order to maintain the property in good order. Some of the jobs included fencing repairs, cutting bracken fern, grubbing tussocks, marking calves, spreading fertilizer, cutting firewood and assisting with general repairs and maintenance of the house and farm buildings. The afternoon milking commenced at about four o'clock and it was usually close to seven o'clock when we returned to the house for an evening meal. Having been out of bed at five o'clock and working all day, despite being a pretty fit young lad, I was usually ready for bed soon after eating. There was of course no television in those days, and most nights I would read before going off to sleep. My wages were one pound ten shillings a week ($3.00) and my keep. After a few months I decided there was no future in this and I left.

I then decided to try life in the City and one of my aunts, who lived in Victoria Parade, Collingwood, said I could board with her while I saw how things would work out and whether I could settle down or not. There were plenty of jobs available in those days and I started almost immediately at Duncan's Match Factory in Abbotsford. I had to operate a machine which made the outer casing of the match boxes. I could not get used to standing at this machine all day and after a short while actually hated the job. Yarra Falls, a short distance away were advertising for staff so I decided to leave and try my luck with them. This job paid better as there was overtime available two nights per week, but I could not get used to the factory environment, and after a few months I decided to go home again. I quite enjoyed some aspects of the City life, particularly going to the boxing at the old West Melbourne Stadium of a

Friday night, and seeing the Collingwood Football team play of a Saturday. These attractions however did not outweigh my love of the country life and I returned to Nyora.

My return coincided with the grass hay harvesting season and the arrival in the district of the first pick up baler. This machine had been built by H.V. Mckay Massey Harris at the Sunshine Harvester Works and was hauled by a Fordson Tractor.

Pick up baler and tractor.

It attracted enormous interest in the district as hitherto most grass hay had been loose stacked involving considerable skill in building the stack and much hard labour in forking it up and then again feeding it out in the winter months.

The owner of the baler, Bob Hutchinson, had engaged a tractor driver but needed another person to ride with him on the wooden seat on the other side of the baler to cut and tie wire for each bale. This was a far cry from the more modern balers which automatically cut and tie twine. This was hard, onerous, repetitive work, riding over bumpy paddocks on the backless wooden seat with dust and grass seeds blowing in your face and down your neck, and if you did not concentrate, the wire would cut your hands. Every now and again Gilbert, the tractor driver, who had to look back all the time checking the flow of hay up the elevator would call out 'snake!' and I can assure you, that bale when it came through, had the wire carefully cut and tied. The hours were long as we worked each night until the dew caused the hay to compact too much and we had to knock off. The only days we had off was when rain occurred and the hay was wet.

Ray, wire cutters in hand on the far side of the baler.

Bob paid me two shillings and sixpence an hour and I made what seemed to me to be a fortune in the ten weeks or so of the season.

Bob was an exceptionally good bloke to work for. He always included Gilbert the tractor driver and myself in away from work activities. One day after rain when it was too wet to bale hay, he said we should have a day out at the Pakenham races. I thought this was great as I had not previously been to a race meeting. Shortly before this we had baled hay for several farmers in the Bass area including that of the horse trainer – Tom Harrison. On arrival at the track we noticed that the Harrisons' had starters in two races and I decided to back them. It was a great thrill for me and I recall quite vividly, firstly "Old Red" winning, and then in a later race, "Old Bailey" winning. At my first attempt at punting on race horses I came home a winner, quite by accident of course as I had no experience of "studying the form". Incidentally, the Harrison family later shifted to Cranbourne where Tom became a top metropolitan trainer. His son Doug still trains there. Another son, Kevin, was a successful jockey for several years and his son, Travis, became a top apprentice jockey, but was tragically killed in a car accident. The Moonee Valley Racing Club honour him by naming a race after him each year. Another grandson of Tom's is present day world class jockey, Craig Williams, who has won many of the richest races, not only in Australia, but all over the world. Another example of Bob's inclusiveness was that each year, when harvesting was finished, he hired a boat at Corinella and took us for a day of fishing on Western Port Bay.

Bob's brother, Bill, had a Bedford tray truck and was a general carrier in the district. When the hay season was over I started working with him as a "jockey". Again, this was very hard work for a teenager. Bill had a circular saw and we would cut firewood in the bush and then deliver in the district. It was not a tip truck, so after loading it in the bush, we would have to unload it by hand at the destination. At this time there was considerable building activity in the district and we used to cart a lot of sand to constructions sites. We had to shovel the sand on the tray at the sand pit, and at the destination we would drop the side boards and then shovel the sand off again.

The upside of this was that you all got a spell driving to and from the bush or the sand pit. I recall frequently we would have to remove yards of overburden to get to the better quality sand. This was certainly hard work. I worked with Bill throughout the year and when the next hay season started, went back to tying bales with Bob.

The year was a most enjoyable one as on Saturday nights there was a 50/50 dance in the Poowong Hall with Drakes three-piece band. Mr Drake played the drums, his mother the piano, and his wife the saxophone. On most occasions we could get a lift to the dance but if we couldn't we would ride our bikes. There were also dances held from time to time in the Loch Hall, and at Nyora a monthly euchre and dance. At first, I would play euchre with the 'oldies' but as I learnt to dance a bit, I favoured the dancing. Nyora Football Club played in the now defunct Bass Valley League and was reasonably successful at this time, but sometimes struggled to fill the team. I was only fifteen and a pretty ordinary footballer but was able to get a game to make up the numbers on some occasions. I enjoyed it very much. I played in the back pocket and would usually manage to get a few kicks. After the 1950/51 hay baling season I decided to go fruit picking at Mildura, thinking it would be a real adventure being so far from home.

Four of us went from Nyora. George Anderson, Mac Dobel and Gilbert Walters were all much older than me, and George was the veteran of many picking seasons. We went on an overnight special pickers' train which was a real eye opener. I was possibly the youngest bloke aboard. The train stopped at all the main stations and without exception, police officers were on platforms to greet it. Although there was some drinking of alcohol, most of the itinerants tried to sleep. One chap in our carriage had a .22 rifle in the rack and when daylight came he amused himself by shooting at rabbits out the window. On arrival at Mildura, Police lined the full length of the platform immediately interviewing some passengers as they alighted. The locals stated that this was done each year and some passengers who were known to the police were directed to return on the train that night as they were not welcome in the district. How different was the world in my teenage days?

George knew the owner of a block at Koorlong, a few kilometres south of Mildura, straight out Benetook Avenue. We were picked up at the station and driven to our workplace. The pickers' quarters were fairly primitive with a community kitchen and huts, each with two beds. The buildings had dirt floors. There was a Coolgardie safe and cold showers. About one hundred yards away was a long drop toilet with hessian walls. The general store and Post Office was just a few minutes' walk away. This was a whole new world to me with heat, mosquitoes and red dust, but I was eager to accept the challenge the next few weeks would bring. The block had about forty acres of vines, predominantly sultanas and a few citrus trees. The owner, George Skelton, had a disability as a result of a road accident and was permanently on crutches, but despite this he was very active and it was surprising what he could do. Mrs Skelton was also a tireless worker. Pay was decided on the number of dip tins of grapes you picked each day. The picking knife used had a parrot beaked blade and it was prudent to be either just ahead or just behind the person picking on the other side as speed was of the essence, and if you both went for the same bunch you were likely to get your hand or fingers cut. I also quickly learnt to swap sides for each row you picked, otherwise you picked in the sun all day and the other person in the shade.

After a couple of weeks, the chap on the cart left and the boss asked me would I like to do that job instead of picking. It involved driving the horse and cart to the dips (all grapes had to be dipped before being spread on the racks for the drying process to take its course), and then bringing back the empty tins and assessing the crop as you threw the tins along the next rows, the pickers would work on. It was important to get the spacing of the empty tins right as the pickers would scream if they were too sparse and they lost picking time through having to walk for them, and if they were too thick and not used, the cart would be delayed whilst the tins were retrieved, as of course the pickers would not collect them for you. The pickers would place the full tins under the vines in the shade for collection and the most responsible part of the job was recording the number of tins picked by each individual for their pay purposes. The man on the dip and the man on the rack spreading, as well as the man on the cart were paid on the basis of how many tins were spread overall each day and I was more than pleased with the money I was earning. So much so, that I opened a bank account in Mildura. The banks were open on a Saturday morning in those days.

As the picking was drawing to a close, George the owner asked if I would like to stay on as there was still plenty of work to do shaking racks, boxing the dried fruit, loading it on the trucks taking the product to the packing sheds and many other routine tasks that had to be attended to. He said "You will be doing a man's work, so I will pay you the adult wage." I immediately agreed. I really enjoyed the work on the block over the next eight months until I went home again for the next hay baling season in November. I learnt how to cincture the currant vines, back the soil off along each row, silly plough around each vine and put the irrigation water on to wash the salt away from the roots, cut out (pruning), pull out and then wrap on the remaining laterals (canes) of the sultana vines. I was also responsible for the two draught horses, Duke and Prince, who participated in many of the activities described. Much of this work was heavy going for a teenager but I mostly enjoyed it. On one occasion I recall George the boss and his wife had to go to Mildura for medical appointments and other business. In their absence, a truck that had been booked to take sweat boxes of dried fruit to a packing shed arrived. The driver and I loaded the consignment and the truck left, only to return an hour or so later, still fully laden. The driver explained that the quality control officer at the shed had rejected the fruit on the grounds that it was "a bit green". This meant that the boxes would have to be unloaded from the truck and then tipped out one by one onto long strips of Sisalcraft and raked over to colour up evenly in the sun. Eventually the fruit would be re-boxed for loading and transport again – a lot of work. I had no experience in judging the readiness of dried fruit for the shed but the boss did and he obviously thought it was ready. I asked the truck driver for his opinion as to the chances of the consignment being passed if he took it to another shed. He replied that it looked reasonable to him and he was surprised that it had been rejected so I told him to take the load to another packing shed. I was quite nervous about this as I had taken the risk of it being rejected again, thus incurring double the cartage costs. Luck was with me however and it was accepted. George the boss was quite pleased that I had taken this initiative but I have sometimes wondered how he would have reacted had the load been rejected a second time.

During the year Mum had written to me to say there was going to be a further addition to the family. My youngest sister, Pamela, was born in September 1951.

I had made some good friends at Mildura and used to go to the dance at the "Old Mill" every Saturday night. Occasionally we would go to the dance at the Workers Club on Wednesdays, but transport was a problem on week nights. On Saturday's there was a late bus to Cardross, which of course went through Koorlong. Once a month there was a dance in the little hall at Koorlong, virtually opposite the block I worked on. The corrugated iron building would be stifling hot but we always had a great time. On Sundays, after I had done my washing and other chores, I would go down the road to George Ponngraz's place. Other boys would come there and we would finish up playing around on their Ferguson tractor or on Bert Evans' motorbike in the scrub at the back of their block. The biggest bit of excitement I had while batching was when a snake slid under my bed on the dirt floor and went down a hole beside the corner stump. I had to pull the bed out, then dig the snake out to ensure my safety that night. Despite political correctness and modern day thinking, I still believe the only good snake is a dead one.

I had regularly saved money at Mildura and decided that as I had never had the opportunity to fly before, when returning home I would try it out rather than go home by train. To me it was quite an experience. The plane was a DC-3. While I had no idea at the time that I would one day live in the area, I can recall the pilot pointing out the memorial cross at Mount Macedon as we passed by it.

The hay baling team was the same as the previous year with Gilbert driving and Bob and me cutting and tying the wires on each bale. I probably enjoyed it more though, as when moving the machinery from one property to another, on the longer trips, I was now allowed to drive the tractor while the other two refreshed themselves with a couple of beers at the nearest pub. Both Mum and Dad had long expressed a wish that I get myself a 'permanent job' instead of floating from one labouring job to the other as I had since leaving school. As I had always been very keen on the railways it seemed logical that I should try them. There were not many other options anyhow as most government jobs, semi government jobs and the banks required you to hold at least an intermediate certificate (Year 10) to join their ranks. I promised Mum that although I was committed to go back to Mildura for the forthcoming picking season, I would give serious consideration to joining the railways if they would have me when the picking season concluded. I thought long and hard about this over the next several weeks while again working on the cart and decided that I would like to become an engine driver. I was aware that this involved starting as an engine cleaner, then qualifying as a fireman before eventually qualifying as a driver and then waiting probably some years to get an appointment on a seniority basis.

When the picking season ended in April 1952 I travelled by overnight train to Melbourne. The next train to Nyora was in the afternoon so I decided to go to the railways employment office to enquire about employment with a view to becoming an engine driver. I was informed that the minimum age for an engine cleaner was seventeen and a half, and therefore I would have to work as a lad labourer at Newport Workshops for the next few months until I reached that age. I had no objection to this, so I was sent to the railway doctor to do a medical test. I was absolutely shocked when they declared after a urine test that I was unfit for employment. I really did not understand as I had been doing quite heavy work for some three years without any problems. I caught the train home and discussed the matter with my family that night. It was decided I should go to Korumburra on the train the next morning and see Dr Lappin. He declared after a comprehensive examination, including a urine test, that he could find nothing wrong with me and if I still wanted to start in the railways he would give me a letter that should help. A couple of days later I went back to the City, was given a second medical and passed with no further trouble.

I then went back to the employment section where the clerk said that the wage for a Lad Labourer was three pounds ten shillings per week, but since I came from the country I would get a living away from home allowance to bring the weekly earnings up to five pounds ($10.00). He thought I would not get board and lodgings under at least four pounds a week, so therefore I would find it impossible to get by financially. He stated that a Lad Porter's base wage was the same but they got penalty time for weekend work and heaps of overtime was available, so it might be better if I went that way. I could transfer over to engine cleaning when I reached the appropriate age. I agreed to do this and my railway career started in the porters' class the following week.

4

Life In Railways

I OBTAINED board in Sydenham Street, Moonee Ponds, and after attending the Porters' induction class and being issued with a uniform, I was given written instructions to report to the Stationmaster at Essendon at 9.00am the following Monday. I arrived at Essendon station about 8:00am and sat on a platform seat for an hour watching the staff and the peak traffic before going to the Stationmaster's Office and meeting Mr Davis, who turned out to be a terrific supervisor and mentor. He was very strict but fair, took a deep interest in the development of his junior staff and gave them every encouragement to study and progress in the job. I think everyone needs a measure of luck in life but the secret to success is being in a position to take advantage of whatever luck comes your way, by obtaining qualifications and experience and ensuring that your performance record is good. My first piece of railway luck was being posted to Essendon where most aspects of railway operations occurred and could be learned. It was a busy passenger station with separate parcels and goods office, a goods yard, sidings, train crews and a large signal box. The next bit of luck was having a boss like Mr. Davis, as not all new starts were so fortunate. I was not put on the roster immediately but rather spent a couple of days on the platform learning to read the timetables, so that correct hanger boards were always displayed on relevant platforms and experiencing the general operations and duties involved.

I was then required to learn Block Recording in the signal box. I really felt inadequate the first days up there, as bells, which I thought I would never learn, seemed to be continually ringing. The trick was to recognize the different tones of each bell signal. The system of safe working was called double line block. The "Is Line Clear?" signals were sent to the signal box in advance and acknowledged by bells, as were train departure signals and train arrival signals. The gatekeeper at Pascoe Vale Road North Essendon (now Strathmore), was advised a train had departed by a bell signal, and there were automatic approach bell signals for trains in each direction when approaching the station. In addition to this, there was the signal box phone, the direct line to the station phone, the block phone, the yard phone, the station to station phone, the North Eastern Controller phone and the Suburban Controller phone. It was the Block Recorder's task to record in the Block Book when "Line Clear" was given, train departure from the station in the rear, train arrival and departure from Essendon station and train arrival at the station in advance. In addition, the block recorder was required to enter other one-off train running information in the relevant column, answer telephones and report train running information to the relevant train controller.

Although awestruck at first, after a few days learning I came good and about a week or so later a Block and Signal Inspector came out and observed me recording during the evening peak. He passed me as competent, and so I had been successful in my first railway examination and felt very relieved. As time went by I became quite competent in operating the sixty-eight lever frame and the dual set of gates over Buckley Street. Officially it was illegal for a Junior Block Recorder to operate the block instruments, the interlocked signal frame or the interlocked gates, but old Ted Pound, who retired about a year after I arrived at Essendon, made sure you learnt very quickly. Hours in the signal box for recorders were 7:00am to 9:00am and 4:00pm to 6:30pm each weekday. Ted would sit in his chair close to the fire reading his paper or having breakfast when you started early in the morning or reading the Herald of an evening, and as the trains were belled on, call out the numbers of the levers you had to pull. This way you certainly learnt all the roads in no time. One of the relieving signalmen who came there from time to time would always say to you, 'you work the frame and I will do the book'- a reversal of roles. I also became familiar with more intricate aspects of signalling such as track locking, back locking and how to illegally cancel it out, and the running of time releases. This knowledge and experience of signalling was invaluable in my later railway career and is something that a lad porter at a location with no signal box, or only a small signal box, would not have had the opportunity to learn. Hence, I was lucky to obtain such a background. The Block Recorder was also the signalman's 'legs' and got the job of delivering the caution order when a signal failed or clipping the points when necessary. I remember feeling rather nervous very early in my recording days when the home departure signal on number one road failed for the passage of the *Spirit of Progress*. I had to climb up to the footplate of the streamlined 'S' Class locomotive to deliver a Caution Order to the driver who looked quite formidable in his "big wheel" garb and goggles. A Caution Order was written authority, issued in certain circumstances to pass a home signal when it was at the stop position.

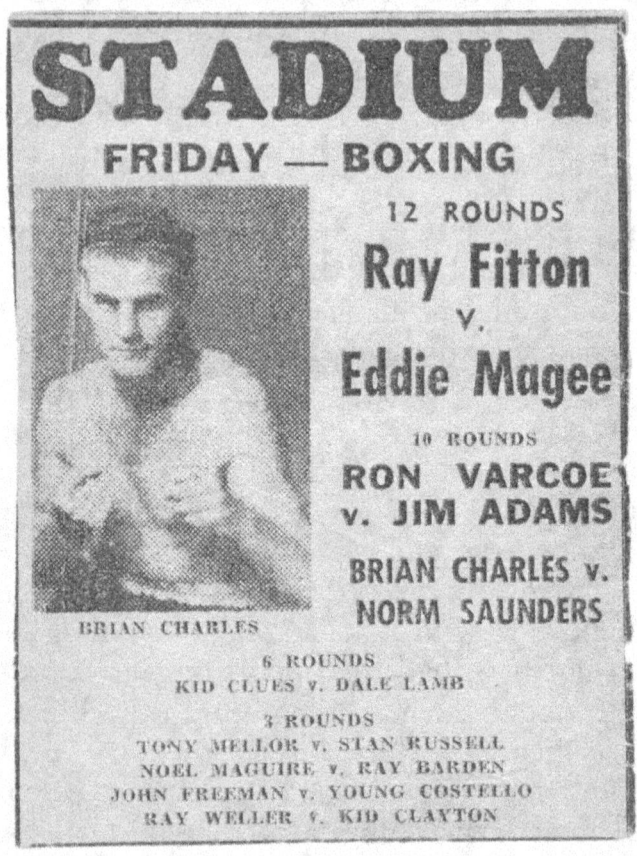

News cutting listing my first fight at the Stadium.

I HAD for some years been keen on boxing and now that I had settled in the city, I decided to go to the gymnasium and take it on seriously. Mick McMahon had a gym in a loft at the back of a house in Sydney Street, Ascot Vale. He coached me for a while and I won an amateur bout in the Richmond Town Hall. He then entered me in the light weight division of the Newport and Williamstown Amateur Championships held in the Williamstown Town Hall. I won two elimination fights but was beaten on points in the light weight final. It was quite difficult to do the proper training when working shifts as you missed out on sparring and specialist training every second week. I could do fitness training at home or running around the park, but this wasn't really enough. However, I persisted and a short while later was listed for a three-round novice fight at the West Melbourne Stadium. The old stadium, which was on the site of the present Festival Hall, was later destroyed by fire in 1953. I was overwhelmed by the atmosphere of the place. The heavy smoke haze, the hundreds of glowing cigarettes in the darkened bleachers; the blazing lights over the ring; the raucous music blaring out as you walked to the ring; the blood splattered canvas you saw when you entered the ring; and the ritual the ring announcer went through when introducing the boxers. We must have put on a good show as the Sportsman Review gave us best novice performance in their weekly write up, but I was disappointed losing on points in what was apparently a close decision.

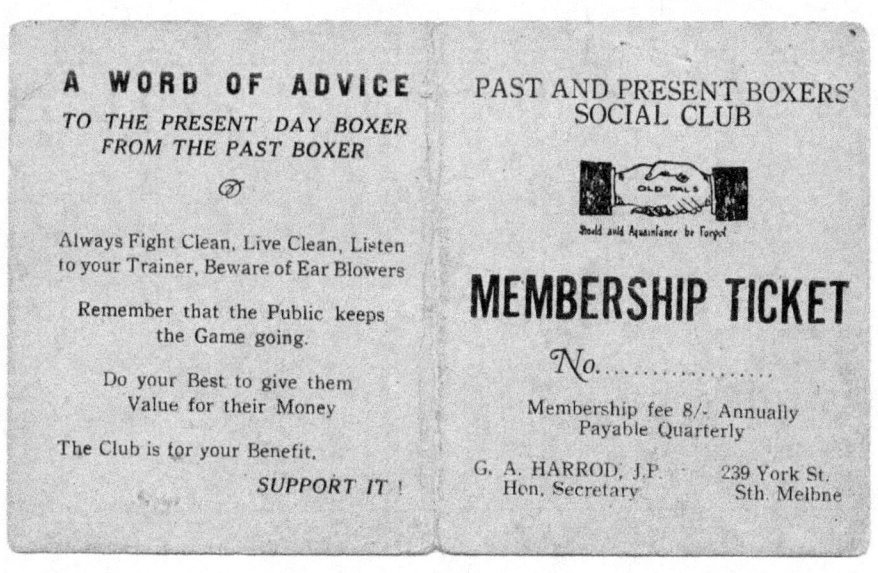

Membership ticket Past and Present Boxers Social Club. Note the words of advice, some of which could apply to railway employees.

I came out of it unharmed except for a depleted ego and I had to change shifts for a rematch the next week. Again, I was beaten on points so I decided to have a break from boxing to consider my future.

A Man of Principle

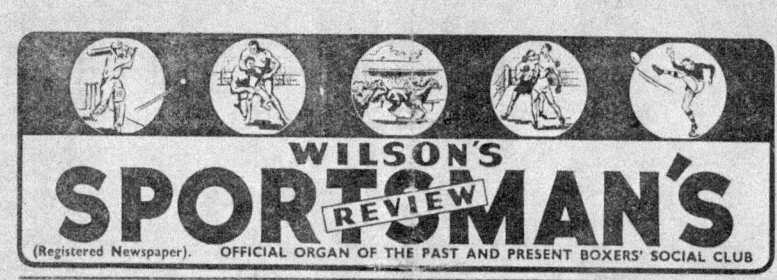

Newspaper write up of my first fight at the stadium.

MEANWHILE, I had met a girl named Carmel at the Saturday night dance at Essendon Town Hall in Moonee Ponds. I had one dance with her and then she disappeared. I did not see her at any of the dances held over the next couple of months that I went to, but an extraordinary coincidence occurred. A fellow Lad Porter, Lawrie, invited me to his home at Pascoe Vale one Saturday afternoon when we had finished work. I could not believe my eyes when he introduced his sister who turned out to be none other than Carmel. She told me that she and her older sister went to the Moonee Ponds dances regularly on both Wednesday and Saturday nights, but rarely did they go upstairs to the 50/50 dancing which I preferred. This explained why I had not seen her. They mostly stayed downstairs which was all modern dancing. Unlike me, Carmel was, and still is, an excellent dancer. A short time after this, we started keeping company. Incidentally, the dances I have referred to were promoted and advertised as 'Gaiety on Parade'. Such a title would have entirely different connotations today.

Mick the boxing trainer considered that I should continue on with boxing. He pointed out that I was still quite young and had some growing and strengthening to do yet. I was subsequently matched for another bout at the stadium which I again lost on points. My opponent was much taller than me and I had great difficulty getting in close as he would back-pedal and jab as I came at him. He caught me with a solid punch between the eyes and the next day both my eyes were black. This upset Carmel's father as he claimed people would think I was a brawler. It also upset the Stationmaster who said he couldn't let me work with the public looking like that, so for a few days I was confined to working in the signal box, cleaning duties and sweeping out 'off' trains, so ended my boxing ambitions at the ripe old age of seventeen years.

A Man of Principle

ESSENDON WAS the supervising station for two small stations, Glenbervie and North Essendon, which were classified as 'Porter Class 1 booking'. Mr Davis knew that I was doing the first aid course and also studying ticket checking and telegraph. He said that when I qualified in ticket checking I should do some private study on station bookkeeping and fare calculations, as a little later it would be necessary for someone to relieve the staff at these two locations for their holidays. On the afternoon shift, after working in the signal box for the peak traffic and then relieving the porter on the platform for a meal, the roster required you to have a meal yourself then go to North Essendon and take over from the 'Porter Class 1' until the last train. I used to go down early and Mrs MacKernan, the booking porter on my shift, would set me some exercises to do such as calculating a school term ticket fare or a pro-rata periodical ticket fare. She also instructed me regarding the various books of accounts and the end of month returns required. Meanwhile, I had applied to transfer to an engine cleaning position as the clerk at the employment office had suggested but was unsuccessful. The reply simply said "You are required in your present position". Mr Davis convinced me that I should forget about the engine driving now, as he considered that the opportunities for promotion in the Traffic Branch for a lad like me were far superior to those in the Rolling Stock Branch.

I must point out that whilst I thoroughly enjoyed the aspects of the job at Essendon that I have described in some detail, there were other duties which were not so interesting. I refer to the cleaning roster. After finishing the morning peak block recording you were required to perform station cleaning. The first job was to clean the men's toilets. This involved scrubbing the wooden seats with sand soap and then rinsing off. Occasionally a toilet would be blocked and you would have to bomb it with buckets of water to clear it. Not a pleasant job. The urinals also had to be cleaned and the floor washed down daily. On completion, you then took the wide broom and swept the asphalted sections of the three platforms and the copings for the full length. The latter was a safety matter, because if pebbles accumulated on the coping they could roll under a passenger's foot when joining a train, which could cause them to go down between the train and platform.

The next task was to sweep the three subways and the ramp/and or steps leading to them. All papers and rubbish had to be taken to the incinerator and burnt. In addition to these daily tasks the cleaning roster included weekly tasks such as clean windows on Monday, (Bon Ami was the cleaning agent), clean brass on Tuesday (Brasso), clean pits on Wednesdays (pit spike provided to pick up litter such as cigarette packets and lolly papers), clean station name plates on Thursday, clean cobwebs from interior of station building and under the verandahs on Friday, mop out waiting room floors, parcels office floor and porters' room floor on Saturdays. All kerosene signals lamps, gate lamps and hand lamps were cleaned by an adult Shed Porter.

The Ladies Waiting Room Attendant cleaned the ladies' toilet and was also responsible for those facilities at Moonee Ponds, Ascot Vale, Newmarket and Kensington stations. My attitude to these cleaning duties was that while I didn't like them, they had to be done. I considered them in fact to be a big incentive for me to study and qualify for a promotion so that I had either no cleaning to do or much less cleaning.

Jobs were fairly plentiful at this time, and the turnover of Lad Porters was quite high. It was claimed that this was due, at least in part, to the fact that many lads could not hack the cleaning duties. However in my case, having previously worked on the land and also in factories, I appreciated that working conditions on the Railways were quite good by comparison. I accept of course that many of the duties allocated to junior staff in my day, would be totally unacceptable today on the grounds of occupational health and safety.

Me, Dot Davies Porteress, and Bill Graham,
Booking Clerk on No. 2 Platform at Essendon.

I HAD REALLY ENJOYED my time working at Essendon, with the exception of one occasion which extremely embarrassed me and was the only time I can recall that Mr. Davis reprimanded me.

The key to the lamp room located at the down end of No. 1 platform was attached to a length of chain as a precaution against staff taking it home in their pocket and when not in use hung on a hook behind the door of the Stationmaster's office.

I had just despatched a train on No. 2 platform, when the Shed Porter standing on No. 1 platform called to me to get the key and throw it across to him.

I did so but unfortunately, I threw it a fraction too high and the end of the chain hit the overhead contact wire of the middle track (since abolished) and twirled around it several times.

This meant that the middle track, fortunately not required for traffic at that time, had to be "booked out" until the Overhead people attended, removed the chain and certified that the contact wire was fit for traffic.

The Shed Porter, being an adult, received a much more severe blast from the Stationmaster than I did but I doubt that his embarrassment was greater.

BY NOW I had turned eighteen and had to register for the National Service Training. I relieved the two ladies at North Essendon for their holidays.

Whilst I found the moderate amount of clerical and accounting work a challenge, I coped alright and tended to like it.

There was not a lot of business at the station, although it certainly livened up on the evenings when there was greyhound racing at Napier Park (now the site of the Strathmore Secondary college), or Bike racing at the North Essendon board track.

A Man of Principle

Ray, standing behind the platoon 'donga' at Puckapunyal during National Service training.

I HAD by now passed my ticket checking and first aid examinations and was progressing with the study of telegraphy. Next, I relieved at Glenbervie for two lots of leave before going to Puckapunyal for National Service Training (Intake three 1953).

On return I was sent to Jolimont to relieve the booking porter there for several weeks. I would ride my bike from Moonee Ponds on the early shift as you had to open the station at about 5:00am, then come home on the train at completion of my shift. When this period of relief cut out I did not go back to Essendon but was sent to North Port on the Port Melbourne line where there was a vacancy for a 'Porter Class 1 Booking'.

After a few weeks I was appointed to the position - my first official promotion.

OVER THE PREVIOUS year or so my family suffered two rather traumatic setbacks.

Firstly, Mum was diagnosed with breast cancer. She was referred to a specialist - Mr. Victor Hurley (later Sir Victor) at the Royal Melbourne Hospital. He was obviously a very skilled surgeon as he amputated her left breast and although these were early days in the treatment of cancer, she survived. About a year later, Mum was seriously injured in a motor car accident on the Bass Highway near the Corinella turn off. She suffered a fractured skull, fractured nose and cheek bone, and a fractured leg. She was in the Alfred Hospital for several weeks but once again, her recovery was complete. I think Mum exemplifies the courage, resilience and toughness of her generation.

Mum at 95 years of age.

A Man of Principle

SHE NOT ONLY SURVIVED THESE two hospitalisations but navigated her way through a lifetime that involved two World Wars, the great depression, and the raising of six children in a period when assistance from the state was minimal or non-existent - a far cry from the situation today. Sadly, mum passed away seven weeks short of her 97th birthday.

5

North Port

NORTH PORT HAD ONLY RECENTLY BEEN CLASSIFIED down from 'Stationmaster Class 8' to 'Porter Class 1', and once again I had been lucky as it was made to order for someone wishing to learn all aspects of station accounting and management, with the exception of goods accountancy. Trains going to and from Flinders Street crossed at North Port so I had a Lad Porter to run the 'down' trains and to do the station cleaning. Ticket sales were not heavy but consistent. Parcels traffic was steady with most 'Inwards' parcels being for traders in the Bay Street shopping strip. 'Outwards' parcels traffic was heavier, the two biggest customers being Kelvinator and Moore Road Machinery. Each weekday, both of these firms consigned spare parts all over Victoria and some interstate, particularly to southern N.S.W. and South Australia. COD (Cash on Delivery) parcels were regularly consigned. There were two signal boxes. 'Ingles Street' Class 3 had interlocked gates and controlled the points in and out of the Montague Shipping Shed. 'Bridge Street' was Class 4 and controlled the crossing gates and signals only. We were supervised by the Stationmaster at Graham who called in each day. When I first arrived at North Port the supervising stationmaster position was vacant, but it was filled shortly after by the transfer of Mr. Tom Bregazzi from the relieving staff. Whilst he had an entirely different personality to Mr. Davis, he had similarities too. He gave staff supervised every encouragement to learn, obtain qualifications and to take promotions. At about this time I qualified in telegraphy and received five pounds ($10) bonus. He immediately suggested that in addition to studying for my first "Safe working" certificate (Staff and Ticket System), I should also enrol at the Victorian Railways Institute classes in Junior Station Accounts (Assistant Stationmaster, Class 5).

Mr. Bregazzi lived in North Melbourne and like me rode a bike to work each morning on early shift. There was a group of five mature ladies who always caught the first train to the city to do office cleaning. They would return just after 9.00am. A couple of them used to go back to the city again at about 5.00pm and return at about 8.30pm. They found the weekly ticket which they bought each Monday morning great value as most of them would also go with their shopping jeeps to the South Melbourne Market once a week after buying an extension 'Flinders Street to South Melbourne'. I got to know them quite well. They were happy with me being at North Port as they claimed that on the other shift, before I was transferred there, the station was sometimes in darkness for the first train and as there were rarely any others catching it, they feared for their safety. I made sure I was always on time on Monday mornings, but riding from Moonee Ponds in all kinds of weather, it got harder and harder to be punctual right through every week. Mr. Bregazzi said that if I got an extra key cut to the office doors, inner and outer he would drop in on his way to Graham and switch on the lights. He risked being disciplined himself with such an arrangement, but this action showed what a good bloke he was. Now, during extremely wet weather, I would catch the train on early shift, except for Mondays. Some months later a public complaint was received to the effect that the complainant had been unable to purchase a ticket on the first train from North Port and therefore was delayed having to go to the booking office at Flinders Street to obtain a ticket to continue his journey on the other side of Melbourne.

I am not proud about this and felt guilty the rest of my railway career, but I had to tell a lie to not only save myself being disciplined, but also the Stationmaster. I told the Inspector investigating the complaint that I definitely was in attendance and I thought this could probably be verified by the ladies who always caught the first train. Apparently they told him they could not recall with any certainty that they had actually seen me on the morning in question, but that I must have been there because they would remember if the lights had not been on. I heard no more about the complaint, but made sure afterwards that come hail, rain or shine I was always in attendance at North Port for the first train. My guilty conscience never allowed me to speak about this until now.

My railway knowledge increased enormously under the supervision of Mr. Bregazzi. I became confident and well-motivated. Certain duties which were the prerogative of the Stationmaster only, such as taking bundles of tickets from stock, ordering new stock and checking off the new stock, he left to me. I would compile the Account Current (a summary of all station business) each month and lay it on the counter for his visit. He would say "Is it right?" and then sign it without checking over it at all. I was amazed that he had such faith in me but I never let him down. Stores and stationery requisitions were another Stationmaster only job, but I even used to sign them for him and we were never queried. With station staff, group staff and signalling staff at the two signal boxes, there were about twelve time-sheets and payrolls to be made out each fortnight and these should have been done by the Assistant Stationmaster at Graham, but again, I was permitted to compile them. All of this was great experience and equipped me well for my studies of Station Accountancy. I felt quite privileged as few others would have a Stationmaster who trusted them as I had.

There was no doubt that 1954 was a better year for me. Carmel and I had become engaged, and in November of that year, I passed with credit the Victorian Railways Institute written examination, in Station Accounts and Management, Junior Grade. I was awarded the Woodruff prize for obtaining the highest marks. The next year, 1955, was shaping to be an even better year. Early on Carmel and I decided on the 24th September for our wedding day. In May I passed my first safe working examination, 'Staff and Ticket' and in June I passed the preliminary 'Assistant Stationmasters' written examination. At about this time it was advertised that there would be a full Stationmasters examination in June the next year. The advice was given early on to allow candidates to step up their study and prepare over a reasonable period of time. The Stationmasters examination was fully written, conducted over two days in the VRI Ballroom at Flinders Street Station. The prerequisites to be eligible to sit for the examination which was only held on an "as required" basis often years apart were - must be at least twenty-one years of age, must hold ticket checkers', first aid, telegraph, and at least one signalling and safe working qualification of Double Line Block or Electric Staff. Before appointment to a Stationmaster's position you must also have passed examination and proved competent to operate an approved interlocked signal frame. Because of the dearth of applicants on this occasion, for the first time, it was later decided to invite candidates who did not hold a telegraph qualification to sit the examination on the clear understanding that even if they passed, they would not be eligible for the appointment to 'Stationmaster' or 'Assistant Class 4, until such time as they qualified in telegraphy. Meanwhile, people who held the telegraph qualification and accepted promotion would gain seniority over those who were yet to qualify. This ruling subsequently advantaged me greatly on the Stationmasters' seniority list and in part, I owed this advantage to my first two

Stationmasters who had advised me so well and encouraged me so much to study.

I was determined to pass the forthcoming Stationmasters examination still at that time about a year ahead, and rarely missed a class of instruction at the VRI at Flinders Street. The class instructor, Mr. Cassell, said to me that he usually was able to get a very young student through at each examination and if I applied myself, he thought I could be the youngest one yet. I was extremely busy with work, study and an approaching marriage. A hiccup occurred when a lady wrote a complaint about my alleged rude conduct. She had come to the booking window during the morning peak to purchase a date to date ticket to Geelong. I quickly calculated the fare and issued her an interim pass as such tickets were not held in stock. Interim passes always had the station of issue printed on them in bold type so when issuing them to save time and perhaps delaying a train it was common practice to write "Here" in the 'station from' space, and in this case Geelong, in the 'station to' space to speed up the transaction. The pass was available for up to ten days in the suburban area and up to fourteen days to country stations after which it was exchanged for the freshly printed ticket which had been requisitioned. The lady came back after seven days and asked for her ticket. I advised her that it had not yet arrived and that she should check again in a few days. As she turned away she proclaimed quite loudly to the women with her, "No wonder the ticket has not arrived, this fool has written 'here' on the pass, how would anyone know where 'here' is?" I know I should have ignored her insulting remark but unfortunately, I instantly retaliated something like "Get yourself some Coles & Garrard's (spectacle makers) madam, the station of issue is printed in bold type just above 'here'". There was no doubt I was guilty of equally insulting remarks albeit under provocation and I readily admitted this. The Stationmaster pointed out in his comments that he had spoken with several business people in the area who all spoke highly of me and had never encountered any rudeness when dealing with me.

Further, only a few months earlier I had passed with credit the 'Station Accounts and Management' examination and any suggestion that I had incorrectly endorsed the pass was not acceptable to him.

The upshot was that I was instructed that under no circumstances should I enter into an altercation with a member of the public in future and should I fail to heed this warning and offend similarly again, disciplinary action would follow.

CARMEL and I married on the 24th September 1955 at 4.30pm in St. Monica's Church, Moonee Ponds. Carmel's bridesmaids were a workmate Maureen, and my cousin Janice. My best man and groomsman were two railway workmates, Sam and Mario. I was some years later, best man for Sam at his wedding.

Our reception was held at "Cidwood" in Wilson Street Moonee Ponds and like the ceremony before it, the reception went off without a hitch. We all had a great time, none more than four bachelor boys from Nyora who travelled down to celebrate with us. Neither Carmel nor I had ever been out of Victoria, save for in Carmel's case, walking over the bridge from Wahgunyah, where her grandparents lived, to Corowa and in my case, walking over the bridge from Mildura to Buronga; so we were quite excited about our planned honeymoon in Sydney.

We left Melbourne on the *Spirit of Progress* the next day and thought we were "toffs" travelling first class with sleeping berths from Albury to Sydney. At that time I was only entitled to a second class pass so I had to pay for the change of class and sleepers.

Carmel about to leave home on our wedding day.

Carmel and Ray leave the church after the ceremony.

I guess by today's standards it might seem pretty dull and low key (two of our grandchildren are married and both had overseas honeymoons), but we had a royal old time in Sydney.

We went to places we had only heard of, and some we had never heard of. Our pass provided on application in Sydney, free train travel in N.S.W. so we did day trips to Katoomba, Newcastle and Nowra, in addition to bus trips to Bondi and Palm Beach, and ferry trips to Manly, Luna Park, Taronga Park and around the Sydney Harbour. We walked over the bridge, visited Kings Cross and many other historical sites in Sydney itself. I don't think we could have enjoyed ourselves more had we gone to Paris or New York. We were only a couple of kids. I was twenty and a half and Carmel turned nineteen nine days after our wedding.

On return from Sydney Carmel and I took up residence in rooms in Gore Street, Fitzroy, just off Victoria Parade. We later moved into rooms in a terrace at 175 Victoria Parade. Carmel went back to her work in Flinders Lane and I returned to North Port station. I passed my examination in the Double Line Block system of safe working in which I had obtained such a good grounding in at the Essendon signal box. I was very proud of the fact that when my certificate of competency arrived it was endorsed, "Not permitted to operate this system until he attains the age of twenty-one years". I now had all the pre-requisites required to sit for the Stationmasters' examination which was scheduled a short time after my twenty first birthday the following year, 1956. In November 1955, I was offered and accepted promotion to Assistant Stationmaster Class 5 at Rosanna. This was possible at my age because there was no safe working involved. Some trains did terminate there under the Electric Staff system on the Heidelberg-Macleod staff, but the driver simply retained the staff until the train returned to Heidelberg. Rosanna was a rapidly growing residential area at this time and the passenger traffic was quite heavy. It was necessary when on afternoon shift, to come on duty for two hours on the Monday morning to open the second booking window for periodical bookings.

6

Married Life

THE MELBOURNE OLYMPIC year of 1956 was an extremely important one for us. In chronological order, I turned twenty-one, bought an FJ Holden utility, passed all subjects of the two day fully written Stationmasters' examination, was promoted to Assistant Stationmaster Class 4 on the Albert Park Group, passed the Electric Staff safe working system examination and on the eighth of October, our first child Joanne was born at the Royal Women's Hospital. It was a great thrill for both of us as she was a beautiful healthy baby. Just after Joanne's birth I transferred from the Albert Park group to Relieving Assistant Stationmaster Class 4 under the Metropolitan Superintendent. I made this move as firstly it meant I could earn more as there were staff shortages at this time and if you wished, on the relieving staff, you could always work thirteen days per fortnightly pay period. We were saving like mad to hasten the day when we could buy our own home. Secondly, I would relieve at a variety of stations right throughout the Metropolitan area and gain further experience to better fit me for later promotion to Stationmaster. Thirdly, I enjoyed meeting new staff at each location and the challenge of the different jobs. Some were straight passenger traffic stations, some had parcels offices, others had goods traffic and goods sidings and some had signal frames in the station office and yet others, had designated signal boxes which were still part of your responsibilities.

Carmel and I thought long and hard about our future as I contemplated a railway career as a Stationmaster. In those days there were virtually only two options open for those being promoted to the grade. Stations were classified from the base grade Class 8 through to Class 1 at provincial cities such as Geelong, Ballarat and Bendigo with Flinders Street and Spencer Street having a classification of Special Class. New appointees were required to go to a country station, often in the Mallee, or go on the relieving staff, as vacancies for Class 8 in the suburban area were filled by transferring people who had already spent some time at country locations, or on the relieving staff. The relieving job meant that you were away from your family sometimes for long periods if a stationmaster was on extended sick leave, or if there was a delay in filling the vacancy you were relieving in. Despite the disadvantages of the relieving position, we decided that when the offer of

Cutting from VR Newsletter re passing the Stationmasters exam just after my 21st birthday.

promotion came, we would take the relieving option, and in time realise our plan to buy our own home in Melbourne. In November 1957, I was promoted to Relieving Stationmaster Class 8, care of the Staff Office, Spencer Street.

7

Life as a Relieving Stationmaster

I WAS VERY conscious of the fact that although I had the necessary qualifications for the position, in many ways these were theoretical, and I lacked practical experience all round, but particularly in the areas of goods accountancy, goods shed operations, yard operations and shunting. These were vital aspects of the Stationmaster's duties at the lower grade country stations where often there were no other staff members and all duties right down to the cleaning were performed by the Stationmaster. Most of my colleagues were very helpful and gave me great encouragement, but there were some who expressed doubt that I could make the grade with only five years' experience, all in the suburban area. This of course made me all the more determined to succeed and it overlooked the fact that I had grown up in a country railway station environment at Nyora. In those days the Stationmaster at country stations in particular was regarded very highly in the local communities. Like the School Principal, Bank Manager and Policeman, he enjoyed some status. Sometimes in a small country town he would be the only official authorised to witness signatures on various documents.

St Kilda station – combination Swing Door and Tait carriage train. Note the driver is resetting the trip apparatus. Ray relieved at St Kilda several times as a lad porter and later as an assistant stationmaster, then as stationmaster. PROV VPRS 12800/P1, Neg H4170. Reproduced with permission of the Keeper of Public Records

Despite the concerns that I may have had about handling the challenge of inexperience in certain aspects of the job, I settled in well and thoroughly enjoyed the new life. Relieving at suburban stations presented no problems at all and when relieving in the country districts, I found that being away from my family, I had time on my hands in off duty hours and when necessary, would go back to the station at night to ensure that all accountancy work was kept up to date. Some jobs of course were much more demanding than others even though they had similar classifications. Foster, in South Gippsland was a case in point. I had two periods of relief there in 1958. The first occasion was filling a vacancy. The second was for annual leave over the Christmas period. The first stint coincided with their superphosphate season which was extremely heavy, and the re-laying of the track from Foster through to

Yarram. At that stage diesels were not permitted beyond Foster, which meant that twice a week a special train consisting of double headed 'T Class" loads of ballast arrived at Foster and terminated. The ballast then had to be fed out as required on the down side on scheduled goods trains creating enormous problems with storage space in the yard, not to mention the extra shunting.

Most nights I would have wagons of ballast or superphosphate stored up on the turntable track, the rest of the yard being full to capacity.

Staff at Foster consisted of a Stationmaster, a Signal Assistant and a Labourer. Virtually all accountancy and clerical work was done by the Stationmaster as well as some of the signalling, safe working and shunting. Foster served a wide area down to Wilsons Promontory not only for farming supplies such as superphosphate, but also foodstuffs and general merchandise all of which went by rail.

When I went back for my second stint that year, I was amazed at the increase in the perishable traffic from earlier in the year. This was brought about by the hundreds of holiday makers who moved into the Wilsons Promontory/Waratah Bay area for the Christmas period.

The general store at Tidal River became the station's biggest customer at that time of the year. I believe that any doubts I had about my ability to manage a station with relatively heavy goods accountancy, shunting and yard work were completely dispelled after my two periods of relief at Foster.

Williamstown Pier pilot at Williamstown. Anne Street signal box at rear. As an RSM I relieved several times at three of the four stations at Williamstown. **PROV VPRS 12800/P1 Neg H 1139 Reproduced with permission of the Keeper of Public Records**

WHILST MOVING around the State I came into contact with many characters. One such fellow was Mr Wally Yole, Stationmaster Class 1 at Williamstown Pier. He had of course a wealth of experience and some time later became Stationmaster at Flinders Street. One morning when I was relieving at Williamstown he called into the office and said that the biggest oil tanker to visit Melbourne would dock at Williamstown Pier that morning and if I would like to see it, I should come down at about 11.00am and he would arrange for us to go on board. I left the Class 2 Booking Porter in charge whilst I went down to the pier. Walking along the pier we noticed a railway tarpaulin had been run over and cut into three pieces by the shunting locomotive. He criticised the shunters for not having moved it clear and then said something like, "It is Wednesday today, the day that the Commissioners do suburban inspections. I had better get rid of it. Give me a hand to roll up the pieces." He then rolled each piece over the side of the pier, saying as the last piece fell into the water, "Dead men tell no tales." I suppose there was a lesson in this for me but I thought that the pieces should have been retained and used for other purposes.

During my three years on the relieving staff, I was promoted to Relieving Stationmaster Class 7 in early 1959 and I learnt a lot about life in general. I met and dealt with a diversity of people including dairy and cattle farmers, sheep farmers, grain growers, orchardists, grape growers, timber mill operators, timber and sleeper cutters, general business men and women and the public generally. The rail at that time was still a "common carrier" and had to accept all freight offered. All grain produced, by law, had to go by rail except of course for local journeys and all groceries, beer and general merchandise to country areas went by rail. I worked at stations as widely apart as Nowa Nowa in the South East, Port Fairy in the South West, Wahgunyah in the North East and Goroke in the North West, and many other places in between. I usually stayed at the hotel nearest the station and have fond memories of many of them. Probably my favourite location was Murchison East where I worked for several weeks over Christmas/New Year period in 1959/1960. It was the junction for Colbinabbin and Girgarre lines and my stay coincided with the wheat harvest overflow period, the overflow being the tonnage of wheat forecast in excess of the capacity of the local silos. Staff at Murchison East consisted of two Assistant Stationmasters Class 4, one Porter/Guard, one Engine Driver and his Fireman. We had a D3 steam locomotive to make up and run the branch line services. Trains were scheduled to Girgarre on each Monday and Thursday and to Colbinabbin each

Wednesday, but during the overflow period we ran two extra services to Colbinabbin each week.

I REALLY ENJOYED the work at Murchison East as it involved a lot of shunting, assembling branch line trains and sorting loading off the branch line to be picked up later in the night by the main line goods trains. Apparently, there had been considerable difficulty the previous wheat season in obtaining a regular and adequate number of empty wagons for both Murchison East and Colbinabbin, but luck was with us this season, and the supply of empty wagons was very good. Somehow the Silo Manager and the Publican, who took a keen interest in what was going on across the road at the rail yard and what he heard from his wheat farmer customers, seemed to think the improved wagon supply had something to do with me being there and every night when I finished work, there would be a pot of beer sitting on the bar for me when I returned to the hotel. Their belief was completely fallacious and I told them so. All I could do was report the statistics and order the wagons. I had no control over the number of wagons subsequently supplied, but they could not be convinced. I did a little bit of 'moonlighting' at Murchison East as some nights after the evening meal the publican's wife would ask me to take over the bar when she considered her husband was too drunk to continue serving. On my last night at the hotel they gave me a little "send-off", which was really a great surprise as I had only been there about eight weeks. I had never experienced anything like that at any other of the many locations at which I had relieved.

It was now time to seriously consider my future in the railways. I was really conscious of the fact that being away from home for relatively long periods on a regular basis was grossly unfair to Carmel, even though she never really complained.

Stations at which I worked as a Lad Porter

NOTE: I always made myself available to work at other locations on my off-Roster days, thus increasing my earnings.

Essendon, Glenbervie, Strathmore, Pascoe Vale, Moonee Ponds, Ascot Vale, South Kensington, Anstey, Yarraville, Richmond, St Kilda, Dandenong Parcels Office, East Richmond, Elsternwick, Jolimont, North Port.

Stations at which I worked as an Assistant Stationmaster

Rosanna, Albert Park, South Melbourne, North Melbourne, Middle Park, Graham, Gardenvale, Balaclava, Ascot Vale, Kensington, South Yarra, Prahran, Hawksburn, Armadale, Malvern, Gardiner, Hawthorn, Glenferrie, East Camberwell, Nunawading, Mitcham, Ringwood, Belgrave, Lilydale, North Richmond, Collingwood, Clifton Hill, Alphington, Northcote, Croxton, Thornbury, Bell, Royal Park, Moreland, Tottenham, St Albans, Yarraville, Williamstown Beach, Williamstown, St Kilda.

Stations at which I relieved clerks

Flinders Street 'A' & 'C' Booking Offices, Sunshine Goods Office, Sale Goods Shed, Caulfield, Essendon, Richmond, Moonee Ponds.

Stations at which I relieved as Stationmaster

Trentham, Spotswood, Anderson (4 times), Foster (2), Royal Park (3), Loch, Kensington, Newmarket, Ascot Vale, Show Grounds, Footscray, West Footscray, St Albans, Goroke (2), Yarraville, North Williamstown, Williamstown Beach (2), Williamstown, Graham, South Melbourne, St Kilda, Windsor,

Ripponlea, Brighton Beach, Lindenow (2), Bunyip (3), Malvern, Cheltenham, Aspendale, Edithvale, Stony Point, Carnegie, Murrumbeena, Nowa Nowa, Heyfield, Cranbourne, Burnley, Burnley Goods, Tooronga, East Malvern (3), Glen Waverley (3), Lilydale, Fitzroy Goods & Public Weighbridge (2), West Richmond, Alphington, Northcote, Bell, Thomastown, Jewell, Brunswick, Moreland, Coburg, Flinders Street, Murchison East, Port Fairy, Mooroopna, Daylesford, Wahgunyah, Tatura, Thornbury, Westgarth.

Total 125 locations in different capacities. Once qualified in an interlocked signal frame, you tended to get sent back to those locations as required.

THERE HAD BEEN two wonderful life changing events in late 1958. On the 25th October we were blessed with the birth of our second child, a beautiful healthy daughter we called Rhonda. Shortly after, we bought our first home, a modest three-bedroom, weatherboard at 30 Fenacre Street, Strathmore.

I had earlier told the Stationmasters' relief clerk the anticipated date of Rhonda's arrival and he assured me he would keep me in the suburban area for a few weeks over that period. He obviously overlooked this however when he sent me to Tatura to cover sick leave shortly before the due date. I was reluctant to remind him of my situation, stupid as that may seem now, as I didn't want to create the impression that I was pushing some of my country work onto others. I was hoping he would remember and pull me out. When nothing happened after a few days I had no alternative but to ring him. He apologised profusely and sent relief up the next day. Rhonda was born three days after I arrived home. I recall it clearly as Carmel was experiencing pains in the evening but did not want to go to hospital too early. I sat up with her knowing that I had to go to Aspendale to open up the station and signal box for the first train. She finally agreed to go to the Royal Women's' Hospital around the three o'clock mark. Our first daughter Joanne was with my mother while Carmel was hospitalised. Rhonda was born at 7.30am that morning.

WE SHIFTED into our new home early in 1959 - Carmel, me and the two girls. I'll never forget the wonderful feeling that we were at last in our own home. Financially it had been a real struggle. At that time the bank would only loan a percentage of their valuation which was always less than the actual sale price. This meant that you had to have a fairly substantial deposit to make up the difference. Carmel's mother and father had a few years before, bought their house at Pascoe Vale with finance being provided through the Coburg Co-operative Housing Society. On her dad's advice we had been wait listed for membership of the Housing Co-operative for some time and were fortunate to eventually obtain most of the required finance through that organisation, whose rules for a loan were less stringent than those of the banks. The price of the house and land was three thousand, nine hundred pounds. We had saved a deposit of nine hundred pounds and the Co-op was prepared to loan two thousand, eight hundred pounds. The balance, or second mortgage, was arranged at a much higher interest rate through a solicitor and had to be paid off within two years. I was quite concerned at the time about our ability to pay this off as although my income was adequate, provided we stuck to a very tight budget, it did depend on a lot of overtime which might not always be available. Carmel of course had not gone to work since a couple of months before Joanne was born. The concern however was unfounded as we were able to pay off the second mortgage in about fifteen months. Shortly after we moved in we received notice that the road would be made and each land owner would have to pay their share. This was good news particularly as the Council would finance it allowing us to pay it off through the rates system.

At that time my ambition in the Railways was to become a senior Stationmaster at Flinders Street or Spencer Street, but this would take a lifetime if I went off the relieving staff as for family reasons I knew I must do. We had previously settled for home ownership in the suburbs rather than frequent transfers from one country station to another to obtain promotion.

Our home at Strathmore shortly before we shifted to Gisborne.

THE SOLUTION to the problem seemed to be to seek promotion to either Train Controller or Traffic Inspector. Appointed Stationmasters who became Train Controllers remained on the Stationmasters' seniority list until offered a Stationmaster Class 4 position. If he knocked it back and remained a Train Controller his seniority was no longer carried forward. Alternatively, if you were promoted to Traffic Inspector your Stationmaster seniority was carried forward until Class 1. This seemed to be an ideal solution for me as it kept open the option to become a senior Stationmaster a few years later, should I desire to do so. I was quite proud of my performance as a Relieving Stationmaster having often relieved at locations with classifications much higher than mine. I once went to Footscray which had a Class 3 rating, supposedly to fill in for a couple of days but remained there for two weeks during which time all end of the month work including the Account Current was satisfactorily completed. At Lilydale, then a class 4 classification, I took over from Mr. Jack Beddoe when he retired. The significance of this was that when I joined the railways in 1952, he was the Stationmaster at my home town, Nyora.

I WAS ALWAYS determined to give my wife and children much better living conditions and opportunities in life than our family had, and the improved economic conditions now, a generation later, helped make this possible. Hence, I was keen to seek promotion as it would increase my earning capacity thus making it possible for our kids to pursue not only a good education, but also to take advantage of any special talents they might have, or to chase their dreams so to speak. This had not been possible in the circumstances experienced by my family and many, many others in our generation. For instance, Carmel, after obtaining her Merit Certificate (Year Eight) wanted to do a commercial course including typing and shorthand as a couple of her friends were doing, but her family could not afford it so she had to go to work and pay board out of her small pay packet.

8

Train Control

I MADE the application for promotion to both Train Controller and Traffic Inspector and was subsequently transferred to Head Office, Spencer Street, to learn the suburban train control system in September, 1960. The learning involved a full round of shifts sitting in with an experienced controller, then a weeks' travelling during which time you visited key operating points such as Jolimont Yard, the drivers and guards rostering depot, Flinders Street platforms at peak periods and key signal boxes in the suburban area. To be an efficient suburban controller it was absolutely essential to have a sound knowledge of the geography of the suburban area, facilities at terminal and junction stations, locations of wired crossovers and wired sidings and the types of signalling and safe working systems in use on each line. Personal attributes required included the ability to quickly analyse a problem situation, make a decision on the most expedient way to deal with it so that delays and cancellations are minimized and localized, and make clear and concise directions to staff concerned to implement a recovery plan. At all times the safety welfare and interests of the travelling public are paramount. The Train Controller's decisions during service disruptions should reflect this. Delays could very quickly spread to other lines if swift, positive action could not be implemented and trains and crews were out of position because of late running and cancellations. Causes of disruptions were many and varied, including equipment failures, accidents, suicides, human error, vandalism, fires, floods, lightning strikes and industrial action amongst others.

One of the most novel and memorable incidents I recall as a Suburban Train Controller occurred in late shift on the Broadmeadows line, when a Melbourne bound electric train was derailed near the Pascoe Vale Road level crossing at Strathmore, (now a road overpass), due to striking and killing an elephant which had escaped from a circus located on the nearby Cross Keys oval. I had seen the circus tent, vehicles and animals when travelling to work that afternoon so I did not question the report, strange as it was, when it came in. We had a direct line to D24 (police) and when I relayed the information to the officer there he immediately asked "Have you been drinking?" He had some difficulty for a few moments accepting that the report was genuine. This resulted in train services being suspended between Essendon and Broadmeadows for a considerable period while the train was re-railed and the dead elephant removed. Fortunately, it was after the evening peak so substitute buses were able to cope reasonably well. The *Daylight Express* from Sydney (on broad gauge from Albury in those days) had to be re-routed around the goods loop from Broadmeadows to Albion thence into Spencer Street that way. Given the widespread use of nick-names within the railway fraternity it is no surprise that the Electric Train Driver involved in this incident became "Sabu, the elephant boy". I settled into the suburban train control job fairly quickly and was able to cope with the almost daily dramas involved quite well. I have no doubt that my early grounding in train running as a block recorder at Essendon Signal Box, and later years on the relieving staff as an Assistant Stationmaster and then Stationmaster where I gained an intimate knowledge of operations at many suburban stations and signal boxes, equipped me well for this position. I thoroughly enjoyed the challenges of the job.

My early days in Suburban Control had been somewhat distracted as on the 4th November 1960, our third daughter, Sharon was born at Vaucluse Hospital in Brunswick. She was perfectly healthy as was Carmel. My mother looked after Joanne and Rhonda while Carmel was hospitalized. It was a great feeling however, knowing that I would be home with them even though I was working shifts, and would not be required to be away from home as I had previously when Rhonda was born. Carmel would certainly have her hands full with three children under school age.

Photo of train controller J Martin, 15.1.1948. Suburban Train Control Desk at Spencer St Head Office. Source PROV VPRS 12800/P1, Neg H591. Reproduced with permission of the Keeper of Public Records.

Suburban train controllers were classified as Class 3, country controllers at Seymour, Bendigo, Ballarat, Ararat and Geelong as Class 2 and controllers located in Head Office who controlled traffic on the country lines between Melbourne, Seymour, Bendigo, Ballarat, Geelong and the Gippsland lines beyond Dandenong were classified as Class 1. The new standard gauge line Albury to Melbourne was scheduled to be completed and commence operation in 1962. This would require four additional Class 1 positions to operate the Centralized Traffic Control system of signalling and safe working between Wodonga and Melbourne. The points and signals at all the crossing loops en route would be operated remotely from a control room in Head Office. These new additional positions would normally be filled by the transfer and promotion of suitable Class 2 Train Controllers from the country. Things were moving a bit too quick for my family because this meant that to get people trained and in position for the additional Class 1 jobs some Class 3 people would be required to transfer to country Class 2 positions. We had settled into our new home with our young family quite well and were extremely happy. We certainly did not wish to shift anywhere at that time, but the dilemma was that I also did not want to knock back the opportunity of promotion which on the longer term, would benefit my family due to increased earning capacity.

In late 1961, I was offered promotion to either Bendigo or Ararat with a departmental residence at either location. After much discussion and deliberation, and on inspection of the house available in Golden Square, we very reluctantly decided to accept Bendigo. The thinking was that in all probability we would not be there very long before promotion became available back in Melbourne, and in the meantime, we could rent out our Strathmore home. A series of events which were completely unforeseen then took place which altered the whole landscape. Firstly, two candidates for suburban train controller's positions pulled out about halfway through their training periods. Then one class 2 man who had accepted promotion to class 1 decided not to proceed with it, and yet another one could not get a recommendation from his District Superintendent as to his suitability for promotion. This exacerbated the problem of getting people in position and trained for the additional jobs on the new standard gauge board.

A week or so after, the learner I had with me decided not to proceed with his training to become a Train Controller. I was on afternoon shift on the South Suburban board when Mr. Kenny, the Chief Train Controller entered the room. He said that since it was reasonably quiet, he wanted to have a talk with me. He stated that he had been asked by the Staff Office to give an opinion on whether I would be suitable for promotion from Class 3 to Class 1, without having experience at class 2 in one of the country districts. He further stated he had been quite happy with my performance as a Train Controller and had no hesitation in recommending me for such promotion, should it work out that way. I felt quite flattered and excited as if it came about, it would mean that we would not have to leave our home that we were so happy with. He went on to say that because of my experience as a Stationmaster and now Train Controller at such a young age, he thought that there could be quite a bright future for me for further promotion, provided I continued to apply myself and take opportunities as they came along.

The conversation with Mr. Kenny certainly motivated me and made me even more diligent if that was possible, in discharging my duties as a Train Controller. It meant a lot to me to take promotion, but it would mean a lot more to my family if we did not have to shift out of our own home. We now had to be patient and await the final decisions on transfers and promotions required to fill the four new positions. Meanwhile on the home front, we received notice that sewerage work had been completed and house owners in our street could make arrangements to connect up. This was good news and we immediately obtained quotes from three different plumbers to carry out the work. In each case I asked what the savings would be if I dug the required trenches myself. Two of them said they would not allow the home owner to dig the trench, but the third one would give a discount of twenty-five pounds ($50.00). As the quotes were all about the same we gave him the job.

It may seem strange in this day and age to take on such a job for the sake of $50.00, but at that time it was not an insignificant amount. After all we had a mortgage, three kids, and were saving to carpet some rooms. Initially the house had polished boards only. Moreover, I was on shift work and had time at home during the day. The trench started at the side of the home, (kitchen sink) went halfway across the back of the house (taking in the toilet, bathroom and laundry), then to the easement at the back of the block. At the start it was 18 inches deep and then tapered to 4 feet deep at the easement. I was on night shift and being favoured by good weather dug it within the week. Our eldest daughter Joanne had the time of her life running along the trench disappearing out of sight as she neared the deeper end. Today no doubt having her on the work site would be considered a safety issue, but life was different then. I recall I was anxious to get the job finished and the back yard cleaned up and restored in case the transfer to Bendigo eventuated making it necessary to rent the house out.

Time over the next several weeks really dragged waiting for news of whether we would have to move or not. The decision had been complicated due to one Class 3 man who was senior to me in the grade and had previously declined promotion, saying he would now accept promotion, if he could go straight to class 1. After what seemed an eternity, the decision came through in my favour. We were so happy, but I was mindful of the fact that I would need to perform really well at class 1 level to obtain 'confirmation' of my appointment and justify the confidence the Chief Train Controller had shown in me. It had been decided to alter the traditional groupings of the class 1 jobs when the standard gauge board took effect. To this end I learned the Geelong and South East which were temporarily together due to space constraints, and the Bendigo and Ballarat. Ultimately the groupings were to be Standard Gauge standing alone, Bendigo and Seymour, Eastern and South Eastern, Geelong and Ballarat. All class 1 controllers were required to learn and be competent in the Standard Gauge board primarily to cover weekend rosters when other rooms were closed and switched into it. I was to spend the next three years operating on the Geelong-Ballarat board with an occasional shift on the Standard Gauge.

The country Train Controller's job was entirely different to the suburban job. The Geelong line was a single track between Newport South and Corio with manned signal boxes, and crossing facilities at Laverton, Werribee, Manor, Little River and Lara. There were remote controlled crossing loops at Rock, controlled by Newport South, and Drome, controlled by Werribee. The safe working system was Automatic and Track Control (A.T.C.), otherwise known as the 'Geelong System'. The Train Controller was not only responsible for arranging the priority of trains, the clearance of loading, the supply of empty wagons, the changeover of engine crews and guards, as per the award ensuring engine crews had sufficient standing time to partake of a meal within the appropriate hours, the arranging of relief crews where late running or delays occurred, arranging substitute services when necessary due to equipment failures, accidents, fires and floods, alerting appropriate authorities, technical staff and emergency staff when their services were required, but when signal failures occurred giving authority for the signalman to issue a caution order for a train to pass a defective home departure signal at the stop position by the exchange of messages written and repeated back. The A.T.C. system of safe working varied from the traditional systems as the rules clearly stated it operated under the direction of the Train Controller.

The Ballarat line was also a single line between Sunshine and Warrenheip. The safe working system was Electric Staff (token system) except for the Bacchus Marsh-Ballan section where a remotely controlled crossing loop at Bank Box had replaced the old crossing facility at Ingliston and was controlled by the signalman at Bacchus Marsh under the Centralised Traffic Control system (C.T.C.). The infrastructure along this route was hopelessly inadequate for the volume and type of traffic being handled. With few exceptions, crossing loops generally were too short to accommodate the interstate express freight trains for crossing purposes. It was common practice to hold passenger trains or shorter local freight trains at the platform or in the yard until the interstate freight train, which was being held at the home arrival signal on the main line, then passed through. Contrary to traditional practice, the freight train got priority over the passenger train in such circumstances, simply because there was insufficient room to put the freight train aside.

All kinds of traffic had to be catered for on the Ballarat line. Apart from the aforementioned interstate freight trains, there was the interstate passenger train (*The Overland*) with a second division operating during holiday periods, commuter services from Bacchus Marsh, coal trains from Bacchus Marsh, intrastate passenger services, fast intrastate goods services and roadside goods services. There were also switch trips from Bacchus Marsh to Parwan because of the ruling grade between the two locations. Half the coal train would be taken up to Parwan and then the locomotive would return for the second half. On arrival back at Parwan the two sections would be joined together making one train to Melbourne. Although policy dictated that priority wherever possible be given to passenger trains, ironically this was often impossible with the rail motor which operated primarily for students from Ballan to Ballarat each morning and return each afternoon. Because it operated against the general flow of traffic at very congested times it was a near impossible task to find or force a path for it. A minor activity that also caused train controllers much frustration and interrupted the efficient flow of traffic was van goods time on goods trains discharging cream cans for the Wallace butter factory.

Looking back, it never ceases to amaze me the volume of all kinds of traffic handled on both the single lines to Geelong and Ballarat. Wheat and grain traffic from the North East including Oaklands and Tocumwal in N.S.W. and a proportion of the grain traffic from north of Bendigo went to Geelong via the Brooklyn loop. There were train loads of cement and superphosphate coming out of Geelong. Livestock trains operated as required on both the Ballarat and Geelong lines. The intensity of the work was such that often you did not get around to eating the sandwiches or meal you had brought with you. Often a colleague would make a pot of tea and bring you a cup, but so intense was your concentration on the job that it was often left to go cold. I compare the scenario then to that of today, where the Geelong line has been duplicated with the bi-directional signalling. The new standard gauge line to Adelaide goes via Geelong taking all the interstate freight trains off the Ballarat line, and in fact the latter line operates almost exclusively for passenger traffic. The amount of intrastate freight traffic handled on the system now is quite minimal although of course the volume of passenger traffic to the provincial cities has increased.

The time spent as a train controller was invaluable to me in shaping my railway career. Much of the knowledge and experience gained in what was commonly referred to as the 'nerve centre of railways' could not be gained elsewhere, and therefore, I believe, people who had this experience behind them had an advantage over those who didn't. A small, but important part of this was that not only did senior officers of the Traffic Branch seek information on train running each morning from you, but also those from other Branches and sometimes Commissioners. The Chairman of Commissioners, Mr. George Brown, visited the Chief Train Controller's office most mornings and sometimes came into the rooms. This gave you an interesting background into their thinking and policies which sometimes conflicted. It was useful to have been exposed to this and to 'take it with you', an opportunity to learn the 'Head Office' culture that those outside did not have. At first, I found the class 1 job fairly heavy going, but after a couple of rounds of shifts I had settled in and was able to cope quite well.

On informing me that he was pleased with my performance on the Geelong-Ballarat board, and that my appointment to class 1 would be confirmed, Mr. Kenny further stated that he felt I should now be looking beyond Train Control for future promotion. He felt that I should be aspiring to senior positions in the Traffic Branch with on the long term eventual Head of Branch status in mind. He then sounded a note of warning. He said times were certainly changing and in the years ahead it might not be possible to become Head of Branch (Chief Traffic Manager) on the basis of internal railway qualifications backed up with experience and proven performance records in senior Branch positions as had traditionally been the case. He felt the Branch might already be at a disadvantage because its leader could not always match it with his peers who had tertiary qualifications in such disciplines as engineering, commerce, accountancy or finance. They therefore were better able to argue their case and support their submissions with facts and figures, when trying to convince the Commissioners, or Minister of Transport of the value of particular projects competing for limited funds. He felt that because Traffic Branch employees rarely had outside qualifications better than intermediate standard, it was likely that future Chief Traffic Managers could be recruited from other Branches, other railway systems, or even outside industry. I should therefore think long and hard about embarking on a course of studies which would give me the pre-requisites to do tertiary courses later.

I was somewhat bewildered as I had no idea that he rated me so highly as a train controller, or that he thought I had the potential to aspire to senior positions in the Branch, or even to

Head of the Branch. Up to that time such thoughts had never entered my head. The conversation with Mr. Kenny was continuously on my mind over the next week or so. I just couldn't believe that a person I had only known for a little more than two years had formed such an opinion of me, and of course it was not a matter I could discuss with other railway colleagues. Our next-door neighbour at Strathmore, Barney Egan, was a teacher at the local High School. I decided to approach Barney to get his thoughts on how I should go about commencing studies the following year at Intermediate level (year 10.)

Yet another shock was in store for me. Barney said it would be a waste of time and effort to do intermediate. He believed at twenty-seven years of age with experience of life generally, including over thirteen years in the workforce, my ability to concentrate and absorb information would be far superior to most teenage students, and therefore I should start at the then School Leaving level (year 11 now.) He said provided passes were obtained in two subjects when studying part time, you could hold them to the following year, when to get the School Leaving Certificate, I would need to do three more subjects. He was teaching Economics and Commercial Principles and would provide me with the papers to study straight away. There were still a few months of the school year left, and he felt I would be able to swat up and pass these subjects by examination time. Anything I was having difficulty with I could bring to him. Barney had a saying it was no good knowing people "if you did not use them" and I certainly did use him, as the occasion demanded.

Barney's prediction turned out to be quite accurate and I was able to pass the two subjects, Economics and Commercial Principles, at the end of the year examinations. The next year I chose English, British History and European History to complete the requirements for the School Leaving Certificate. The local High School had night classes for English, but I had to do the other two subjects by correspondence with Taylors Business College. Inconvenient as it was studying with three young kids in the house and working shifts (night shift every fourth week), I knuckled down and actually enjoyed it. I felt a sense of achievement having passed the two subjects in a short space of time and this had motivated me to keep going. The fact that Mr. Kenny kept checking on my progress and encouraging me also helped greatly, as apart from the self-satisfaction I was experiencing, there was no way in the world that I would let him down by failing at the end of the year, or not completing the course. Nevertheless, it was a great relief when the study year was over and I received notification that I had passed the three subjects thus giving me the School Leaving Certificate.

Mr. Kenny quickly pointed out to me that Matriculation (Year 12) was the required entry standard for university courses and now that I had established that I could study part time, and could be successful, it was a must that I keep going. Meanwhile, the Chartered Institute of Transport in conjunction with the Royal Melbourne Institute of Technology had offered a four-year course titled Transport Administration. Exemptions were given for English and Economics for students who had passed these subjects at Matriculation level. I discussed the possibility of doing this course with both Mr. Kenny and Barney Egan. We came to the conclusion that I should register for the Transport Administration Course but do the English and Economic subjects at Matriculation level, rather than at the Transport Administration course level, as I then would be halfway toward Matriculating.

I registered for English Expression at University High School night class, History of Transport at R.M.I.T. and Barney provided me with the papers he set for his students in Economics at Matriculation level. At the end of a fairly tough year I passed all three subjects. But a much tougher year was ahead in 1966. I was in too deep now to pull out of the education trip I had embarked on, but the situation had become complicated due to me being offered and accepting promotion to the position of Traffic Inspector in the metropolitan area in

September 1965. This meant that in 1966 1 would be still settling in to the new job as Inspector in addition to doing three subjects in the Transport Course at R.M.I.T., and the final two subjects I had chosen to complete my Matriculation, British History and Social Studies, which I did by correspondence with Taylors. This was without doubt one of the toughest years of my life, but somehow, someway, I got through it all successfully. I now had my full Matriculation qualification and had also completed two years of the Transport Administration course at R.M.I.T. I had also received confirmation of my appointment to the position of Traffic Inspector earlier in the year. In order to complete the Transport Administration qualification, I needed to successfully complete three subjects a year over the next two years. Tough as it was, I was able to do so and completed the course successfully in 1968.

Matriculation Examination

THE VICTORIAN UNIVERSITIES AND SCHOOLS EXAMINATIONS BOARD

This is to Certify that

RAYMOND THOMAS BARDEN

at the Matriculation Examination held in the years indicated passed in the following   FOUR   subjects

DECEMBER, 1965 : 1. ENGLISH EXPRESSION
                 2. ECONOMICS
DECEMBER, 1966 : 1. BRITISH HISTORY
                 2. SOCIAL STUDIES

thereby passing the Matriculation Examination

The passing of the Matriculation Examination does not in itself necessarily satisfy the University entrance requirements of the Board.

Secretary

Certificate – Matriculation Exam.

9

Traffic Inspector

THE DUTIES of the Traffic Inspector were many and varied. He was in fact a bridge between the field managers, the Stationmasters and Senior Branch Management, but his role was often maligned by the disaffected, or discontented, who saw him as a type of policeman not to be trusted. However, the vast majority of Stationmasters who were competent and diligent had nothing to fear from the Inspector and in fact would welcome you to their station. Inspections involved checks of station accounts and returns, checks of station cleanliness, checks of progress of junior staff and the general performance of other staff, checks of overtime wagons, goods or parcels, interviewing staff to establish their suitability to transfer to positions they had applied for, check that rosters as they stood were still appropriate for the duties to be performed and if not, discuss with the Stationmaster before recommending changes, and examining staff competency in ticket checking, booking and other duties.

In times of disruptions to traffic due to accidents, equipment failures and other emergency situations the Inspector was required to immediately go to the scene and take charge.

Flinders Street Station, main entrance. Photo, Adrian Ponton.

He would make frequent and regular contact with the Train Controller to report progress and update the estimate of when normal traffic might resume. Disruptions caused by natural occurrences such as fires, floods, landslips or equipment failures were stressful enough, trying to minimize the delays to passengers using substitute bus services, some of whom became quite agitated and aggressive, but the stress level was even higher where fatalities had occurred (suicides were common) and even worse still, when the victims were seriously injured, perhaps had lost a limb, but still conscious and caught beneath a train, or in a crushed vehicle. I was fortunate in that I was able to cope with the stress of these situations fairly well and did not allow it to affect my judgement in the discharge of my duties, or to carry over to my off-duty hours.

Jolimont Railyards viewed from Swanston Street. PROV, VPRS 12800 P3 ADW 1063

Other responsibilities of the Traffic Inspector, depending on what shift he was working, included supervising peak traffic at Flinders Street platforms, conducting special race traffic from Flinders Street and return traffic from Flemington, Caulfield and Sandown and conducting return football traffic from suburban stations at Moorabbin, Victoria Park, West Footscray, Essendon, Richmond and Jolimont. Richmond was always a challenge, at finals matches in particular, ensuring the special trains allocated were brought to the platforms at the optimum time, thus maximizing crowd clearance and minimizing delays to regular services. Overcrowding or crushes on platforms could very quickly become a safety issue. It was always difficult to accurately judge the time that a match would finish. I enjoyed very much opening up the Flemington Race Course line to conduct night trotting traffic at the Showgrounds and was lucky enough to act as Stationmaster Show

Grounds for two Royal Shows which I found to be a pleasant diversion from the grind of the Inspector's usual duties. I also enjoyed very much acting as Stationmaster at Flinders Street when on late shift from 9.00pm till the last train and picking up a full Sunday shift as Stationmaster Flinders Street when rostered. A uniform had to be worn when performing Stationmaster's duties.

DURING THE PERIOD I was a Traffic Inspector under the Metropolitan Superintendent I was allocated responsibility at different times for three different sections. Initially I had responsibility for the Eastern section which comprised the Epping, Hurstbridge, Warburton, Healesville, Belgrave, Alamein and Glen Waverley lines. After a few months in the position the Metropolitan Superintendent called me to his office and asked me would I have any objection to taking over the Northern section which comprised the Upfield, Broadmeadows, St. Albans, Werribee, Altona and Williamstown Pier lines. This section took in the large marshalling yards at Tottenham and Newport, the Brooklyn loop sidings, the Somerton sidings and Ford works at Upfield, Maribyrnong sidings and Newmarket livestock sidings. Mr. McInnes thought it would be advantageous to me living in my section at Strathmore, but also because of my Train Control experience on the Geelong and Ballarat boards in particular, I had a much better appreciation of the marshalling yards and their problems than would an officer without such experience. I readily accepted this move.

The third section I was allocated to in 1967 was the day shift job at Flinders Street, Spencer Street, plus the St. Kilda and Port Melbourne lines. Although a very compact section it was also quite challenging. It involved almost daily liaison with the Stationmasters at Flinders Street and Spencer Street, the Yardmaster at Jolimont yard and the O.I.C. at the Guards Depot, Jolimont. The correspondence component of this job was extremely heavy involving public complaints about performance of staff in both the parcels and passenger areas, trains docking late to the platforms from the yard, signalman's errors, guards not in position due to misreading their rosters, cash shortages in the various booking offices and a host of other miscellaneous matters which were forever arising in this labour-intensive area.

NO MATTER what section he was operating in, a large and disproportionate amount of the Inspectors time was taken up with public complaints. It was the policy of the department at that time for all complaints appertaining to Traffic Branch operations or employees, to be referred to the appropriate Traffic Inspector for his investigation and settlement with the complainant. The prime objective of this policy was to avoid whenever possible the necessity to reply to the complainant in writing. Rather, the Inspector was to initially make contact by telephone and if possible, settle the complaint. After clarification of certain points, a full explanation of the situation that obtained at the time and an apology if appropriate. An offer was usually made to visit the person for a more detailed interview, either at their home, or at their place of work should they desire. It was amazing the number of complaints which were settled on the telephone but of course a considerable amount of valuable time had always been expended beforehand interviewing staff, obtaining written statements and gaining a full appreciation of where our staff or systems had failed. Some complaints were of a most serious nature, others were minor or frivolous, but in my experience, the majority of them were justified. There were occasions, fairly rare, when the Inspector could not finalise the complaint but in the vast majority of cases he did and was able to complete his report by stating:

The complainant was satisfied with the investigation and explanation and does not require any further communication on the matter.

The Traffic Inspectors' responsibilities were many and varied and particularly in the Metropolitan area, extremely demanding. He operated alone and often felt very lonely and highly challenged. The sheer volume of work and the fact that it was extremely difficult to get discussion time and clear direction from superiors brought this about. In contrast, the Inspector in a country district spent many hours each week travelling with his Superintendent and his correspondence load was much, much lighter. He often had his Superintendent with him when performing station inspections and interviews and almost always had his superior with him when attending derailments or accident scenes. I believe that many of the duties that fell the way of the Metropolitan Inspector could have, and should have, been performed by the Stationmaster. Surely the Stationmaster should have been the officer to examine a learner clerk to establish his competence in booking or goods duties. Likewise, his recommendations in most cases, as to whether an employee was suitable for promotion should have been accepted without the necessity for the Inspector to interview the person concerned and make a further recommendation. The supervising of special traffic in many cases could also have been left to the Stationmaster instead of the Inspector taking over. I always recall how irate Mr. Davis at Essendon used to get as he remained in his office whilst the Traffic Inspector handled the return football traffic on No. 1 platform.

THE TRAFFIC INSPECTOR was sometimes made the scapegoat when things went wrong and it is little wonder that many officers appointed in the Metropolitan area failed to have their appointments confirmed and others, after a short time in the position decided that the job was not for them. This wastage was really not surprising as prior to 1973, there was no training course for aspirants who with few exceptions, came from the grade of Stationmaster, or Train Controllers who had previous experience as Stationmasters. Mostly they were recruited from the base or lower classifications of Stationmasters so they lacked experience. Some appointed to the Metropolitan area had no experience as Stationmasters other than in the country. The salary was around the middle range of classification for Stationmasters so it was not an attraction for the more senior and experienced people in that grade. The only "learning" the new recruit Inspector was given was a few days in Head Office where they had discussions with senior 'Traffic' Branch officers and others such as the Claims Agent, followed by one week in the field with an appointed Inspector. I recall at one time speaking to Mr. James, the then Chief Traffic Manager, about the selection and training of Traffic Inspectors but he said he preferred the 'sink or swim' method. He claimed that by throwing them in at the deep end it very quickly separated the men from the boys. I believed it was a very necessary and long overdue change of thinking, when after Mr. Crute became Chief Traffic Manager; he initiated a training course for aspiring Inspectors.

10

Into Middle Management

IN LATE 1967 I was called to Head Office where the Chief Traffic Manager Mr. James told me he needed a handy man to do some foot work for him and implement various ideas that he had. He thought that I could fit the bill. If I was interested I would remain in the grade of Traffic Inspector, but to give me a bit of 'clout' when out and about, I was to use the title of Personal Assistant to the Chief Traffic Manager. I was quite apprehensive about this but of course could not afford to knock back the opportunity. I would be located in his office. Shortly after I was transferred. There was no job description and I found great difficulty in settling in on a day to day basis. I felt embarrassed on occasions when interviews took place with staff members or senior officers and left the room as I felt I was eavesdropping. Clearly Mr. James had not thought the job out. He would give me tasks on an ad hoc basis sometimes emanating from correspondence that he was signing, or from a report he had just read. There were times when I had nothing to work on. Once I recall he was reading train running performances prior to the District Superintendents Conference, and out of the blue he said, "I want you to review through and connecting rail motor services throughout the state and where they are running late consistently, put another five minutes into their schedules."

This was clearly a job for the then Superintendent of Train Services (later titled Manager of Passenger Operations), who was responsible for timetabling and train control and was also the officer that District Superintendents reported to on train running and timekeeping matters. It was the responsibility of his Timetable Officers to review and analyse timekeeping in their respective sections, highlighting poor performance and making recommendations for corrective action. I immediately sensed I was between a rock and a hard place as the Train Services people would feel I was 'white anting' them but Mr. James would want results. He had spent some time as Superintendent of Train Services himself and was very critical at times of the performance of the division. It was an old trick to put a margin or 'tail' into the schedule of a train to statistically improve the timekeeping performance but that did nothing for our customers. Their journey to the terminal had been lengthened in terms of time and those detraining at intermediate stations would still be late. If the extra time was spread over the entire journey the rail motor would be waiting time at intermediate stations on occasions when there had been no incidents to absorb the extra time.

I spoke to the relevant Timetable Officers and obtained all their data after explaining what the C.T.M. was thinking. I also spoke again with Mr. James and told him of my suspicions in some of the cases, but he did not want me to involve other Branches other than by way of seeking information on say how long a speed restriction might remain in force. It was not uncommon for speed restrictions to be in force on some bridges for months or even years. In my experience it was not unusual for train crews to ask the Stationmaster at some depot stations where there were no Rolling Stock Branch officials other than a driver in charge, to show them 'over the pit' five minutes later than the actual time. This does not seem much but on pay day, the few minutes each day would cover the cost of a few pots. I suspected that in a few cases at least, crews were showing themselves in late by a few minutes, when such was not the case. I personally rode on several of these rail motor trips and questioned staff about particular time-keeping problems as they saw it.

I did not agree with the proposal of the C.T.M. to insert the extra time in these schedules, but after much deliberation, in most cases, this was done. I honestly cannot recall whether the percentage of on time performances of these services markedly improved performance as it should have done, as I was seconded to several other roles still operating from the Chief's office, but not spending near as much time indoors. The Assistant Chief Traffic Manager, Mr. Black was nearing retirement and Mr. James stated that a direction had come from the Chairman of Commissioners that urgent action was to be taken to arrest the wastage of junior staff at suburban stations and at the same time, improve their presentation to the public. The main points of contention were staff not wearing caps when on the platforms, long unkempt hair which contravened the instruction that hair should not extend below the level of the collar and unsafe, unsightly pointy-toed shoes which had become the fashion of the time. It was proposed to put Mr. Black on special duties to deal with this problem over the next few weeks. I was to drive him each day and generally provide back up and assistance.

I found the next few weeks working as a car driver and message boy for Mr. Black to be boring, frustrating and a complete waste of time, but had no recourse but to go along with it and do the best I could. It seemed he was on a sort of ego trip telling the O.I.C. at each location we visited that the job he was doing was extremely important, it being the idea of the Chairman of Commissioners who had personally directed that he (Black) go on special duties to do the job. I took no part in any of the interviews, nor was I required to write any reports. One day at Box Hill a young Lad Porter who had only been on the job a couple of weeks and was obviously unimpressed

A Man of Principle

with Mr. Black's "pep talk" told him he did not like working in the Railways and intended to leave as soon as he could get another job. Black's response was that if he felt that way it would be better for all concerned if he finished up now. He rang Arthur Ward, the O.I.C. Room 55, otherwise known as the "Magistrate" because he handled all disciplinary correspondence, and the decision was made to terminate the Lad's services later that day.

This gave Mr. Black an additional talking point when speaking to Stationmasters, telling them he had already sacked one young fellow for his unsatisfactory attitude and conduct and would not hesitate to repeat this action if and when it appeared justified. A short time later it was announced that Mr. James would take annual leave and Mr. Black would act as Chief Traffic Manager in his absence. Mr. Black was excited about this as he had not acted in the position before. However, his excitement turned to anger when on his first day in the acting capacity, the painters arrived to paint out the office. He had not been warned that this was going to happen. The painters put a tarpaulin up over the desk but after one day he said he could not work under these conditions and moved next door to his old office displacing the acting Assistant Chief Traffic Manager, Mr. Arthur. Although I could not show it, I found the whole exercise very amusing. Mr. Black spoke to Mr. Arthur in my presence and stated that since the original direction for the high-powered inspections and interviews at suburban stations came from the Chairman, he did not want them to stop while he was Acting C.T.M. and Mr. Arthur was to get out and about at least a couple of times a week. He should take the matter very seriously and not hesitate to make an example and terminate unsatisfactory staff members as he (Black) had done, should the occasion demand it.

It was apparent that Mr. Arthur was uncomfortable with the situation he found himself in but we put in two half days a week on inspections and interviews. On one occasion we arrived at North Williamstown and noted that no station staff attended on the 'down' side for the passage of a train. We walked to the 'up' side and found the office door wide open. On entering we observed that the Assistant Stationmaster was standing at the booking window and the Lad Porter was lying flat out on the bench. Mr. Arthur introduced himself and immediately sought an explanation from the lad as to why he was apparently sleeping on duty in the middle of the day, why he had not attended the 'down' train and why he was not wearing a tie. I knew the lad and had had discussions with him and his supervisor several times when I was the section Inspector concerning his unsatisfactory performance, but I did not speak on this occasion. The lad responded to the queries rather aggressively and quite rudely, criticizing the railways in general and those who ran it in particular. Mr. Arthur asked him why, if he was so unhappy with his employment, he didn't leave. The lad replied that he intended to do just that, when it suited him. Mr. Arthur stated something like 'it might be more appropriate if the department initiates action straight away instead of waiting for you to make the decision'. He then spoke to the Assistant Stationmaster for the first time telling him he would hear from Head Office later in the day and we left the station office.

Back at the car Mr. Arthur was making notes when I pointed out to him that this was an entirely different situation to that at Box Hill that Mr. Black so often talked about. This lad had about three years' service and had been appointed to the permanent staff. His uncle whom he lived with was a yard Foreman in the railways and an active unionist. I thought it likely that any attempt to terminate the lad's services would be strongly opposed. I thought it would be much better to deal with it in the Branch, fine him the maximum amount of $10.00, and transfer him to a location where the supervision was much stricter. If such action was taken he might decide to resign anyhow. I also thought that in part at least, the lax supervision had led to some of the lad's problems. Why had the supervisor allowed him to lay along the counter instead of running the down train? Why had he allowed him to work incorrectly attired? I believed in fact that the supervisor should also be disciplined. On return to Head Office Mr. Arthur and Mr. Black discussed the matter with the discipline clerk and decided to recommend to the Staff Board that the boy's services be terminated.

A couple of days later I was sitting at my desk with my back to the door when J.J. Brown, the State Secretary of the A.R.U. burst into the office. He said something like "You have gone too far this time Rex (Mr. Arthur), wanting to sack the kid at North Williamstown. Take no notice of that Traffic Inspector Barden — he had had it in for him for a long time. I tell you if action against the kid is not immediately withdrawn, there will be hell to play and you will regret it."

I did not speak but stood up and walked out of the office. I thought to myself this is another case of the Traffic Inspector being made a scapegoat. I had not opened my mouth in the office at North Williamstown and nor had I participated in discussions with the disciplinary clerk after our return to Head Office. Even though I had warned Mr. Arthur of problems which I could foresee if the lad was sacked and had suggested an alternative course of action, the advice had been ignored. I was pretty sure what the outcome would be now as Mr. Black would not want any industrial problems while he was acting C.T.M. On my return to the office Mr. Black informed me that the decision to sack the lad had been reversed, not because it was the wrong decision, but because Rex (Mr. Arthur) had not handled it properly. Therefore, the lad and his supervisor had got away absolutely free of any discipline, and no doubt the lad was now even more disrespectful of authority. I was disgusted with the way this matter, which was really simple and straight forward, had been handled.

I had worked very closely with the three top men in the Traffic Branch in recent times and got to know them reasonably well, but I was far from impressed with any of them. I remember thinking if ever I became a senior officer my modus operandi and style of management would be entirely different to theirs. I had no doubt that much of the morass in the Branch was being caused by the lack of clear cut decision making, the seemingly inability to focus on important matters and a general lack of leadership. I think one of the major problems was that in most cases heads of branches were in their sixties, or close to it before being appointed. This meant that most of them did not want to 'rock the boat' and were quite content to see out their time to retirement by maintaining the status quo and running their branch in much the same way as it had been run over the years they had been in the railways. To me we were going backwards as the world around us was changing rapidly, particularly the transport scene. I dared not mention my thoughts to anyone for fear of being side tracked which was not an uncommon occurrence in the Traffic Branch.

On return of Mr. James from annual leave he gave Mr. Black an additional job to do which resulted in the suburban interviews and inspections being relegated and eventually fading out. They were a lot of huff and puff and I doubted very much if anything at all worthwhile was achieved. A decision had been made to construct a new batch of GJX wagons, but it had not been decided whether the construction should be of aluminium as was the first lot, which gave a greater payload because of the lighter tare, or of steel with a reduced payload because of the heavier tare. With the lighter tare many more tonnes of grain could be carried each season for a given amount of locomotive power but concern had been expressed that metal fatigue would set in much earlier in the aluminium wagons as against the steel. Apparently, the engineers were looking to the operations people to analyse the situation and give them a lead on which way to go. I found it incredible, given Mr. Black's background, that the Chief Traffic Manager should have selected him to do the exercise as he had not worked in the Freight Operations Division on his way up and had never had to plan a season's wheat shift. Again I was to stay with him and run up and down to Freight Operations at his every whim getting him the relevant statistics on tonnages, storages and shipping over several grain seasons.

He was very determined and independent and would not let me write up any section of his report. He claimed he had been given the job and he would do it. It was my job to source the information and keep it up to him. Of course the report took probably twice as long as it should have because he was spending a considerable amount of time each day calculating his superannuation payout for his forthcoming retirement. At that time, he could take a full fortnightly pension or he could convert half of the pension to a lump sum. He spent many hours talking to other people in his age group finding out what they intended to do and how they had come to their conclusions. He spent many more hours calculating what a lump sum might earn him at various interest rates and what his tax situation might be in the different scenarios he had worked up. A lot of this time I had nothing to do but he did not like to be left on his own, other than when I was running errands for him. I have no idea whether his report influenced the final decision on the GJX wagons, but they did settle for steel construction. Likewise, I have no idea whether he converted half his pension or not, but the sad thing was that like so many railway people of his time, he did not live very long after his retirement.

I was still notionally working from Mr. James' office but had become a sort of go to man, or spare part to be utilized on any, or it seemed everything that cropped up. An inter-branch committee had been formed to formulate procedures for the safer handling of L.P. Gas by rail and I became the Traffic Branch representative. Incidentally some years later the Railways won a Safety Award from a large insurance company in recognition of safety procedures with L.P. Gas. The Minister of Transport stated there was a need for a Transport Information Centre where information on Train, Tram and Bus schedules and fares could be obtained by ringing one number at the Victorian Government Tourist Bureau.

Victorian Government Tourist Bureau. PROV VPRS 12903/P1, Box 393048. Reproduced with permission of the Keeper of Public Records.

I became the Rail representative on that committee. The Chairman had what was called a Special Investigating Committee whose job it was to analyse and report direct to him on different tasks he had handed them. I was the Traffic Branch representative on that for a period. The Public Relations and Betterment Board decided the Railways should have a panel of speakers and I was nominated as the Traffic Branch speaker. This scared me no end as I had had no experience or training in public speaking and have never felt comfortable or competent in such a role. Nevertheless I managed to get by, speaking on railway operations at community groups such as Apex and Lions Clubs but was very happy when I was promoted and went off the panel. There were heaps of other day to day matters that were directed my way such as escorting interstate visitors or consultants and showing groups over Train Control,

Dynon Goods Terminal, Signal Boxes and other operating facilities.

In 1968 a Work Value Case was conducted by the Conciliation and Arbitration Commission comparing the value of the work done by Stations Assistants in Victoria with that done by comparable grades in N.S.W. To that point I had no idea of the detail and the trouble the officials went to in comparing the work in order to reach their decision. Management nominated locations which should be visited and likewise the Australian Railways Union nominated locations they chose for examinations of the Staff. There was an enormous entourage to each station we visited and one Stationmaster was heard to say 'the circus has arrived in town.' The number of people involved, to me, was incredible. The Commissioner from the Conciliation and Arbitration Court had his personal staff including his driver and short hand machine operators. The Victorian Railways had their Industrial Advocate and his assistant and an officer from the Traffic Branch which for inspections in Sydney suburban and Victorian suburban and country was me. I was required to advise on technical matters on signalling and safe working and other duties performed and also comment on the accuracy or otherwise of the evidence given by the staff member being interviewed. Evidence was led and then as required the witness was cross examined.

The N.S.W. Government Railways had similar representation as Victoria and because any decision made finally by the court could have an effect on other states. I recall Tasmania and South Australia had management representatives there as observers. On top of this the Unions, any of which had coverage of these grades, had representatives and observers present. The trip to Sydney was the first I had made interstate on railway business. I cannot recall all of the locations visited during this fairly long drawn out exercise but some of the Victorian locations included the luggage hall at Spencer Street, Hurstbridge, Springvale, Echuca, Bendigo and Ballarat. Whilst I felt the procedures involved were very much 'over kill', I also found them very interesting and of course the experience gained was no load to carry.

During this period, I was required to learn the Assistant Goods Superintendent's job at Dynon. I decided it would be of advantage to me if I could do a couple of these learning days on the night shift at South Dynon, as too often time was expended when you arrived on day shift trying to sort out what had happened, or had not happened, on the night shift. I thought that if I could experience it myself for a couple of nights, at least I would have a better appreciation of the tasks and the problems that beset the staff overnight. I spoke to the yard Foreman, Jim Hornbuckle, who was to be on the night shift the following week. He was adamant that the shunters would think I was spying on them and would not agree to me being in the yard. He stated that those before me had not done a night shift when learning and this would make the shunters more suspicious. I pointed out to him that Dynon was a 24-hour operation and if I was to be competent and effective when I took over, I needed to know what happened 24 hours a day, not just on the day shift. It could in fact be to his and the shunters advantage in certain circumstances. I gave an undertaking that they would know what I was doing every minute of the shift as I intended to ride on the pilot with them for every move and would also eat my meals with them in their tucker room. He must have been a good advocate for me as to everyone's' surprise, the shunters agreed to me being with them. I really enjoyed the experience and came out of it with a better knowledge of the night shift operation and also the culture of the shunters, which was entirely different when they did not have an active union official with them, or in the area.

I was also required to learn the position of Assistant Superintendent, Freight Operations in Head Office. This job had been a relatively recent creation and had not been properly structured. There was no job description provided and the lines of authority were not clear. The Superintendent would give you tasks to perform and there were some set things that you learned to check each day and follow up on an as required basis. During the time that I relieved in the position the Superintendent, Mr. Butler, was not enjoying good health. He was frequently off sick and when this occurred relief was not provided. This meant that some of the daily routine matters, such as signing off on correspondence prepared in various sections of the division, became the lot of the acting assistant. I was quite nervous signing off some of these files as clearly the clerk who wrote them had much more experience and, in some cases, superior knowledge of the subject than I had. However, I survived this situation and the experience proved invaluable during my later career as I would never sign off on anything I had any doubts about, or did not fully understand, without questioning the author to enlighten myself.

Just after 7.00am on the 7th February 1969, a head on collision occurred on the standard gauge line on the Melbourne side of Violet Town between the overnight sleeping car train from Sydney, the *Southern Aurora*, and a Sydney bound goods train. The result was horrific. Five passengers were killed and three crew members — one conductor and the electrician on the *Southern Aurora*, and the driver of the goods train. It was later established that the driver of the *Southern Aurora* was not killed in the collision but had died of heart failure a short time before hand. That was the prime cause of the disaster although it could have, and should have been avoided, had the fireman and the guard of the *Southern Aurora* not been derelict in their duties. When I arrived at work in the Chief Traffic Managers' office that morning Mr. James told me to go to the Control rooms to help out in whatever capacity I could but said that when the members of the Enquiry Board and their transport was finalized, I should be prepared to accompany them to take notes and generally assist as required. Consideration was given to flying the board members to Violet Town, but then it was decided they would be driven in the Chairman of Commissioners car and that the Chairman and Transport Minister would fly up.

Board Members were Mr. McCallum, Assistant Chief Civil Engineer as Chairman, Mr. Keane, Chief Mechanical Engineer and Mr. McInnes, Acting Assistant Chief Traffic Manager. A scene of devastation greeted us at Violet Town. The locomotives were complete wrecks as were some of the *Southern Aurora* carriages and freight vehicles off the goods train. About two hundred metres of track was destroyed. The board members surveyed the situation and conducted some informal interviews but of course many people who would be important witnesses had left the scene. The Secretary of the Victorian Division of the Australian Federated Union of Locomotive Enginemen had instructed the fireman of the *Southern Aurora* before he was taken to hospital, that on no account was he to speak to anyone about the accident, before he, his union official, was able to discuss the details with him and give him advice. The union official, Mr. Carey was therefore very reluctant to reverse his instructions, but he realized the gravity of the situation and in the spirit of co-operation, he wrote a note authorizing an interview. The fireman had suffered burns and other injuries that were not life threatening. He had been taken to the Wangaratta hospital.

Later in the afternoon we went to Wangaratta where the medical superintendent at the hospital gave us permission to interview the fireman. Mr. Keane engaged in a short session of question and answer type interview. I stood behind him and recorded as best I could what took place. This was not easy as I do not do shorthand. It was decided about tea time that we should return to Melbourne and continue the enquiry the next morning. I was directed by the Chief Traffic Manager to remain with the board until further notice. My job involved liaising with relevant branch officials and N.S.W. officials and arranging the diary for daily interviews of witnesses. There were many other random matters such as escorting the police sergeant who was preparing a brief for the Coroner over the set of *Southern Aurora* carriages and vans when they were in Melbourne through the day. He was particularly interested in the brake van and how the guard was able to view signals from it. The other important duty I had was to make the tea and run sundry messages. The experience I gained and the protocol I learned was not a load to carry a few years later when as Assistant Chief Traffic Manager I was usually required to be the Traffic Branch representative on main line boards of enquiry.

Meanwhile in order to have much closer supervision of suburban train services and much greater emphasis placed on timekeeping, a new position titled Superintendent, Metropolitan Train Running had been created, with a staff of two Traffic Inspectors, two Train Running Officers, two clerks and a typist. The office was located in the station building at Flinders Street. The first appointee to the position, Mr. Ronald was due to go on annual leave after which he was to be utilized on 'special duties'. I was required to learn the Superintendent's duties and then take over from Mr. Ronald. I acted in this position for several months, thoroughly enjoying the challenge. Again, the experience gained would prove very beneficial in my future career. Then suddenly, out of the blue, came a direction to report to the office of the District Superintendent Eastern, have a week learning the duties, and then take over from Mr. Rae as acting Superintendent until further notice. I was thrilled with this latest move as it meant that I would spend several days each week in the part of the state in which I was born in and grew up in, Gippsland.

The routine for the Superintendent was to go into the district by road each Monday morning and return to the office each Thursday afternoon, then spend Friday in the office. After settling in over a few weeks I decided that it could be an advantage to vary the routine thus obtaining a better appreciation of what the demands of the district were on a Friday or Saturday. I was not only interested in station rosters including parcels and goods staff, but also freight trains timetabled at weekends and of course yard pilots at places like Warragul and Traralgon particularly. A problem in railway operations I had noted was that although traffic often varied in volume, type and emphasis, staffing rarely did. If there was new or increased traffic, or changed emphasis on particular days, application was quickly made for adjustments to meet that demand, by way of altered rosters or approval for overtime but if the change was the other way and traffic and volume reduced, it was not unusual to maintain the status quo sometimes for years after.

This proved to be an interesting exercise. Staff were extremely surprised to see the Superintendent in the district on a Friday and even more so, on the odd occasions that I ventured out on a Saturday. When in the district on any day I would sometimes visit locations where yard pilots were operating (Warragul and Traralgon) after tea. This was possible being away from home as otherwise I would only be sitting in a hotel room reading books to pass the time. On one occasion the staff at Warragul had asked for a roster change to deal with the heavy volume of parcels received off the paper train so they could be checked off quicker and be available for earlier delivery. They got the surprise of their lives when I fronted up at 4.30am to see the situation first hand for myself. They could not believe it when I turned up at the same time but on a different day the following week. I did this because it had been claimed that the volume of parcels had been down on the morning of my first visit.

Warragul was a major depot and it interested me greatly. Situated 60 miles (100km) from Melbourne it would have been absolutely essential in the days of steam locomotives, but the latter had been superseded in the 1950s by electric locomotives and the branch line which ran out to Noojee had been closed at about the same time. It seemed to me that the operations and staffing at Warragul had not changed much, if at all, in the almost fifteen years that had elapsed since. I believed that a complete review of freight train timetabling with emphasis on through loads, also the three shifts each day that the yard pilots operated, was long overdue. In many instances through loading was being delayed by trains going into Warragul yard, working there, and then departing some hours later. This had an adverse effect on customer service and wagon utilization and increased the number of train crews and yard staff required. Electric locomotives did not require servicing en route as steam did and clearly management had not taken advantage of this.

I believed that apart from local requirements train crews should be progressively eliminated at Warragul allowing Traralgon (97 miles from Melbourne) and South Dynon crews to either work through or changeover. There was potential for enormous savings, but at the same time, speeding up services to our customers. I mentioned my ideas to Mr. James the Chief Traffic Manager who said he would think about it but would have to confer with the Chief Mechanical Engineer as the train drivers were of course his responsibility. A short time later I was told to forget about my proposal as the C.M.E. would not agree to it. I was disappointed but the knowledge I had gained on Warragul was not wasted. I could store it away and use it at a later date should the opportunity arise. I was convinced that my ideas were sound and practicable. Perhaps my studies of economics and management at the R.M.I.T. course had caused me to see things a little differently from the Traffic Branch officers who preceded me.

As previously stated there had been some restructuring within the Traffic Branch in the 1960s including the creation of the Assistant Superintendent, Freight Operations position and that of Superintendent, Metropolitan Train Running. This was surely an indication that the Commissioners were unhappy with the performance of the Branch in some areas and were trying to bolster it up. Notwithstanding, that a 'rose by any other name would smell as sweet' they modernized the titles of the Superintendent, Train Services to Manager, Passenger Operations, still retaining responsibility for timetabling both passenger and freight train services including suburban services and Train Control. The Superintendent Freight Operations became the Manager, Freight Operations. The Assistant position in Freight Operations was abolished but a position of Superintendent, Freight Train Running was created. In the passenger division a position of Superintendent, Country Train Running (Passenger Division) was created. What a mouthful that was! The salary range for these two new positions was the same as that for District Superintendent.

In December 1969 I received a wonderful Christmas present when advised that as from the 24th December I was promoted to the new position of Superintendent in the Passenger Division. The T.R. (transfer) notice stated your duties and responsibilities will be as follows:

> *Responsible to the Manager, Passenger Operations, for the operation of all country passenger services.*
>
> *Responsible for research and submissions for improvements to services. Exercise oversight of Traffic Branch servicing of all country passenger services.*

There were two important omissions in this list of duties and responsibilities. Firstly, the interstate passenger services we operated at the time, the *Southern Aurora* and *Spirit of Progress* overnight trains and the *Intercapital Daylight* to and from Sydney and *The Overland* overnight train to and from Adelaide were added to my responsibilities and secondly, parcels traffic, which was considerable on both interstate and intrastate passenger trains and influenced timetabling and timekeeping considerably, was also added to the list. Much as I really enjoyed the period of relief as District Superintendent Eastern, this suited me more as in the ordinary course of events, I would be home every night. Furthermore, I would be able to influence directly the quality of these services to the people of country Victoria. The status of the position was such that I was presented with a Victorian System gold pass for the first time.

Very early in my tenure as Superintendent Country Train Running I requested each District Superintendent to arrange for their Traffic Inspectors and Block and Signal Inspector to do train running checks within the district at least once per week. Over time the information detailed on their running statements which were to be forwarded to my office with relevant and explanatory comments would give me valuable information when contemplating timetable improvements. I expected that it should serve to improve timekeeping when train crews and station staff realized that regular timekeeping checks were being done and if van goods were not properly dealt with, or signals not promptly cleared, they would be required to justify the reason. I also travelled and did timekeeping checks myself on as many trains as I could, given the demands on my time. I found it quite valuable to talk to train crews and get their thoughts on how services and particularly timekeeping could be improved.

By far the most difficult services to improve were the shorter distance country commuter trains from Geelong, Ballarat, Bacchus Marsh, Kyneton, Seymour and Gippsland. Services on these lines were required to arrive and depart Melbourne during the peak suburban services and of course share common tracks with stopping electric suburban trains. Any delays to suburban services generally snowballed to the country commuter trains morning and night. As stated earlier, the Ballarat line facilities were hopelessly inadequate to handle the volume of mixed traffic, the very long interstate express freight trains being the main offenders. The long stretch of single track on the Geelong line also presented major problems to running efficient commuter services from Geelong and Werribee.

It is little wonder that the vast majority of complaints received concerning country and interstate services emanated from people using these commuter services. There were relatively few complaints received concerning the longer distance country train services and with the exception of *The Overland*, very few complaints about interstate services. The most amusing complaint I recall concerned the antiquated carriages we were using on some Geelong services. The rolling stock in use was certainly old but there was no alternative. We simply had no spare carriages during the peak periods. The complainant stated that on wet days he frequently had to use his umbrella when inside the carriages to avoid getting wet. The situation was no doubt exaggerated for while I accepted that occasionally the roof of a carriage would leak, it certainly was not a widespread problem, as evidenced by the fact that during the period of time I was in the Passenger Operations division, no other complaints on this subject were received, and no reports from staff concerned water entering carriages.

After a process of education, much stricter supervision, adjustments to some train consists and some altered van goods arrangements, we did improve the timekeeping marginally, but this was largely negated due to major works in Melbourne Yard with late and out of course running of goods trains having a knock-on effect in some instances with passenger traffic and the quadruplicating of track work between Footscray and South Kensington to mention just two problems. Much worse was to come later on with restrictions on track work in the Spencer Street area due to preparation work for the Underground Loop. A worthwhile achievement was the provision of an extra train to Geelong just after 5.00pm in the evening peak. We adjusted the consists of some other trains and used some P.L. stock to provide sufficient carriages, much to the chagrin of older time-tabling staff who claimed we would receive an avalanche of complaints using such antiquated stock. The complaints forecast did not eventuate and the feedback indicated that Geelongites were generally happy with the extra service, not only because some got home a little earlier, but because at last the railways were doing something positive to improve their lot.

Another initiative I was required to take was the writing of the rules for the later introduction of a Green Star parcels service. I personally carried out this task as if not carefully planned, such a service had potential to cause delays, particularly to suburban services, as transfers between Flinders Street and Spencer Street could not wait for parcels coaches. For a surcharge to apply we had to make sure that users of the service got a speedier and more reliable service. To ensure this, I believed we had to receive a signature each time the parcel changed hands. Furthermore, the sending station was to telephone the junction station or terminal station details of dispatch so that parcels were not delayed on platforms and trains were not delayed awaiting signatures. The commissioners had become aware of the Red Star service on British Rail and rightly thought it could become a good revenue earner on our system. The service was eventually introduced and was quite successful. I was a little disappointed some years later when I was in the U.K. and found that signatures and phone calls were not involved for their Red Star Service because of the large volume. They simply relied on staff to respond to the Red Star when they saw it.

Shortly after my appointment to the Country Train Running position I was required to go to Flinders Street for one month to act as Metropolitan Superintendent as the arrangement previously made for the occupant's annual leave could not be implemented. Again, this was a wonderful opportunity to widen my knowledge of railway operations and staff management. The Metropolitan Superintendent was responsible for the administration of the entire suburban area. It was the senior position of all the District Superintendents and this was recognized in the occupant's rate of pay. Most of the office staff had been there when I was one of the Traffic Inspectors a few years earlier and this made my period of relief so much more enjoyable. Whilst I found the job demanding I was able to cope quite well and had no problems. I felt a measure of self-satisfaction when on my last day, three of the Traffic Inspectors came to my office and complimented me on my management style. They claimed that my accessibility, firm prompt decision making and flexibility where required had helped them considerably. I think they were "gilding the lily" a bit but I thought that the number of suburban locations I had worked at in my earlier career and the fact that I had been a Suburban Train Controller and a Metropolitan District Traffic Inspector, plus more recent exposure to the 'Head Office' culture should have equipped me well for that particular job, and was experience broader than most other occupants would have had.

On return to Head Office I resumed responsibility for Country Train Running, but not for long. One interruption was the Victorian Industrial Safety Convention conducted at Monash University over three days early in June 1970. The Superintendent of the Metropolitan Train Running, Mr. Ronald had been working with Engineers and the Chief Safety Officer to produce a paper on "Service With Safety" which resulted in a comprehensive outline of the evolution of safe practices in all aspects of train running, and rail maintenance to that time. The intention was that he would represent VicRail and deliver the paper at the conference. However, because of other commitments he was not able to do so and it became my lot to replace him. As previously stated I am never comfortable when required to speak publicly and in this case was even more uncomfortable knowing the large number of "high flyers" and "high powered" speakers and delegates from general industry, corporations and government departments who would be present and no doubt have questions during the discussion panel which followed the presentation. I survived however and was certainly glad when it was over.

Mr. Lalor had been appointed Manager Passenger Operations, the number three position in the branch, shortly before I was appointed to the number two position in the passenger division in late 1969. He was an extremely knowledgeable railway man and in fact a bit of a railway buff. His background was one of Stationmaster, Traffic Inspector and District Superintendent. I first met him in 1958 when he was Stationmaster at Nyora and I was relieving the Station Master at Loch which was the banking station for Nyora. There was no doubt that he was a very capable operator. He was a very polite well-mannered person rather reserved and almost shy. After working alongside him for a few months I formed the opinion that although he was certainly worthy of his promotion, it had probably come a little too late in life as he seemed to struggle from time to time when the inevitable pressure went on. We had an excellent relationship and I always did what I could to help him, but over time it seemed that his health was deteriorating. When he took sick I used to step into his job and this was great experience for me. On some occasions no relief was provided in my job and that made the going really tough.

11

The Crute Days

IN LATE 1970 the Chief Traffic Manager Mr. James retired and his replacement was Mr. Crute. This appointment was rather a surprise to most people as Mr. Crute was in his early sixties and it was tipped that Mr. Ronald, only in his mid-forties would be preferred. This decision however, was destined to have an enormous influence on my future career although I did not realise it at the time.

Mr. Crute was unlike any other senior Traffic Branch officer I had known. His background was really quite different to others who had aspired to this position. Whilst early on he had been a Stationmaster and then a Traffic Inspector at Albury (transshipping days), in the Eastern District and for a period in the Metropolitan District, he had not occupied any of the senior Branch positions in Head Office. Instead he had been the Assistant Goods Superintendent at Dynon for some time where he also stepped up to act as Melbourne Goods Superintendent as required. He was a "knock about" type of bloke, well read with a sharp intellect, sharp wit and on occasions, a sharp tongue.

A Man of Principle

Jack Crute with his two sons, stepping into his new role. Picture, Ray Barden's collection.

In the 1960s, in an attempt to gain greater efficiencies and much better co-ordination of operations between Melbourne Goods, Melbourne Yard and Dynon, he was promoted to a newly created position of Manager, Melbourne Freight Terminals. Soon after he accompanied Commissioner, Mr. Reynolds (a civil engineer by profession), on a study tour of marshalling yards and freight terminals in the U.S.A. and Canada. He then played the major role from the Traffic Branch aspect in the planning for the re-organised operations of the terminals and the installation of an automated hump shunting facility in the Melbourne Yard.

IN JANUARY 1970 he was appointed to the position of Assistant Chief Traffic Manager, but in fact, he never actually took over. The freight terminals were in chaos trying to provide a semblance of normal services while major works were in progress including new goods sheds and buildings, new and altered track work, new bridges over Dudley Street and of course the provision of the hump and all its associated equipment. With the new technology to be used there was also a need for new staff, and training of existing staff. All this was happening in the "home" of the most militant sections at that time of the Australian Railways Union (Victorian Division). I refer to the Metropolitan Shunters Section, the Metropolitan Guards Section and the Yard Foremen's Section all of which had restrictive work practices in place but were also capable of "wild cat" actions that were not necessarily sanctioned by the executives of the union. It was therefore imperative that Mr. Crute be released from his Managing position to concentrate on overseeing and programming these special works as there were no other senior officers with his "know how" and experience on yard matters.

Actually, the problems arising with the construction work in the yard caused a review of freight train operations throughout the state so that the number of trains and wagons entering the yard could be reduced to relieve congestion. This resulted in the discontinuation of some wasteful practices, e.g. equipment such as tarpaulins, rope lashings and packing bags being returned to Melbourne Goods, usually in very lightly laden wagons from each station. Instead the originating station would card and envelope the wagon and roadside stations would treat their return equipment as van goods and load into the same vehicle en route. This reduced the number of wagons for Melbourne Yard on each train. A similar situation applied for skins and hides and empty returns where possible. Empty wagons were consolidated at depots or sidings short of Melbourne and sent direct in a block to the location required. More block trains by-passed Melbourne Yard, e.g. briquettes for the Geelong area and Boorcan. Other trains were terminated short of Melbourne and loading consolidated before being sent on. This altered working helped marginally in Melbourne Yard and most of it was retained even when the construction crisis was over.

During 1970 Mr. Blencowe who had been acting Manager, Melbourne Freight Terminals was required to go to Sydney to complete a course he was doing at the University of N.S.W., but somehow his relief arrangements had been overlooked. I was informed on the Friday afternoon that I would be required to take over the Manager's position at the West Tower, Melbourne Yard, the following Monday although I had not had any learning time. It was really a unique job so different to other senior positions in the Branch. I recall going in in my own time on the Saturday morning when Mr. Crute gave me a very quick "crash course" on the major problems I would likely experience and introduced me to the senior staff who were on duty, and a couple of section Union Officials. Obviously I struggled a bit early on, but I must have done reasonably well as I was required to relieve in this position several times subsequently. Because of the nature of the job, continual industrial relations problems, bans and occasional stop work meetings, none of the District Superintendents, one from the Eastern District and one from Ararat who were transferred to it, could settle down and requested to be released. Fred Blencowe was eventually appointed to the position in 1971 and held it down until he replaced me as Manager Passenger Operations in 1974.

Shortly after Mr. Crute took over the Chief Traffic Manager's position he called me to his office and said he intended to change the practice of the next man stepping up to relieve the Managers of the three divisions in the Traffic Branch in Head Office, i.e. Passenger, Freight and Stations Operations, to cover annual leave, prolonged sick leave or vacancies. He felt that the second in charge was inclined to simply mark time in the absence of his manager and if someone from outside the division was utilized with a fresh outlook and perhaps fresh ideas it could be quite productive. To this end he intended to transfer me to be his Personal Assistant. I would be utilized to do the relief in all the senior positions in the Branch except his in which case the Assistant Chief Traffic Manager would still step up and I would fill the assistant's position. In addition to the Head Office positions, I would also relieve the Metropolitan Superintendent and the Manager, Melbourne Freight Terminals. With my own leave I would be occupied eight months of the year on annual leave requirements. In theory there would be four months each year to cover other absenteeism or special projects that he would want me to do. I had of course relieved in all these positions previously with the exception of the Assistant Chief Traffic Manager and the Manager Stations Operations.

This move caught everyone by surprise including me. I certainly did not see it coming and while it was a wonderful opportunity for me to prove my worth, it would also be a very testing situation as some of the senior officers and others in the Branch, were suspicious of Mr. Crute's motives particularly as he was an "outsider" to the bulk of Head Office staff. Although I had relieved in most of the positions beforehand I

A Man of Principle

realized that now I would be very closely scrutinized by some staff members before I was fully accepted. I had met Jack Crute back in the late fifties when he was the Traffic Inspector in the Eastern District and I was a Relieving Stationmaster. I was relieving at Loch and had a truck of lambs to be picked up in the stock siding which was on the 'up' side of the main line at the 'down' end of the platform. It was a loop, staff locked at the 'down' end and Annett locked at the 'up' end. I stopped No. 38 roadside goods short of the Annett locked points, cut the engine off, then signalled it forward to clear the points, made the road into the siding then signalled it back. Next, I heard thump, as the wheels of the tender derailed. I could not understand how this could have happened as being inexperienced in shunting, I had looked along the track after making the road, to ensure the point blade was fully closed.

The District Superintendent, Mr. Clark and his Traffic Inspector Mr. Crute were travelling by car and were at Nyora at the time. They were quickly on the scene as I had the main line blocked. Mr. Crute inspected the derailment site while I was talking to the District Superintendent. He came back and said indications were that the points must have been open allowing the flange of the wheel to go between the blade and the stock rail. He thought there could have been some foreign matter holding them open. I immediately refuted his theory stating firmly that I had checked that the points were fully closed before authorizing the driver to set back. Mr. Clark then asked why I would do that stating that when he was shunting he would simply pull the points over and step away and it was his experience that most people did the same, without checking if the blade was fully home. Both officers tried hard to convince me that I could not have checked that the points were completely closed, but I knew that I had and flatly refused to accept responsibility. Many months later when I was relieving at Spotswood a very thick file arrived concerning the derailment. The last minute on it read something like this:

'It is considered Mr. Barden R.S.M. is at fault in that he did not ensure the points were properly closed before authorizing the move. He is hereby instructed as to future care.'

My blood pressure immediately rose and I determined I would challenge the decision. However, I thought about it for a day or so and then decided that since there was no disciplinary action and no entry on my history sheet, it might be more prudent to simply note it and return it.

MY NEXT ENCOUNTER with Mr. Crute was not long after when I was relieving at Aspendale. A Station Assistant there responded to an advertisement in the Weekly Notice calling for applications for staff to transfer to the Commercial Branch to become Railway Investigation Officers. This employee had an appalling record for being late for duty or being absent without leave and I endorsed his application accordingly, believing he was totally unsuitable for the position. Shortly after on a Saturday morning he again failed to report for duty as rostered or advise his inability to do so. After daylight broke I went down to the road crossing and brought the gate lamps up to the signal box but forgot to extinguish them. Mr. Crute alighted from the next 'down' train. He had recently been transferred to the Metropolitan Superintendents Office. He asked me why the platform was unattended for the 'down' train. I told him I was alone doing the 'up' side booking and operating the signal box as the Station Assistant had not reported for duty. He then said he was allergic to kerosene fumes and asked why I had not extinguished the gate lamps. I immediately blew them out saying it was an oversight on my part. I was astounded when he said he had come to interview the Station Assistant about his transfer application and he could not understand why I did not recommend him. I told him I thought the answer to that was obvious given his punctuality and attendance records. He retorted, "Exactly, we don't want him so why not send him to Charlie Pilgrim (the Chief Inspector). He will soon get rid of him if he doesn't measure up." I replied something like no wonder the Traffic Branch has so many problems if they don't face up to them and push them off to others. He dropped the subject and caught the next 'up" train.

At that stage I certainly was not impressed with Mr. Crute and thought that he was probably not impressed with me. I will never know if he was serious about this transfer or just stirring me but I thought one thing was certain, I was far from his favourite Relieving Station Master. Later on, when I had got to know him much better, I realized that it was part of his personality to prickle people a bit, stir them up and leave them in doubt as to whether he was serious or not. He really had a sense of humour, but it was somewhat different to that of most other people. Now that I was his Personal Assistant, I would certainly have to quickly learn how to "read" him better. In the twelve years or so that had passed since the two incidents I have described occurred, I had, off and on, had many dealings with Mr. Crute and we had got on quite well. I now hoped that this situation would continue.

Early in 1971 I was advised that I had been selected to attend the No. 4 course in Railway Administration at the Residential Centre of the University of N.S.W. at Little Bay. The live-in course ran for six weeks from May to July then back for two weeks in November. The course concentrated on organization and management, human behaviour, marketing and distribution, financial planning and control, and the social, economic and political environment. I was really pleased to be given this opportunity as I considered the knowledge I could gain would equip me much better to hold down senior positions in the Branch, and to hold my own with senior managers in other Branches and with managers from outside the industry. Course members comprised six from Victoria, six from N.S.W. four from Queensland, four from Western Australia, two from South Australia, two from Commonwealth Railways and one from Tasmania. I was quite looking forward to this break from the day to day grind of Head Office.

The new arrangement for me of officially being the personal assistant to the Chief Traffic Manager and providing annual leave and other relief for the top seven officers of the Traffic Branch proved extremely interesting and challenging. The relief part of the job presented no great problems, nor did the longer-term projects set me by Mr. Crute. However, some of the shorter-term tasks did as they would often be given to me one day with the answer required by the next day which could also involve the writing of a report or a letter for his signature. This meant that sometimes I had to defer important matters in the division I was acting in at the time, to accommodate these priority tasks. It could also be embarrassing when I needed to obtain statistics or other information from other divisions where the manager would quite reasonably feel that the file should have been referred to him. There were occasions of course, where the file had been dealt with in a particular division, but the Chief was not happy with it and then referred it to me to tidy up and expand.

Mr. Ronald had been appointed to the Assistant Chief Traffic Manager's position in which he had been acting for some time, in December 1970. His background was a prominent farming family in the Pakenham area. His brother Peter had been a local shire councillor. Peter had also been the Ringmaster at the Royal Melbourne Show in the middle sixties when I was Stationmaster Showgrounds for the Show and he later became the President of the Royal Agricultural Society of Victoria. Mike had been a railway buff from childhood and joined the railways as a Lad Porter at Brighton Beach after completing his college education at Melbourne Grammar.

He qualified as a Stationmaster but did not take an appointment to that grade preferring to become a Train Controller where at that time, 1952, qualified officers automatically went on to the Stationmasters seniority list. This practice was discontinued some years later when the Stationmasters' Section of the ARU convinced the C.T.M. of the day that it was unfair to their members. From that point if you were not an appointed Stationmaster when you became a Train Controller, you did not go on the seniority list, irrespective of your qualification.

Mike was promoted to Traffic Inspector in 1958 in the Metropolitan Superintendent's' office. As previously written this was an extremely demanding, unrelenting and lonely job and unfortunately, after a couple of years, Mike developed a serious health issue and had to take time off for treatment and recovery. During this time, he did a private trip to Asia, including Japan, where he was very impressed with their railways especially the bullet trains. He did not return to the Metropolitan Superintendent's Office but instead, was transferred to Head Office where he undertook special duties which included among other things, membership of the Chairman's Special Investigative Committee. A bit further down the track he was appointed to a newly created position of Assistant Superintendent Freight Operations. Later on, he spent time at Ararat as District Superintendent before coming back to Flinders Street to the new position of Superintendent Metropolitan Train Running. I took over from him there when he went on leave and then back to Head Office on special duties in early 1969.

Mike and I had common interests in various railway operations and had been friends for some years. He had a warm friendly personality and was an outgoing and at times generous person. However, I noticed a change in his attitude with my new appointment. He became very cool towards me and in conversation he often was quite terse. Social activity such as having a beer after work where we used to discuss many railway problems had ended. I put it to him that I perceived a change in our relationship and asked if I had in some way unknowingly offended him. He denied that there was any problem and passed it off saying that we were both a lot busier now. My gut feeling told me that something was definitely wrong, but I could not at that time work out what it was.

Mike's office and the Chief's office were connected by an inner door which was mostly ajar. It was common practice for people wanting to see the Chief to come into the corner of Mike's office and peep around the inner door to get the nod or otherwise from the boss. One day Mike said to me "You are spending a lot of time visiting the boss". I agreed with him saying he had given me several projects to do and of course the Manager of Passenger Operations position, in which I was relieving answered direct to the Chief. He then said in future I was to give him a copy of everything except routine matters, of correspondence I had prepared for the boss. I told him I would be quite happy to do so if the boss cleared it and he should speak to him first. As his Personal Assistant I did not want to breach his confidence. It was a sad day not only for me, but I believe the whole Traffic Branch, because after that discussion Mike really "sent me to Coventry" and the situation slowly but surely deteriorated over time. He would only speak to me briefly when in company or on rare occasions on work matters that could not be avoided.

I thought long and hard about this problem but could not come up with a solution. My gut feeling again told me that it was probably an extension of the problem that existed between Mike and Jack Crute, who never spoke to one another except on urgent railway matters or for 'appearances' when there was no alternative in company. I have no idea what caused their rift, but I do know that Mike was very disappointed when Mr Arthur retired and Jack Crute was appointed to ACTM. Mike had expected to be appointed to the position, and it probably added insult to injury when Jack Crute never took over but remained in his capacity of overseeing the changes required with the modernization of the Melbourne Freight Terminals. Mike acted in the ACTM position for most of the year knowing that in all probability when Mr James retired in December 1970, Mr Crute and not Mike would then replace him. And so it came to pass.

In May 1971, I attended the Railway Administration course at the University of NSW residential centre at Little Bay. We lived in for six weeks, less a weekend home after three weeks, and then went back for two weeks revision in November. Overall, I enjoyed this course and felt I had derived considerable benefit from it. I particularly liked the sessions on organization and management, industrial relations and human behaviour. The visits to Long Bay Gaol and the Gladesville Psychiatric Centre created great interest and certainly opened my eyes. An extremely valuable side benefit of this course was the contacts made with interstate officers and also the better understanding of, and closer friendships developed, with the other representatives from Victoria.

Also in 1971, I was nominated to be a Commissioners' Representative on the Victorian Railways Institute Council. I later became Junior, then Senior Vice President, but knocked back the chance to become General President in the early nineteen eighties due to the extremely heavy workload I had, feeling I would not be able to spare time to do justice to this important position. In 1984 Honorary Life Membership was conferred on me. The VRI had about seventeen thousand members when I started on Council. It had been formed early in the century to further the educational, cultural, social and sporting activities of staff. The administrative staff were located in the Flinders St Station buildings as was a library, gymnasium, billiard room, ball room, and several class rooms. The larger country locations had VRI Halls, some housing a small library and a billiard table. Some of these locations entered teams in local sporting competitions such as bowls, tennis, cricket, golf and billiards. The VRI also entered teams in interstate railway sporting competitions.

The library was reputed to be the largest in the state. In pre-television days, each week literally hundreds of books were either loaned direct or sent to every corner of the State by train. Some Shire councils paid the VRI a fee to allow their ratepayers access to books. Demand tapered after the arrival of television, but I recall the Shire of Walpeup using the library service at Ouyen in the seventies. Classes were held at Flinders Street for Ticket Checking, Telegraph, Station Accounts - junior and senior, Signalling and various forms of Safe working, the Westinghouse Brake and Short-hand and Typing. There were also a number of smaller clubs including, Camera and Fencing. Correspondence courses were available in most, but obviously not all the subjects mentioned above, ensuring that staff at even the remotest of small country stations could study for qualifications.

Meanwhile the Eucharistic Congress had been scheduled to be held in Melbourne in early 1973. The venue was the Melbourne Cricket Ground where a huge crowd was expected, particularly if the Pope attended as had been mooted, but not confirmed. The State Government formed a Services Committee which was headed by the Under Secretary, Mr John Dillon, who proved to be an extremely capable chairman. Planning meetings were held regularly in the old Treasury Building at the top end of Collins Street. I was nominated as the Railway representative on this committee along with Bob Drummond, Traffic Manager for the Tramways, Bob Sitch Commonwealth Cars, Melbourne City Council Representatives and Transport Regulation Board representatives and a host of other apparently senior people, including Mick Miller the Assistant Police Commissioner, later Chief Commissioner. My main task was to organize the scheduling of special trains, both country and suburban, or the strengthening of existing timetabled trains to and from the event. The program was developed and updated regularly as estimated attendance figures were supplied from the Catholic Church representatives from their schools throughout the state.

This proved to be a major exercise not only in transport, but also in logistics. In some instances, for a variety of reasons, buses were more suitable than trains from some locations in both the suburbs and country. Marshalling points had to be set up in the parks outside the ground in chronological order of departure for the smooth movement of children to Richmond or Jolimont railway stations or buses. Through the year I was informed that I had been selected to attend the Eighteenth Summer School of Business Administration at the University of Melbourne in early 1973. This was good news but, unfortunately the date clashed with that of the Eucharistic Congress. I continued working with the committee until Christmas break after which Fred Blencowe took over from me. I was somewhat disappointed that I would not now be involved at the Congress to see firsthand the results of our planning. By all reports the program worked well, the Railways carrying about one hundred thousand people to and from the Congress which incidentally, the Pope did not attend.

The Summer School of Business Administration ran from January 15th to February 23rd 1973. Those attending lived in. I had a room in Trinity College. I found the course tough going, particularly the syndicate work. By far the majority of those attending were University Graduates and held quite senior positions in industry, commerce and government. I worked hard however and was able to contribute in a reasonable fashion in most areas. A highlight was not only the status and quality of the Directing Staff, but also that of the visiting speakers who were usually listed for the last session in the afternoon and some of them stayed on for the evening meal. One of these was Mr A.G. (Bill) Gibbs, the first Australian to head General Motors in Australia. He later became the Chairman of the VicRail Board. Although I struggled with some aspects of this course, there is no doubt that I benefitted greatly from having been exposed to the people running it and my fellow attendees.

This business administration course had been structured to make the absolute maximum use of time available. There were sessions after the evening meal each night and on Saturday mornings. Locals like myself could go home at lunchtime on

Saturdays but had to be back for sessions on Sunday night after the evening meal. I often worked late into the night, or sometimes into the morning, to keep on top of syndicate work as it was important to me not to fall behind or to be seen as "not up to it". Whilst I was attending this course Mr Lalor, the Manager Passenger Operations retired due to ill health and I was appointed to the position. In actual fact it made no difference to my situation as I was still required to relieve in the other senior positions in the Branch as previously and do projects for Mr Crute as they came along.

Traditionally the Chief Traffic Manager had a seat on the board of the Grain Elevators Board Victoria as the Railways were responsible for all grain movements, (local trips excepted) whether it be to ports, mills or inland storages such as Dunolly, Marmalake or Warrackside. During 1973 Mr Crute was required to be away for a week when he accompanied other Board Members on a trip through the State's grain growing areas. This coincided with Mr Ronald being interstate. In his usual way Mr Crute told me to "mind the shop and 'take care of any fires" that might flare up. On the second day of his absence I received a call from the Acting Manager, Melbourne Freight Terminals, that there had been an incident in the yard and that the ARU Shunters Section were demanding an immediate meeting with the Head of the Branch. I took the second branch car and drove myself from Head Office to the West Tower car park. On arrival I noticed the shunters' representatives in discussion in the car park with J.J. Brown, the State Secretary of the ARU.

Jack Brown immediately called me over and asked something like "what are you doing driving the car?" It seemed a strange question and I asked him what he meant. He said "You're acting Chief Traffic Manager are you not?" I replied that I was just "minding the shop "while the boss and his assistant CTM are away. He raised his voice a little and said "I know that and when I was talking to Mr Crute last week he said that if any problems arose while he was away I should talk to you." I explained that that was the very reason for me coming to the yard at this time. I was having difficulty in understanding what he was questioning me about. He then said something like "Well what are you driving yourself for? If you are acting Head of Branch you should have a driver. You are doing a man out of a job." I could not believe that he was serious. I thought he was either "grand standing" in front of the shunters, or he was trying to upset me before the meeting, or both. I tried to explain to him that the Chief was not on leave or interstate but simply in country Victoria with his car and driver with him and if anything really serious occurred we could track him down and call him back. In such circumstances it had never been the practice to have someone officially act in his position. He would usually telephone each day to see if there were any major problems. Jack Brown would not accept this explanation and said as far as he was concerned I was acting CTM and had done the wrong thing. I could not believe that he was making an issue out of such a trivial thing. However, the meeting went on and we were able to settle the problem, without any industrial action taking place.

J.J. Brown was the original firebrand union leader of the modern-day ilk. He was the architect of the long strike in late 1950 from which the railways in Victoria never recovered. When attending the management course at the University of NSW in 1971 an executive of Thomas' Nationwide Transport, (TNT) was a guest speaker at one session. He openly stated that his company largely owed its' rapid expansion and great success in the last two decades to the long rail strike of 1950. He stated that it not only provided a wonderful marketing opportunity to show the quality of the service road transport could give but forced courts and governments to change legislation allowing them to legally compete. I believe that history certainly proved his assertions to be correct.

I BECAME a member of the ARU on my first railway pay day back in 1952 and remained one for my entire railway career. At no time during those years did I ever request help from them on any personal matters. I recall an amusing incident concerning my Union membership, the fees for which were deducted from my pay. As a result of a dispute in the early 1980s the Railways stopped payroll deductions for ARU fees. A few paydays later there was a knock on my office door and a Shunters' Section union representative who would not normally collect fees in Head Office, sheepishly asked me would I like to pay my Union fees before I got too far in arrears. I didn't hesitate and paid him for six months membership although I thought something strange was going on. Rumour had it later that he did it for several bets he had made with shunting staff who dared him to front the Head of Branch for his Union fees. Rumour further had it that he had far too much to drink that pay night after producing the copy of my receipt and collecting his bets.

Politically both my mother and father had strong socialist leanings. In fact, it used to be said of Dad that if he wasn't red, he was certainly pink. This was the atmosphere our whole family was brought up in. Mum, even though she was in her middle nineties, was thrilled to bits when Australia got its first female Prime Minister who was not only the leader of the Labor Party, but also a red head like her. My three sisters are all very keen "left wingers", the youngest one is still working full time in the office of a large union. My ex locomotive driver brother David is not so keen on politics but definitely left leaning. I shall discuss my other brother Max, now deceased, later on. I have never had much interest in politics and certainly never been a member of any political party but given my upbringing did vote Labor early in life but after being exposed to many militant union leaders and politicians of all persuasions in more recent years, I changed. The reasons will be revealed later.

Dad regarded J.J. Brown highly and he must have been

one of his greatest supporters. Because of this I knew much more about J.J. Brown than what he knew about me. Dad used to bring the ARU Gazette home when I was still a kid and I used to read it as there was not much else to read other than school work. I still recall the logo which was a man with a bundle of sticks tied together and held to his knee. The caption was "Unity is Strength." Little did I know then that I would one day be a member of this Union and would also be featured many times in its gazette as one of its greatest enemies. I never did like J.J. Brown and once I knew him personally I liked him less. I thought he was a loud-mouthed bully who could not be trusted. In meetings he had a habit of continually interrupting and talking over people. I also felt his advice to members was often flawed. The two biggest instances of this were the 1950 strike and ten years later the service grant where he recommended to members to give up their superannuation in return for a very small rise in take home pay. I did not but hundreds did, and most of them regretted it for the rest of their careers. I was absolutely astounded when he left the Union and was given a seat on the VicRail Board. In my opinion he had done more damage to the rail industry than any other single person. If it was thought that he would become some sort of a bridge between the Board and the Union the idea failed dismally as ARU members almost to a man considered him a traitor. So far as operating staff, with whom I dealt with regularly he had lost whatever trust they had previously had in him. For obvious reasons I have never revealed my feelings about Jack Brown until now.

Conversely, Charlie Bone who was ARU President for some of the time that Brown was Secretary and of course later when Jim Frazer became Secretary was a thorough gentleman. He conducted himself with skill and aplomb, was completely trustworthy and was always fair and reasonable to everyone. Whereas Brown came from the Workshops and his replacement Frazer came from the Storehouse, Charlie was the son of a Leading Shunter at Geelong, became a Shunter himself, then a Guard and finally a Yard Foreman. He was completely familiar with Traffic Branch operations. His career had been interrupted by war service where he became a prisoner of the Japanese. He was subsequently sent to Japan to work in their mines. Charlie and I became good friends and kept in contact in retirement. We used to phone one another, have an occasional lunch together and swap tomato seeds and plants. When he went into care in Geelong Carmel and I visited him occasionally. We were greatly saddened when his daughter rang to say he had passed away.

12

Passenger Operations Division

THE MANAGER PASSENGER Operations was a very demanding job. In addition to monitoring the day to day operation of suburban and country passenger trains my staff were responsible for scheduling goods trains and all manner of special trains (livestock excepted), production of the working timetables for each district, wall sheet timetables displayed at all stations, hand out timetables for the public, train control, the central reservations bureau, (interstate and country bookings) and package tours. Special trains included race specials to and from Flemington, Caulfield, Sandown and Moonee Ponds, the latter, usually one train only, which stabled at Essendon after the forward journey and was brought out for return traffic between regular trains soon after the last race.

RACE SPECIALS also operated to country meetings such as Geelong, Ballarat, Bendigo, Moe, Pakenham and Werribee on week days. The Grand Annual Steeplechase/Warrnambool Cup Carnival attracted a special train on the Tuesday and Wednesday and two specials on the Thursday in addition to the timetabled regular train with increased capacity. The Head of the River rowing competition alternated between Melbourne and Geelong (Yarra and Barwon Rivers) each year and several of the competing colleges hired special trains for their teams and supporters.

Football specials included extra trains to and from South Geelong as well as to and from suburban locations of league teams. At one stage league teams in Melbourne hired Rail Motors for their matches at Geelong as they thought they could stretch out better and take more gear with them than they could on the buses. There were usually daily special trains from country locations to the Show Grounds during the Royal Melbourne Show and of course group travel on regular country trains which involved extra carriages to increase capacity or reserving sections of a carriage for smaller numbers. With school excursions we often had to liaise with Refreshment Services Division to provide package lunch boxes for each student. Some annual trade picnic specials also operated as did the vintage train for historical or enthusiast groups. Party trains were popular, sometimes with an extra van so they could play music and dance.

We were also responsible for the hiring out of the "Norman" car which was usually attached to regular trains. It had a dining area which doubled for a conference area, a kitchen, a bar and a smaller area at one end where office staff could work. The State Government used to hire it when they wished to hold Cabinet Meetings in regional centres. The State Electricity Commission also hired it on occasions so they could hold meetings or work when en route to and from the Latrobe Valley. Many other organisations and companies hired the "Norman" car from time to time. The Railway Commissioners always used it along with a sleeping carriage and staff carriage when on their regular inspections tours to country Victoria.

We were also responsible for the State Carriage used on Royal Visits and by Vice Regal people between times.

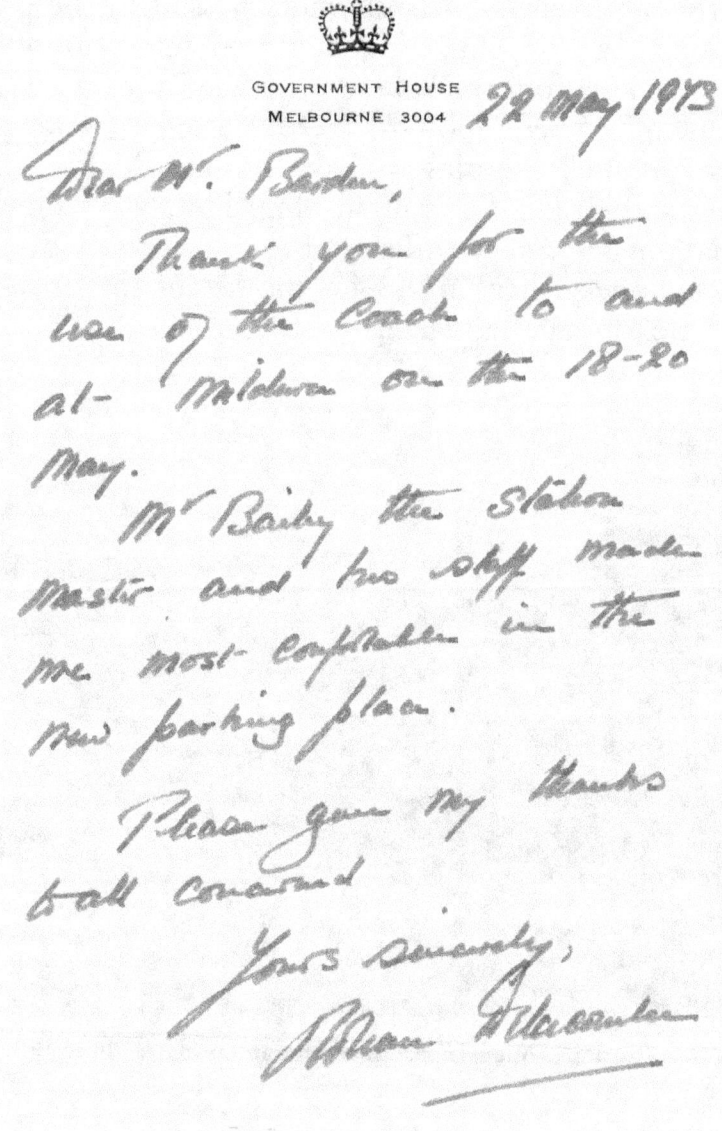

Letter – hand written by the Victorian Governor Sir Rohan Delacombe

Sir Rohan Delacombe, Governor of Victoria was a regular user of the State Carriage. When performing official duties in rural areas he liked to use rail where possible as he preferred the privacy of a rail siding compared to motels. A lot of his unofficial activities for which he always used the rail would be very much frowned upon today. We used to take him to Donald for duck shooting at Lake Buloke, Maffra for quail shooting and Bright for trout fishing. He always showed his appreciation by hand writing a note on official Government House stationery thanking us for the use of the carriage and for the care the staff had taken.

Norman Car. Commissioners Inspection train at Taradale. Photo Bob Wilson.

13

New Head of Branch

IN JULY 1974 Mr. Crute retired. Mike Ronald was appointed Chief Traffic Manager and I was appointed Assistant Chief Traffic Manager. A few days later I approached Mike when he was on his own in his office. I was hoping that he may have thawed out a bit now he had his appointment to Branch Head. I congratulated him and gave him my best wishes saying I would support him as much as I could, as I thought that a good relationship between us was absolutely essential for the smooth running of the Branch. I said I wanted to work with him to make changes in the Branch which were obviously needed in the changing transport scene, and we should make them ourselves rather than wait until they were forced upon us from senior management, when they might well be what we didn't want. I was absolutely shocked with his response.

It went something like this:

"There are somethings you should know. You are not my choice for the Assistant's position. You were forced upon me. Any changes to be made in the Branch will be made by me and you will not be involved in them other than providing answers to any questions I may ask you. I intend to change some things immediately. Crute used to like going down to the yard and had the Terminal Manager reporting direct to him. In future he will report to you and you are to deal with anything the Manager needs advice on, or Union demands to meet with more senior management. Just make sure you consult with me before you enter into any agreements with them. As from next week the Superintendent Safeworking will report to me, not the Assistant Head as has traditionally occurred. All his circulars will go out under my signature not yours. You will not in future go to the monthly business lunch organized by the Chief Marketing Manager. I will select who should go with me after seeing the list of business people invited. I want the three division managers, Passenger, Freight and Stations to report direct to me, so the Freight Operation people who have since Truck Office days, gone to the Assistant Branch Head, will no longer do so. There will be further changes in due course."

Although my normal re-action would be to challenge him on most of his proposals, I did not. I quietly told him I was extremely disappointed in his lack of confidence in me and asked him again the reason for it. He said, "You kicked me in the guts," but refused to elaborate on it despite me asking him a couple of times and telling him that surely I was entitled to know. I returned to my office in a state of shock. I decided to "cop it sweet" and go about my business as best I could without any drama. Any other course of action would only aggravate the situation and help him to feel justified in what he was doing. I searched my conscience, but although there had been several situations over the years where we had differences of opinion, I honestly could not recall any instance which could be described as a "kick in the guts" or justify in any way his vindictive attitude towards me.

A Man of Principle

RAILWAYS SEPTEMBER 1974

people

A RAY OF HOPE

There is every chance of promotion for even the most junior Railways employee, according to recently appointed Assistant Chief Traffic Manager Ray Barden.

Mr. Barden joined the Department in 1952 as a junior porter at Essendon, aged 17, and qualified for his stationmaster's certificate just four years later.

Between 1957 and 1960 he travelled to every corner of the State—from Nowa Nowa to Wahgunyah, and Port Fairy to Goroka—as a relieving stationmaster, before becoming a train controller at Head Office.

Although he left school at eighth grade, primary, level, he decided to start part time studies in 1963, and passed his Leaving Certificate the next year.

He then obtained four matriculation passes, and qualified in the transport administration course at the Royal Melbourne Institute of Technology in 1968.

Since then Mr. Barden has attended a number of other courses.

Study, guidance from his superiors, and his wide experience throughout the State, have been largely responsible for his rapid rise through the ranks, Mr. Barden says.

After five years as a train controller his experience was widened further by his transfer as a traffic inspector in the Metropolitan Superintendent's office.

In 1967 he returned to Head Office, on relieving duties, and was appointed Superintendent of Country Train Running in 1969.

After another relieving spell, when his acting positions included Manager, Station Operations, Manager, Freight Operations, and Assistant Chief Traffic manager, he became Manager, Passenger Operations in January, 1973.

He was appointed Assistant Chief Traffic Manager on July 2 this year—just 22 years after he joined the Department.

Mr. Barden feels study is most important for operating staff.

"While engineers and so on in other branches have technical qualifications, many operating staff rely on experience alone," he says.

Proper guidance for young staff from supervising officers is vital, too—and he gives particular credit to his first two stationmasters, as well as former Chief Train Controller Arthur Kenny, and recently retired Chief Traffic Manager Jack Crute for help in his career.

"Supervisors can also help young staff understand the changing government and public attitudes towards railways," Mr Barden says.

"As more finance becomes available the image of the Railways, and therefore its staff, will continue to lift".

Mr Barden comes from a railway family—his father was a repairer, and later a yard porter in his home town of Nyora.

His wife's father was a relieving operating porter, and goods guard, while his grandfather was a stationmaster.

With many friends throughout the Department—he likes the feeling of comradeship—Mr Barden says there is great satisfaction in doing the job, and knowing it is done well.

"Every Railways job is a challenge—but the biggest challenge is ahead of me now," he says.

One important job, Mr. Barden says, will be to help lift the image of Railways staff.

He has been a VRI Councillor since 1971, and is on the Sports and Library, Lectures, and Classes committees.

September 1974

Perhaps it was the situation I have previously mentioned where he wanted me to provide him with copies of work I had prepared at Mr. Crute's request, and I had refused to do so unless he cleared it with the boss first. I think most average people would consider my request reasonable but Mike did react aggressively and treated me differently from that day on.

The only other situation I could remember was when Mike became quite agitated and aggressive, and dressed me down the next day. It concerned the lengthening of platforms a few feet to accommodate the new suburban trains with seventy-five feet long carriages. At the time Mike was acting Chief Traffic Manager and I was relieving him as Acting ACTM. We were both working back when he called me to his office. He said to Bob Gallacher, the Assistant Chief Civil Engineer, who was heading the Planning Division at that time and had brought plans to Mike's office, "Rays' home station was Essendon, he will be able to give you the best perspective". Bob explained that there was no problem extending the island platform at the 'down' end but it was impossible, without incurring enormous cost, to extend No. 1 Platform because the points into the goods yard were just clear of the 'down' end and the Buckley Street road crossing was at the immediate 'up; end. Mike said he believed that a hinged timber platform extension could be made at the 'down' end which could be wound back out of the way either manually, or with a motor when it was necessary to enter the yard. I pointed out that the platform had extremely limited use; about six or seven 'up' trains in the morning peak, two or three football specials in season, stopping country trains on the 'up" and parcels coaches. Neither of the latter two would be affected anyway. The suburban trains, timetabled and special, could, I believed, easily be run off the island platform. I made the point that in assessing situations such as this, my test was to ask myself if the station was not already there and you were building one for today's and potential traffic, what would you require? In this case I considered the island platform would be adequate. Mike argued that it would inconvenience passengers having to use the subway and ramp. I stated it would be no different to many other suburban stations, some of which serviced football traffic.

First thing next morning he had called me to his office. He was clearly upset because he said I had failed to support him the previous night as he expected his assistant should. I told him I was sorry he felt that way, but he had not discussed the matter with me beforehand and I was not aware he felt so strongly about it. I had simply been asked my opinion and I gave it. Incidentally, for what it is worth, when the new trains entered service, all 'up' suburban trains operated via the island platform and have done so for the last thirty odd years.

14

Overseas Study Tour

I WAS the number two man in the Traffic Branch from 1974 until 1980 and it should have been a most rewarding and happy time, but because of the relationship with Mike, it was the reverse. In April 1975 Jack Emmins, the Design Engineer in the Way & Works Branch called into my office and said he had been expecting to hear from me. I got the surprise of my life when he said that the two of us had been selected to do an overseas study tour later in the year. His boss, the Chief Civil Engineer, had informed him of this about three weeks previously after it was announced at the Heads of Branch Meeting. He could not believe that Mike had not told me. I explained to Jack that Carmel and I were expecting our fourth child in July and although this was great news, I would certainly have to discuss it with her as depending on the departure date, I may not be able to go. I then went to Mike to seek such confirmation of the study tour but he was quite abrupt with his reply. He said it had been mooted but he had told them "upstairs" that he was working on some organization changes in the Branch which could involve the shifting of some senior officers, so it might be that they were sending the wrong man overseas and therefore, I should not start making any plans as it may not eventuate.

I thought his reply and his treatment of me was outrageous but did not let it get at me because, after all, I had become quite used to his attitude over recent years. I kept it to myself and thought the whole thing over during the next couple of weeks. I decided to again raise the subject with Mike as time was slipping away. He told me he had heard nothing more about it and to stop annoying him. He would let me know when anything definite developed. It occurred to me that he was playing childish games and enjoying it.

I had been a fool "copping it sweet" and having sleepless nights trying to figure out what the alleged "kick in the guts" was that had allegedly destroyed our relationship and in my opinion having an extremely detrimental affect not only on me, but, on other staff and the smooth operation of the Branch. I decided that hence forth I would be my natural self and stop "rolling over" for him at his whim. I would not mention the overseas trip to him again but rather, would go to the General Manager and seek confirmation and whatever details were available. Having made the decision, I immediately felt a lot better. Ian Hodges had been third Commissioner in the old VicRail system. He was an electrical engineer by profession and had headed the Electrical Engineering Branch prior to that appointment. When the Railway Board was formed to replace the Commissioners, he became the General Manager. When I met with him he confirmed that the study tour was definitely on. It had been approved by the Board and by the Transport Minister. While details had not been finalised, it would involve travel in our spring, to the United Kingdom, Europe, and North America. We would be away for several weeks. We would be required to study and report on L.C.L. (less than car load) traffic, container traffic, terminal operations, facilities and equipment, and the use of contractors and road vehicles. The antiquated methods of handling L.C.L. traffic on our system were extremely costly and losses were mounting each year. The system in use in some countries where overnight trains, by-passing smaller intermediate stations, ran to major locations from which deliveries were made by road direct to customers in the area was certainly worth looking at.

A secondary task was to look at commuter car parking at stations. Following this discussion with Ian Hodges I decided I would go ahead and make all the necessary arrangements for the study tour without any further reference to Mike Ronald whose behaviour, I thought, had been deplorable.

Jack Emmins, my travel companion, and I met regularly to study protocols and plan ahead in some detail how we might handle the day to day tasks while travelling. From time to time we consulted with Ian Hodges for information and he proved very helpful.

Jack and I decided that while overseas we should give priority to what we had seen throughout each day and what we thought might be appropriate on our system, having regard to work practices and industrial matters - particularly at the Melbourne Goods Depot. We would at all times be mindful that any recommendations must provide improved quality of service to the community and be viable in the longer term. When we agreed on matters which might be appropriate with our system, arising out of our interviews and inspections each day, we would write them up on return to our hotel each late afternoon, Jack the technical matters, me the operational matters and then dictate our reports on to a tape.

This way the reports would be completed while the day's activities were fresh in our minds and there would be no back logs or confusion as to where we had seen what. Every couple of weeks we would post the tapes to our secretaries back home so that they would virtually have a draft of our final report when we arrived home. We would also take photographs to support our recommendations. I can honestly say that we stuck rigidly to this plan while overseas, even though on some occasions it was as late as 9.00 pm before we went for our evening meal.

RAILWAYS MARCH 1976

Observations of study tour

An overseas study tour has discovered that Australian railways' handling of maritime container traffic compares favorably with the methods used abroad.

Ray Barden, assistant chief traffic manager and Jack Emmins, chief design engineer, undertook the study tour to investigate overseas container terminals, less-than-car-load (LCL) traffic, goods handling techniques and innovations, commuter car parking and gas pipelines in railways reserves.

A report of their findings has been submitted to the General Manager, Mr Ian Hodges.

The first stop was Italy, where they visited the modern container terminal at Pomezia, about 32 km (20 miles) south of Rome.

They went on to England where they investigated parcels handling and LCL at Euston (London), Manchester and Leicester. They were impressed by the handling of parcels at Manchester and Euston and the efficient operation of domestic container traffic within England.

They found the service for parcels was door to door with road delivery and pick up made by National Carriers, a subsidiary company of the National Freight Corporation in which British Rail owns 49% of the shares.

Delivery and pick up of containers is controlled by Freightliners Limited, a subsidiary of the National Freight Corporation. Freightliners also hires trains and blocks of rail vehicles from British Rail.

British Rail is unable, under the 1968 Transport Act to operate its own road vehicles, so subsidiary companies were formed to provide the door to door service.

The VR pair travelled on the efficient passenger service from London to the north. The trains reached 193 kph (120 mph), a speed which will increase to 225 kph (140).

In England they met Ray Oakley, who is well known to many Victorian railwaymen. He took Ray and Jack on an inspection of the partially completed London Bridge signalling complex.

Europe

Next stop was Holland where they met Henri Dekker of Netherlands Rail, who was in Victoria last year to discuss the VR's new clearance survey project. (See *Rail Ways*, April 1975.)

They were surprised to learn that Netherlands Rail does not handle parcels and LCL traffic. This is done by its very efficient and wholly owned subsidiary company Van Gend and Loos.

Most discussions took place in Utrecht and another stop was Rotterdam, the biggest shipping container terminal in the world.

The Dutch intercity passenger service is completely electrified, providing a fast, efficient service between Utrecht, Amsterdam, Rotterdam, The Hague and other major centres.

NS does not run goods trains during the day because of frequent passenger services. Goods traffic is a night operation.

After Holland they visited France's container terminals and investigated LCL handling in Paris, Lucerne, Munich and Stockholm.

French railways have formed a wholly owned subsidiary company, *Sernam*, which handles LCL traffic door to door. Rail vehicles are used for longer line hauls.

● *Jack Emmins (left) and Ray Barden, back at head office, discuss their overseas study tour.*

Canada

In Canada the VR representatives had discussions with Canadian National, the government railways system, and Canadian Pacific, a privately owned company.

Both systems are heavily involved in overall transport and have diversified into road trucking, shipping, airlines, hotels and telecommunications. A tower, 520 metres (1750 ft) high, on the site of the old Toronto Yard is owned and operated by CN.

Both companies have headquarters in Montreal and they are in direct competition. It was here that Ray and Jack met Con Bach and Joe Vilagos, two engineers from CN who came to Victoria in 1975.

The volume of freight, including parcels and containers traffic on Canadian railways is a significant factor in their successful and profitable organisations. Another is the necessary long hauls.

With both CN and CP, LCL traffic is part of an itegrated transport system with greater use being made of road transport for shorter hauls.

America

Back to America where Ray and Jack were impressed by huge marshalling yards and the magnitude of the operations.

In the US, LCL traffic is not handled by the various rail companies, but is consolidated by forwarding agents or subsidiary firms. Depending on the distance the goods are carried by TOFC (trailer on flat car) or in box vans, or in the case of shorter distances, sent by road.

(cont. next page)

March 1976   35

Our fourth child Daniel was born on 13th July 1975. It was a great event in our lives and an extremely exciting time as we now had a son after three daughters, with there being a gap of fourteen years between our youngest daughter Sharon, and the arrival of Daniel. Mother and son were both fit and well. My family appreciated the importance of the overseas trip to me personally, and to my future career, and although Carmel obviously would have preferred me to be home a little longer after Danny's birth, she gave it her blessing. The study tour itself was a big event to me as overseas travel was nowhere near as common in those days as it is today. I had never contemplated an overseas trip, let alone one paid for by my employers. To me it was an unexpected chance of a lifetime and I was determined to maximise the benefits and knowledge I could gain from it, and hopefully repay the confidence shown in me, over future years. When finalised, the itinerary revealed we would undertake inspections of rail freight systems in Italy, England, Holland, France, Switzerland, Germany, Sweden, USA and Canada over a period of about nine weeks.

We were able to make minor alterations to this programme if considered necessary. Jack and I had to separate in San Francisco. I came home and he doubled back across the USA to Columbus, Ohio, where he attended a conference on gas pipelines.

The next few weeks were quite frantic. It seemed there were "hundreds "of things to be done before the departure date on the third of September.

WE LEFT Australia on the third of September and had an uneventful flight to Bombay where we were required to change aircraft. I was extremely excited, it being my first international trip, but also a bit sad as I was leaving Carmel at home alone with our four kids, the youngest only seven weeks old. She had been alone with the kids many times previously but that was when I was relieving at country locations and able to get home at least every second weekend, or interstate for relatively short periods. This time I would be on the other side of the world and away for over two months. I promised to write to her frequently and to give her a phone call whenever possible. I felt a bit sad again when I rang her from the hotel in Paris for our twentieth wedding anniversary. I did keep in contact as promised and found that towards the end of the study tour, I was getting quite homesick. Carmel had our detailed itinerary including the hotels we were booked into and knew that if anything was worrying her she could get the railways Chief Telegraph Officer to contact me. Whilst sitting in the transit lounge at Bombay the economy class seat numbers on the changeover aircraft were announced but we did not get a mention. We immediately queried the girl at the desk. Her reply was that she did not have the first class rebooks yet. I tried to tell her that we were definitely economy class but she insisted otherwise. Jack suddenly gave me a kick on the ankle so we moved back from the desk. Jack said you have told her three times we are economy passengers, so if they want to put us in first class why should we argue about it. Shortly after we were allotted first class seats to Rome. Our aircraft had to refuel at Beirut and passengers were bussed to the transit lounge. I found it quite scary looking at bullet riddled buildings adjacent to the airport and even worse, when being checked out of the lounge to the bus, we were frisked by one official while another stood by with a machine gun. On arrival at Rome airport we noticed tanks flanking the tarmac. This sort of "security" was all new to me and a bit unnerving. When booking in at Rome airport for London, we were again allotted first class seats.

THE SAME THING applied Stockholm to New York and in my case, San Francisco to Hawaii. When re-booking in

Hawaii on Qantas the booking clerk said there was something wrong with the ticket. He pointed out that the symbol in the class of travel box was for first class but the amount in the fare paid box was for the economy fare. Being an Australian and working for Qantas he knew the cost in our dollars for an around the world ticket but the staff on foreign airlines we had travelled on until then, would have relied on the class symbol only. I told him that I did not pay for the ticket issued at the Victorian Government Tourist Bureau, but understood it to be economy, despite staff at other airlines insisting it was first class. It was a big letdown, travelling economy for the last leg to Sydney. The first class travel was a great experience, even though I expect it will never happen again.

ANOTHER EXAMPLE of the regard had for Australians was when Jack and I were in an extremely long queue for customs after arrival at New York Airport from Stockholm. A uniformed lady walking along the queue noticed our Australian Government passports in our hands, had a look at one, then said "Come with me gentlemen." She took us to an officer who was obviously much senior to her saying, "These are Australian Diplomats." We were almost immediately passed through. This is an example of how times have changed. It certainly could not happen these days.

THE HOSPITALITY EXTENDED to us in Canada was incredible. We were met at Montreal Airport by Joe Vilagos, an official of Canadian National Railways, who had been to Australia with another official, Con Bach, earlier in the year. We had sent him a copy of our itinerary. Joe took us on a brief tour of Montreal and then to our hotel. The hotel we were originally booked into had been closed for business a couple of weeks earlier due to a fire and Joe had booked us into another hotel on his own initiative. It was a Saturday and Joe said he and Con and their wives were taking us out for dinner that night. He would pick us up at 7.00 pm. They took us to a French restaurant in "Old Montreal" where we had a lovely meal in beautiful surroundings. Joe said it was still early and having seen this side of the City they would take us to a modern "beer barn" in the newer part to see the contrast. The place was packed with Canadians having a Saturday night out. We were not aware of it but Joe had apparently spoken to the host who was a singer, and after one of her songs she asked the patrons to "give a special welcome to Jack and Ray, two Australians who had just arrived in Montreal". This was a bit embarrassing, but worse was to come. She then came to our table and requested Jack and I to come to the stage and sing Waltzing Matilda. We both declined, but after considerable harassment from both her and Joe, I finally agreed when she said she would sing with me. There was considerable noisy applause when we finished and she then said, "You will have to give them another, can you sing *The Pub With No Beer?*" I said I couldn't because I did not know all the words but she brushed that off saying "I will help you." In fact, I did know some of the words as I have always been a fan of country music, and particularly Slim Dusty. It actually went over quite well despite my nervousness, but I was certainly relieved to get back to the sanctuary of our table. On the way back to our hotel Joe announced he would be picking us up early afternoon on Sunday and taking us for a drive through the Laurentian Mountains outside Montreal. We again had a most enjoyable time driving through the Canadian countryside. I was completely amazed at the warm and friendly treatment we received from these Canadians, none of which was expected in any way.

RAY BARDEN

CANADIAN NATIONAL RAILWAY COMPANY

ST. LAWRENCE REGION

RELEASE OF LIABILITY IN RESPECT OF PASSENGERS TRAVELLING

ON LOCOMOTIVES

Permission is hereby given to the undersigned (hereinafter called the "Licensee"), to travel on the locomotive on train.....#20 on October 13, 1975,................ ....between.......Montreal...........and.......Quebec...........

In consideration of the Canadian National Railway Company (or one of its subsidiary Companies) permitting me to travel on a locomotive, between the above points, or for part of this distance, -- which I am not entitled by law to do -- and not withstanding any rights to the contrary, which I may have in law, I DO HEREBY RELEASE AND DISCHARGE the said Company, its successors and assigns, for myself, my heirs, executors, and administrators, of and from all claims of whatsoever nature which I may now or at any time hereafter have by reason of any damage, loss, or injury to person or property, which I may suffer in getting to or from or on or off any such locomotive, or while travelling on any such locomotive, or in any manner as a consequence of the said journey, whether such damage, loss or injury may be caused by negligence or otherwise; furthermore, I agree to indemnify and save harmless at all times the said Company from and against all claims, loss, costs, actions, or other proceedings by whomsoever made, whether arising by reason of accident, damage or injury to person or property or otherwise, in any manner arising out of, or attributable to the existence of these presents, or any privileges granted by virtue hereof.

IN WITNESS WHEREOF I have signed this...10th,...day of....October.............1975.

_____ _____
         WITNESS   LICENSEE

TO ENGINEER OF TRAIN...........#20.......................................

This is your authority for allowing........Mr. R.T. Barden...................... to ride on locomotive between the points above named upon production of necessary transportation documents, and expressly subject to the aforesaid provisions.

CANADIAN NATIONAL RAILWAY COMPANY

By:_____

VALID ~~UNTIL AND~~ ON THE .....13th..........DAY OF......October....................1975.

Cab Pass – Montreal to Quebec

A Man of Principle

The General Manager had written to the rail systems concerned in Europe, England and Canada, and to the Railroad Companies in the USA advising them of our proposed visit, the dates we would be in their area and the rail operations we wished to study, requesting whatever assistance they may be able to provide, and the name and details of the officer in their employ we should make contact with. Many replies had already been received and the warm friendly co-operation quite frankly surprised me. I later realised as the tour progressed, that railway people throughout the world had a common bond, and many friendships developed almost automatically. The regard in which Australians were generally held in the countries we visited also surprised me somewhat, as did the services provided to us. In all the European countries with the exception of France, sufficient English was spoken for us to understand and be understood. In Paris, the SNCF supplied an interpreter who remained with us every working day. Transport was supplied to visit particular depots. The highlight of this was probably in the USA where the Cadillac limousine driven by a uniformed chauffeur, cap and all, was supplied by the Santa Fe Railroad Company in Chicago. It was certainly out of my league. Canadian National Railroads booked us into the dome car when travelling between Montreal and Toronto. They also gave me a cab pass to travel on the locomotive between Montreal and Quebec City. I don't think I have ever been made more welcome on a locomotive than I was by the old French / Canadian driver whose English was not all that good, but we were able to converse. He obviously had a burning ambition to visit Australia when he retired and spoke about "Skippy the Bush Kangaroo," crocodiles, koalas and a host of other Australian features. I gave him my card and asked him to look me up when he got to Melbourne, but unfortunately, I have not heard from him again.

THE RESULT of our inspections of rail freight systems, facilities, equipment, staffing and services offered in the nine countries we visited is detailed in our report produced shortly after our return. We found that our method of handling LCL traffic and the service provided was totally unsatisfactory and the cost prohibitive. If we wished to remain in the traffic and from the financial aspect this was questionable, we had to make revolutionary changes. We should work towards providing door to door services as quickly as possible. Freight should be consolidated, palletised and perhaps where justified, shrink wrapped and containerised when the volume demanded. We felt that a small state like Victoria could support no more than about ten to twelve freight depots in country locations. These should be serviced by rail daily and have proper, modern equipment and facilities. Road contractors should service smaller intermediate locations by road from these depots and from Melbourne Goods. The cost to provide such a service would be considerable but there would be many benefits. Consolidation of loading meant that the task could be performed with a much lesser number of wagons which would be turned around much more quickly. The potential was there to retire many of the antiquated four-wheel wagons, thus saving maintenance costs. The system we were operating meant that many very lightly laden wagons were placed at smaller locations on the main lines or on branch lines where the roadside goods train service was once weekly only, or perhaps bi-weekly, thus completely destroying quick wagon turnaround. Quite clearly there were many other benefits which could follow including locomotives and staff utilization, track maintenance, and longer term, building maintenance. Damage to goods would be reduced. Jack and I were extremely disappointed when early in 1976, the General Manager called us up and stated that the proposal for ten to twelve freight depots throughout the state was politically unacceptable. This was another glaring example of politics overriding management, and with it, common sense.

15

The Freight Branch Created

THE POLITICIANS, however, conceded that something had to be done to cut costs and drastically improve services. Shortly after, the Railways Board decided that to provide tighter control and supervision of the LCL traffic and management of staff, equipment, and facilities at Melbourne Goods, Dynon and larger country locations, a new Branch would be created to specialize in these activities. Staff in these areas, hitherto the responsibility of the Traffic Branch would be hived off to the new Freight Branch. The Chief Traffic Manager, Mike Ronald, fiercely opposed the proposal and devoted a disproportionate amount of his time, and the time of some of his staff, to listing as many negatives as they could collectively think up, and elaborating on them, in an effort to have the decision reversed. On this occasion I certainly agreed with Mike, but not with his methods, actions, and rantings in trying to derail the change. I thought the problems had arisen due to years of senior management neglect in this unfashionable goods section of the Branch, a failure to invest in new equipment and move with the times, and a failure by many country Stationmasters to take much interest in their goods shed. The creation of a new Branch and its bureaucracy would likely overcome most of these problems - but the cost would be astronomical. I liken it to using a sledge hammer to crack a nut. I thought there were simpler, cost effective ways of attacking the problem which over the years was largely one of neglect by management, their attitude and lack of focus. I readily admit that during my periods of relief as Manager, Melbourne Freight Terminals, I always focused on Melbourne Yard and the industrial problems, sometimes on Dynon, but rarely did I visit Melbourne Goods, even though the Superintendent officially answered to me. There were practical problems also with the proposal for a new Branch which could have been fixed with a stroke of a pen, but never were. The General Manager had decreed that employees in one Branch could not be loaned to another Branch on a regular basis. Traditionally staff from the goods shed were used on the passenger side for a short time when the work load there peaked. One example was Bairnsdale with the quick turnaround of *The Gippslander* passenger train daily. The Stationmaster would utilise two shed staff members to clean the train, help unload and check off the van full of parcels received daily. There were many other locations where similar situations occurred. At some locations goods shed staff had qualified in safe working and guards duties and in the wheat season the Stationmaster would utilise them in train running, and when necessary, put on a casual to cover in the shed. With the advent of the new Branch this movement of staff was prohibited - ridiculous as it sounds and was.

IT WAS EVENTUALLY ANNOUNCED in mid-1976 that a task force would be set up to determine the organisational structure of the new Freight Branch, after which positions could be advertised where necessary. A further task was to re-organize the Traffic Branch when the Melbourne Goods area, part of Dynon, and staff at the larger country locations where

"Freight Centres" would be located, moved into the Freight Branch. Incidentally it was stated that there would be over thirty Freight Centres established throughout the State. This to me was an over kill and had a political "smell" about it. It was around three times the number we had recommended and of course the costs to provide office space and equipment, mechanical and lifting equipment, undercover areas for unloading and hard standing areas for the mechanical equipment to work on would also likely triple. To me it did not make sense. In such a small State, road contractors could have covered the area and distances quite satisfactorily from ten or twelve points. Furthermore, the benefits and savings previously outlined would be severely eroded.

CONSULTANTS WERE ENGAGED to assist and guide the task force which worked from offices up town, away from the Railway Head Office. Mr Ronald, Chief Traffic Manager and Mr Bell, Manager Freight Operations were seconded to this group. This seemed a strange decision as Mike had made it clear to all and sundry that he was hostile to the proposal. It suited me however, as I would be acting Chief Traffic Manager until work was completed. However, there were some big surprises in store. The Freight Branch structure was much as I expected although, I thought a little top heavy. The new modelled Traffic Branch was a real "clanger". I have no idea how it could have been approved or justified but it was. My job as Assistant Chief Traffic Manager had been split three ways. I now became the Deputy Chief Traffic Manager and Assistant Chief Traffic Manager Districts. There was an Assistant Chief Traffic Manager Operations, Fred Blencowe, and an Assistant Chief Traffic Manager Suburban, Jack Draper.

THERE WAS no doubt in my mind that Mike had looked after a couple of his loyal servants and tried to push me out of the main stream. The organisation was such that there were many overlaps and anomalies. I was responsible for the country districts but also Melbourne Yard, Tottenham Yard, Dynon and Spencer Street Station which of course had suburban platforms and booking offices. The Operations Division was responsible for "Centrol" (Melbourne Train Control) yet the yard and station at which country and interstate trains originated and terminated were my responsibility as were the lines they ran on once outside the electrified area. I therefore felt the Train Controllers at "Centrol" should have been my responsibly as were the country district Train Controllers. Mike was not impressed saying that was the way he wanted it and that was the way it would stay. I then put it to him that as his Deputy I would have to stand in for him or relieve him on occasions and therefore I had to keep up to speed on the suburban side of things, particularly the development of the Melbourne Underground Loop. He said with this reorganisation you will not be involved with the suburban operation or the development of the Underground Loop.

I said, "Well that means it is going to be pretty tough for me on the longer term as my knowledge falls behind." He looked at me with a wry grin and said "bad luck". I thought to myself, he is enjoying this and I am getting nowhere. It would have been pointless to bring up any other matters. I thought what company or large business organisation would increase its senior managers (two extra assistant Chiefs) and support staff when it was about to lose fifteen hundred staff and responsibility for L.C.L. traffic, Melbourne goods, part of Dynon and all country goods sheds? There was now absolutely no doubt in my mind that the problem between Mike and I was nothing more than professional jealousy on his part. For some reason, only known to him, I think he saw me as some sort of a threat. He seemed to delight from time to time in trying to provoke and/ or humiliate me and even although it was contrary to my personality to "cop it sweet", I felt I should do so as I did not want to allow an incident or an undisciplined action by me to put my career in jeopardy. I had worked and strived so hard and made many sacrifices involving my family. I decided to make the best with what I had and make a detailed study of country depot stations, particularly in the matter of staffing levels and the operations of yards and pilots (shunting locomotives). This would mean trips into the country on a reasonably regular basis but I could not be away too long as Melbourne Yard still was, and probably always would be, an industrial powder keg. The Freight Branch started up in 1977 with a Mechanical Engineer Alf Nicholson, as its head and Stan Bell from the Traffic Branch as his assistant. It operated as a completely separate entity with its own administration. In many cases positions were duplicated with those existing in the Traffic Branch meaning that there was now twice the number of staff supervising and administering roughly the same number of operatives. This ongoing cost, substantial as it was, was dwarfed by the astronomical costs of setting up thirty-five modern freight centres, mechanising them and providing facilities and other equipment, sometimes at locations where the limited amount of traffic could not justify them.

16

Housing and Family Changes

MEANWHILE, on the home front, many serious discussions were taking place day after day. Our situation had certainly changed in the last couple of years. The major change of course was the arrival of Danny, which was creating a need for additional space. There were of course other factors, such as our youngest daughter Sharon's love of horses. We had for a couple of years taken her out to Yuroke each Saturday and Sunday to ride horses and she had become quite competent. More recently we had bought her a pony and it was agisted at Oaklands Junction. She now wanted to go out there each Wednesday night to hand feed it, in addition to weekends. Because of the long hours which I was working this task often fell to Carmel and after some time, became a real tie.

The two older girls, Joanne and Rhonda, had left school stating they had absolutely no interest in pursuing tertiary qualifications. There was no doubt that the same situation was developing with Sharon. This was a great disappointment to us as we had put each of them through St. Columba's Secondary College at Essendon at considerable expense, believing that such an education would be to their advantage, an opportunity that neither Carmel nor I had ever had.

It was apparent to us that we would very soon have to "upsize" but the big question was where? I was keen to go onto a hobby farm which would involve shifting the family to a rural or semi-rural area from where I and the two older girls could commute to work each day. Carmel at first had an open mind on where we should go but we both thought that a rural environment would be a much better upbringing for Danny rather than the City where new problems with teenagers were starting to emerge. The two older girls, Joanne and Rhonda, were adamant they would not shift from the City. They claimed I was out of order contemplating the sale of their home. This was a real concern as neither of them had ever given any indication before that they might move out of the family home. Carmel and I thought that despite this opposition to shifting, when and if the time came, they would relent, especially as we had stated that if necessary, we would buy them a small car to help with the longer commute.

CARMEL and I spent a lot of time at weekends looking at properties that might suit our needs. My work was located at Spencer Street so there was an advantage from the travelling aspect to live on the North or Western side of the City. I personally would have preferred the West Gippsland area but the train services for commuters were not as good as those from the opposite side of the City and if motoring to work, the time taken would be much greater traversing the South Eastern suburbs. We looked at many properties in the Kilmore and Gisborne areas before settling for one approximately half way between Gisborne and Riddells Creek, where the Bendigo railway line formed our northern boundary. The railway line actually running East-West past the property. It was twelve acres in size, divided into two paddocks, one dam, and a brick veneer home with a gravelled driveway about eighty metres in length. The house was about ninety percent completed when a marriage breakdown forced the sale.

Family photograph taken many years later on the occasion of Danny's graduation from Year 12. Back Sharron, Joanne, Danny and Rhonda, Front Ray and Carmel.

There was not one tree on the property. We knew it would be a lot of hard work completing the house and providing outbuildings and fencing but decided to take it. On the credit side, there were magnificent views of the Macedon Range of mountains and Mount Macedon itself, which was only a short distance away. We were only four kilometres from Gisborne Township and the same distance in a different direction, from the railway station at New Gisborne. There was a beautiful bluestone arch bridge, constructed in 1860, over the rail line at less than one hundred metres from the house. We shifted in on the 30th of August 1976. It was an exciting day but also a very sad day. We had failed to convince the two older girls, Joanne about to turn twenty and Rhonda about to turn eighteen that they should come with us. They had together, gone it alone, in rented premises. I felt very emotional and sentimental and obviously Carmel felt the same, leaving the home we had developed, maintained and cherished for almost eighteen years, particularly as it was where the three girls had spent their childhood. They did not remember any other home. We also regretted leaving the wonderful neighbours and friends we had made as at the time we had shifted to Strathmore, Carmel and I would have been the youngest couple in the street.

Aerial view of the property after about ten years' hard work.

17

Management Problems

THE SITUATION between my immediate superior, Mike Ronald and I had not improved. An example of how ridiculous things had become involved Bill Gibbs, the Chairman of the Railways Board. He had expressed a desire to visit every country station when he took up his appointment. He did this utilizing the Board train and usually combined it with other official duties he had to perform. During the time he had been with us he had travelled on most lines with the exception of the Skipton, Bolangum, Yanac and Queenscliff and he wanted to visit these locations, plus Portland where he had official business with the council. A programme was drawn up for him but when he realised the General Manager's inspection tour train had been to Portland only four weeks before hand he felt it would not look good if he took the Heads of Branches with him as was the custom, so soon afterwards. After some thought he decided to proceed with the trip but he would take Assistant Branch Heads rather than the Heads of Branch. Possibly some Branch Heads were relieved that they did not have to go, but Stan Keane the Chief Mechanical Engineer and Mike Ronald protested strongly both claiming that it was absolutely essential that they accompany the train. I am unaware of the reasoning of Stan Keane but he won the day and went on the train. Mike Ronald pointed out to Mr Gibbs that in order to obviate or minimize any delays to revenue trains safe working rules were often eased or actually broken, it being the responsibility of the Chief Traffic Manager, the highest authority on signalling, safe working and train running to authorise this and personally supervise it and therefore he must go as no other officer had this authority. Apparently Gibbs was not impressed and asked Ronald what happened if he was off sick, on leave or otherwise absent. It was pointed out to him that in such cases his absence was promulgated in the Weekly Notice to all staff in the system and they then knew that he was away, and who was officially acting in his position, therefore taking responsibility for such matters. Despite all his efforts Mike had failed to convince Gibbs and he called me to his office on the Friday afternoon telling me that I would be going on tour with the Chairman the following Monday. He told me that he would be at work and therefore any need to disregard any safe working rules had to be communicated to him, and if necessary authorised by him.

Under no circumstances whatsoever was I to arrange, or authorise such working myself, as I was not acting in his position as I had done when he was on leave or on special duties. I stated the obvious that in certain situations this would cause lengthy avoidable delays, not only to the tour train, but revenue trains. This was before the days of mobile phones and he could be uncontactable if a problem arose when he was at lunch or otherwise engaged. He simply said he had made Gibbs aware of this but to no avail. I spent the whole weekend pondering over this and how I would act if a problem occurred. One way or another, I could not win if something went wrong, as either Ronald or Gibbs would be upset.

I did not realise it when departing on the Monday, but this train trip was destined to be one of the most interesting of my career. All went well on the first and second days although I was embarrassed a bit and took some barracking from my colleagues after Gibbs came to the Norman car where we were all seated a short time after we passed through Bank Box, (a crossing loop on the single line remotely controlled by Bacchus Marsh) and commented to all and sundry something like "I got considerable criticism from one or two people for not having the Branch Heads with me but it looks like it is working quite well. I've been through Bank Box five times now, twice with Mr Crute in charge and twice with Mr Ronald and each time our train was delayed. With Ray Barden in charge today we went straight through at full speed and are in fact a little bit ahead of time". This was really a silly thing to say as on a single line the passage a train gets depends entirely on the whereabouts and priority of other trains in the vicinity and this would vary from hour to hour and day to day. It was nothing to do with anything I had done. We were just lucky on this occasion that a clear pathway was available. On the first night out, we stabled at Skipton and the next night at Portland. We carried point clips in the Norman car and when on tour trains I always personally clipped the points of the siding we were to stable in to ensure no vehicles could enter the siding and collide with our train overnight. On the Wednesday morning I left the train and removed the point clip. I then spoke to the Stationmaster explaining to him that the Chairman would want to leave strictly on time and asked him if everything was in order for an on-time departure. He assured me there was no impediment to our on-time departure. His wife who ran a florist shop in town would come down and present Mrs Gibbs with a bouquet of flowers, but that would be well before our departure time of 8.00am. After the presentation of the flowers at about 7.45am the Chairman announced "We had better get on our way as we have a long day ahead of us".

A Man of Principle

WE HAD a telephone connection between the Norman Car and the locomotive and when I rang the driver, Les Haining to tell him we would be leaving in a few minutes I was shocked to hear he did not have the "staff" (token system of safeworking) for the section Portland-Heywood. I immediately went to the Signal Assistant who said the staff was at Heywood as the goods train was running quite late. I now had a dilemma, do I ring the Chief Traffic Manager as per my instructions from him which would probably involve a considerable delay, or do I take the initiative? Within an instant I chose the latter line of action and kept the delay to few minutes. I rang the Stationmaster at Heywood, instructing him to lock the staff in the safe, place the keys in his pocket and then come back to me. I then told him on no account was he to release the staff until our train arrived there and I was able to personally give him permission. Further, he was to write the details of my instructions to him prominently across the figure columns of the block book. We would leave Portland without the staff in the next couple of minutes. I then rang the senior train controller at Ararat, told him what I had authorised, and directed him to ring Heywood and double check that my instructions had been carried out. I was disappointed that the Stationmaster at Portland had let me down shortly beforehand saying everything was set for an on time departure when in fact he had obviously not checked. I had no time to take it up with him then but would have the next few days to ponder how I was going to deal with this matter when I got back to Head Office as Mike Ronald would be checking on the progress of the train and almost certainly would know that I had disregarded his instructions. This day was certainly not one of my better ones. The train came to an unscheduled halt at Glenorchy where it was reported that the electric staff instruments for the section to Lubeck had failed. This would normally involve the issue of a "proceed order" and delay us at least fifteen minutes. I immediately spoke with the officers in charge at each station, checked the phases of the instruments and authorised them to let the train enter the section without a staff or a "proceed order". They were to make an entry across the figure columns of their block books and I spoke with Ararat Control informing them of the situation. Again I had disregarded the instructions of my superior but felt that having already done it earlier in the day, there was no point in reverting back to following his instructions.

WE STABLED that night at Remlaw, a small siding outside of Horsham. The Chairman had a policy of inviting the Stationmaster and his wife onto the train for dinner whenever possible. In this case the Stationmaster from Horsham came on board and it soon became evident that he and his wife had had some sort of disagreement. The Chairman continually tried to make conversation with the Stationmaster on local matters but his wife kept chipping in, frequently contradicting him and correcting him to the extent that everyone felt uneasy and uncomfortable. I had not previously experienced such behaviour and felt really sorry for the Stationmaster. I was extremely relieved when the meal ended.

The next morning, we departed for Yanac, a "no-one in charge" station at the end of the line out from Jeparit. On arrival the crew ran the loco around the train to make ready for departure as there was nothing much to see at Yanac. We were having lunch in the Norman car when someone called out "snake!" A fairly long brown snake was wriggling along the platform. Bill Gibbs jumped straight out of his chair and rushed to the door saying he had never killed a snake whilst Mrs Gibbs kept calling "Don't go out". Stan Keane chimed in saying "Take Ray with you, he is a bush boy". I left the train behind Bill, just in time to see the snake disappear under the "Mallee shed." I commented that it was probably looking for mice and we went back to our lunch. A minute or two later the snake was observed going back along the platform. Bill

A Man of Principle

Gibbs again rushed to the door and I was urged to go with him. I had noticed a bundle of wooden fence droppers at the "Mallee shed" so I grabbed one and gave it to him. Because of its rigidity it was far from the ideal weapon with which to kill a snake. He swung a hefty blow and broke the snake's back but at the same time broke a bit off the end of the dropper. With the snake writhing at the end of the platform he stepped back and said "How do we finish it off?" I took the shortened dropper from him and finished the job. He then raced back into the train to get his camera and asked me to take his photograph holding up the dropper with the snake draped over the end of it. He was really quite excited and got me to take a second photo. Soon after, we departed for the Bolangum line and subsequently stabled overnight at Rupanyup.

Although there was no Stationmaster at Rupanyup, there was at that time, an assistant, quite a young fellow who came on board with his wife for dinner. I recall he seemed rather nervous, perhaps a little overawed at the prospect of dining with the Chairman of the Railways Board, but this was nothing to what was to come a little later on. Bill Gibbs was a great conversationist and after discussing the Assistant Stationmasters background, how he liked living at Rupanyup and what he hoped to achieve in the Railways, he then described his train trip so far, including a detailed account of the killing of the snake earlier in the day. The Assistant's wife, who had very little to say until then, suddenly opened up saying something like "that's the trouble with you city people, you pay no heed to the ecology. The killing of snakes upsets the balance and every now and again we get a mouse plague. Snakes should never be killed". Her husband looked like he wanted to slide under the table, Bill Gibbs looked aghast but quickly recovered, and everyone else seemed stunned. Bill Gibbs spoke direct to her saying he realised that quite rightly the ecology had assumed much greater importance in modern day thinking and his action earlier in the day had been spontaneous, in keeping with what had been the common practice for most of his life. The awkward moment soon passed but I, along with everyone else I expect, felt very relieved when the dinner was finished. I also felt a little guilty myself as being of the "old school" I have always believed that the only good snake was a dead one.

The final day of the tour was uneventful. We departed Rupanyup on time, went through to Queenscliff, then arrived back home to Melbourne on time. I was certain that Mike Ronald would know that I had disregarded his instructions and was apprehensive as to how he would react. The strange thing was he never mentioned it. Based on his previous performances in such circumstances, I just couldn't believe it. A side issue was that at the next Heads of Branch luncheon, Bill Gibbs described the snake killing incident in some detail. A friend of mine sitting near Mike said that he leaned over the table and quietly said to those in earshot "Barden had no need to worry, no snake would ever bite him". To me this was a clear indication of how far our relationship had deteriorated.

IN MY CAPACITY as Assistant Chief Traffic Manager Districts, I had started a personal review of train running, staffing, and yard working at depots throughout the state. It was often difficult to get away because of my responsibilities in Melbourne but armed with a master graph of the timetable for the particular district, I would pick up the District Superintendent and cover as much ground as we could in the limited time available on each of my inspection tours. It was absolutely amazing the number of matters "thrown up" ranging from the amount of overtime being worked at many locations, the regular late running of trains from depot to depot in the district, and the utilisation of yard pilots and whether some rostering of station staff was still appropriate, given changed volumes of traffic, changed types of traffic, changed timetables and social changes which had taken place. For example, banks and many other businesses no longer opened on a Saturday morning but our parcels offices and goods offices remained staffed even though the demand for service had reduced to almost nil in many cases. A check of the timekeeping records M132 often revealed regular overtime being worked at penalty rates when with adjustments to timetables or hours of service, worthwhile cost savings could be achieved. Stationmasters were often reluctant to bring these matters to notice as it could mean a reduction in take home pay for them or some other staff members. The District Superintendents should have been on top of these matters but perhaps they could not see the "forest for the trees". I doubt that any of them had ever used a master graph to more clearly and easily see possible changes to the timetable when checked against the time sheets of staff. Overtime was an important cost factor and I wanted the Superintendent to take a much greater interest in it rather than leaving it to clerical staff in the office. I had developed a habit fairly early in my career when I was working on rosters, timetables, facilities and indeed all other cost factors, of asking myself what I would do if it was my own personal business. Would I incur the cost or would I save the cost? Was there some other way? Although there was a vast difference in the two situations, I found it a useful guide in making decisions.

18

Main Line Enquiry Boards

The double ended Tait car operating between Eltham and Hurstbridge during off peak times and evenings. Photo Bob Wilson

ONE OF THE most interesting and challenging responsibilities of the Assistant Branch Head was to represent the Branch on Main Line Enquiry Boards. As my career panned out I spent more time in the position of Assistant Branch Head (six years) than any other position from lad porter up, during the thirty-four years of my employment. The board consisted of three officers from the Branches whose staff were mostly involved in the particular incident, be it a derailment, a collision, or some other serious mishap or unusual occurrence. The majority of Enquiries involved representatives from Traffic (Operations), Rolling Stock (Mechanical Engineering) and Way & Works (Civil Engineering), but depending on the nature of the incident, this was not always so. The Chairman of the Board was usually selected from the Branch less likely to be at fault. There were three main responsibilities. The first was to fix the cause of the incident, the second was to establish culpability and the third was to make recommendations on how to prevent a recurrence. It was the responsibly of the Head of Branch to take disciplinary action where appropriate, against any staff found culpable. He could caution them, fine them to a maximum of $10, reduce them in grade either temporarily, or permanently, or recommend termination of their employment.

In train running matters the rules, regulations and standing instructions were framed so that more than one person usually had to be at fault before there was an incident. I took part in many Enquiries over the years, too numerous to detail here, but I will outline a couple of them that I found most interesting and challenging.

The first concerns the evening shuttle service running between Hurstbridge and Eltham. The first indication that anything was wrong was when the train Driver knocked on the door of the Ganger's departmental residence at Diamond Creek. He was incoherent, covered in mud and bleeding from the lacerations to his head and face. He was sent to hospital in an ambulance. He had been unable to tell the Ganger what had happened or where his train was. At first it was thought that he might have been assaulted and possibly struck with a blunt instrument. The train was later located in the Diamond Creek/Eltham section, having come to a stand in a depression between two rising grades. The Guard was in an agitated state saying he did not know what had happened but when he could not find the driver he went into a state of shock. He was sent home in a taxi. There were only four passengers on the train. Two of them were a young couple who boarded at Diamond Creek and sat immediately behind the Driver's compartment. The train was commandeered and impounded until the Enquiry Board's needs were satisfied. We took a crew out with us the next day and arranged for train services between Eltham and Hurstbridge to be suspended while we tried to simulate what might have happened the night before. The Driver had obviously powered out of Diamond Creek so we did the same cutting off and allowing the train to coast after we topped the grade just over the road crossing a short distance on the Eltham side. It was certainly a fascinating exercise over the undulating track with the train sometimes almost stopping but then gaining momentum again. It in fact 'seesawed' a few times before coming to a stand a very short distance from where it stopped the night before. Another piece of seemingly important evidence was that there were scuff marks on the side of the train consistent with what you would expect if a person was hanging out of the doorway holding the handrail, and then lost his footing when leaning over too far along the train. The marks were likely the result of trying to regain a foothold before losing his grip on the handrail and falling. We were unable to interview the driver until the following day but it proved fruitless as did subsequent interviews, as he steadfastly maintained that he could recall absolutely nothing after departure from Diamond Creek. Interviews with the Guard were also unhelpful in solving the problem as he defended his inaction by saying he had every confidence in the driver and thought that there must have been some sort of equipment failure that caused the extraordinary movements of the train. He was not aware that the Driver was not on board until the train actually came to a stand.

BECAUSE OF THE sensitivity of the matter a senior Railways Investigation Officer who specialised in interviewing members of the public about such things as level crossing accidents and fires allegedly started by trains, assisted the Enquiry Board by interviewing the passengers and the medical people who attended the Driver. Again, very little came out of the interviews except that the injuries sustained were more likely to have been the result of a fall rather than being struck over the head. After reviewing all of the evidence many times over, it was the unanimous view of Board members that the Driver was culpable in that contrary to Rules Regulations and Instructions, he had endangered the travelling public, members of the public in general and railway equipment by cutting out his controller and allowing the train to coast and not keeping a look out of the track conditions ahead from his cab. We had no proof that he was a "peeping tom" but the scuff marks indicated that he had swung out holding the handrail to look through the carriage window, lost his footing and eventually his grip on the handrail, and fell into the trackside drain which would explain the head injuries and the blood and mud on his face and clothing. His services were subsequently terminated. The Guard was disciplined for his inaction. Given the circumstances it was not unreasonable to expect him to have operated the train brakes from his end of the train or even to operate the whistle to try and attract attention. Instead, of his own admission, he did absolutely nothing until the train came to a stand.

ANOTHER ENQUIRY which I shall never forget, not just for the very serious misconduct of the locomotive crew, but for the incredible "cover up" and lack of application to their responsibilities by other staff members who could have and should have prevented this frightening incident. At that time *The Vinelander* overnight passenger train operating each way between Melbourne and Mildura was run by a Maryborough crew from that depot each morning. The crew then went to rest in Melbourne before running the 9.20pm departure Vinelander back to Maryborough that night. On this occasion nothing untoward had been reported until the train went through Clunes at excessive speed and failed to exchange the staff, (token system of safe working). At this stage it was not known why we had an apparent runaway train. For that reason, it was a great relief to all concerned when *The Vinelander* subsequently came to a stop at Talbot. It was sheer luck that the Train Controller had decided to side track the Melbourne bound *Fruit Flyer* (fast goods train conveying fresh produce to the market) at Talbot rather than send it on to Clunes to cross as he had originally considered, thus avoiding what could have been a disastrous head on collision similar to the *Southern Aurora* smash at Violet Town mentioned earlier. First reports were that the Driver was disorientated, did not know where he was, and had completely missed Clunes but it was not clear why the fireman and the guard had not taken action to stop the train. There was evidence that the Driver had vomited out the window and down the side of the locomotive. He claimed he had knocked his head when the locomotive lurched somewhere on the journey and thought he might have vomited at about that time. The driver was relieved from duty and taken to the Maryborough hospital where he was admitted for observation. Blood tests were taken but proved inconclusive. Over the next few days Enquiry Board members checked the speed chart (black box) from the locomotive and interviewed and took statements from all relevant witnesses with the exception of the driver who was off sick. It was established that both the

Driver and the Fireman had consumed intoxicating liquor at two Melbourne hotels and a private residence during the period from lunch time to about 6.00pm before signing on at 8.20pm to run *The Vinelander*. The speed chart revealed there had been some irregularities in the operation of the driver's side vigilance control button between Melbourne and Ballarat. When departing Ballarat, the train moved backwards a short distance before finally going forward. Approaching Clunes, the train negotiated the 35mph curve at 57mph, failed to stop at Clunes as scheduled and failed to exchange staffs (token system), then rounded the 20mph curve on the down side of Clunes at 59mph.

The Fireman had denied he or his driver had consumed alcoholic drinks when in Melbourne the previous afternoon in a statement made to his OIC at Maryborough in the early hours of the next morning. When interviewed the following day by the Enquiry Board members he again denied they had partaken of intoxicating liquor while in Melbourne but later under cross examination he admitted that they had about ten glasses of beer each. He had been concerned about the Driver's demeanour several times during the journey, particularly going through Clunes, but did not intervene as he feared the Driver would become violent. The Guard also was unimpressive stating he noticed nothing untoward about the Driver when he entered the cab of the locomotive at Spencer Street to give him the load of the train and the stopping conditions. He admitted he took no action at Ballarat when the train moved backwards a couple of times before departure and again at Clunes when the train failed to stop as scheduled and went through at excessive speed. The sign-on Clerk at South Dynon Locomotive Depot noticed nothing unusual about the Maryborough crew when they signed on ex rest at 8.20pm. The OIC at Ballarat admitted he saw the train move backwards three or four times before it actually departed but did not think it necessary to report it to anyone.

The Driver was interviewed five days after the incident. He

said that after a few hours' sleep at the hostel he and the fireman had one or two beers with a counter lunch at a nearby hotel. They then went to a second hotel where the fireman was to meet his Aunt. They had two or three more beers before going by car to the Aunt's residence in North Melbourne. He stated that if the fireman said he had more beer there he could not deny it as he could not remember anything after arriving at this house until he arrived at Talbot many hours later.

After due consideration of all the evidence given, Board members unanimously concluded that the irregular running of the train was due to the crew of the locomotive having unfitted themselves for duty by their consumption of intoxicating liquor.

The Driver was culpable in that he:

(1) By his consumption of alcoholic liquor in Melbourne prior to running *The Vinelander* he rendered himself incapable of performing his duties in a safe and proper manner;

(2) At Ballarat, when given the signal to depart the train he mishandled the controls with the result that the train moved backwards at least three times before departing the platform;

(3) Approaching Clunes station, he permitted the train to pass over the 35mph speed limit curve at a speed of 57mph;

(4) He failed to stop the train at Clunes as scheduled;

(5) After passing through Clunes he permitted the train to pass over the 20mph speed limit curve at a speed of 59mph;

(6) He ran the train from Clunes to Talbot without being in possession of the "staff" for the section;

(7) He overcarried the Creswick to Clunes staff to Talbot; and

(8) He seriously endangered the safety of the passengers, other employees, equipment and the general public.

The Fireman is culpable in that he:

(1) By his consumption of alcoholic liquor in Melbourne prior to running *The Vinelander* he rendered himself incapable of performing his duties in a safe and proper manner.;

(2) He failed to take any action, such as that of allowing the vigilance control apparatus to bring about a penalty brake application to stop the train after the driver had failed to stop at Clunes, and the train had passed through that station at a dangerously excessive speed;

(3) When questioned at Talbot he failed to give a true account of the condition of the driver;

(4) He made and signed a false misleading statement to his Branch Officer in Charge and the Stationmaster at Maryborough; and

(5) He attempted to give false and misleading evidence to the Board of Inquiry at Maryborough.

The Guard was culpable in that he:

(1) Took no action at Ballarat to ascertain the reason the train moved backwards prior to departure or to prevent it moving backwards on at least three occasions; and

(2) He failed to take any action to stop the train as it passed through Clunes at a dangerously excessive speed without stopping as scheduled.

THE OUTCOME of this inquiry was that the services of both the Driver and the Fireman were terminated. The Guard was not terminated but subjected to disciplinary action. It was clear to Board members that this extremely dangerous situation could have been avoided if either the guard or fireman had acted in accordance with Rules, Regulations and Instructions, particularly at Ballarat. We were also of the opinion that some other staff members must have been aware that all was not well, but chose to ignore their responsibilities in this regard, thus "covering up".

19

Rationalisation Attempts

MY INSPECTION TRIPS to the country districts were certainly getting results. Altered timetabling where appropriate to freight train services, thus allowing reductions in overtime worked and altered business hours particularly on Saturday mornings were worthwhile savings in costs but of course very unpopular with the staff affected. Rumour had it that in some districts I was referred to as "razor" and in others "hatchet". This did not concern me greatly as railway staff had always had nicknames for almost everyone. It was not of course improving my relationship with the industrial organisations. An example of how things had been allowed to roll on without any questioning or review was at Serviceton on the South Australian border. I noted comparing the master graph of the timetable with the M132 timesheets that for several hours each Sunday a member of the station staff was booked on when no trains were scheduled. When I queried this, I was told that several years earlier it was agreed that water for the town's water supply storage would be filled each Sunday so the housewives in the small township, mainly railway houses, had good water pressure on Monday's to do clothes washing. The starting and supervision of the pumping system had been the responsibility of the Way & Works Branch who booked staff on for the task each Sunday. Sometime later a new District Engineer noted that station staff were booked on during these hours for train running purposes and sought to save his Branch the costs by training the Traffic Branch staff in the operation of the pumping system which they could do in addition to their existing train running duties. The District Superintendent had readily agreed to this but later on, after timetable alterations, when his staff was not required for train running duties, they were still booked on each Sunday for water pumping duties. Thus, the cost was a debit against the Traffic Branch instead of the Way & Works Branch where it quite properly belonged. After a discussion with my counterpart in the Way & Works Branch, the Sunday pumping at penalty rates ceased. It would now be done on a weekday by staff from that Branch.

THE METROPOLITAN SHUNTERS' section of the ARU was certainly not getting any easier to manage. Hence a disproportionate amount of my time was taken up with Melbourne yard and its environs. The Yard Foremens Section ARU were also difficult as they had restrictive work practices in place. A major problem in the Traffic Branch where, of necessity, people were promoted from within, was that many of them did not make the transition from "one of the boys" to Supervisor. They were quite happy to accept the rise in pay and whatever status went with it but often did not change their thinking or loyalties. We had identified this problem earlier in my career with some Stationmasters who saw themselves as part of management when things were running smoothly but sided with the union if there were industrial problems. The standing time of pilots was a key issue in allocating work and staff to particular pilots thus evening up workloads and improving the makeup and on time departure of trains and pilots to other locations. For some years however, Yard Foremen who supervised shunters in each section of the yard refused to record standing time or the justification or otherwise for it. While we could obtain a copy of graphs of the speed chart on the locomotive we did not know the reason for the non-movement which sometimes ran into hours and in many cases probably meant they had run out of work but we could not prove it, as there were often quite legitimate reasons for non-movement. I considered that there was enormous scope for improving our freight services which, after all, was where the most revenue came from. If railways were to survive in the competitive field of freight services in the future it was clear to me that Melbourne Yard was the key, but I did not have the answer to this shocking underperformance in this vital area. We had several meetings with the Yard Foremen's Section of the ARU to try and convince them that it was an important part of their supervising role to record the reasons for standing time during the course of each shift. By doing this, we could make changes where appropriate in the utilisation of staff and equipment and so improve the turnaround of wagons and the service to our customers. The latter was essential if we were to retain and hopefully increase our share of the freight transport task. Sadly, we were unable to convince them. A major reason for this was that many yard foremen, particularly those that took on union roles, still thought like shunters and were much more closely aligned to the Union than to Management - a major problem in other parts of the railway also.

20

Operations Branch

ONE DAY IN EARLY 1979, I was on an inspection tour in the North East District with the District Superintendent when a message was received from my secretary that I was to return to Head Office as soon as possible as the Chairman of the Board, Mr Gibbs, wanted to talk to me personally. She had no details of the reason for the discussion. I came home late that afternoon and saw Mr Gibbs the next morning. He told me that the Board had approved a massive re-organisation and restructure of Branches within the railway. Some Branches would be abolished, others would be greatly reduced in numbers and new Branches would be created. Of the latter, by far the largest staff- wise would be the Operations Branch - between five and six thousand people and I had been selected to head it. He congratulated me, wished me well and said I should talk with the General Manager, Ian Hodges for a detailed account of the changes, as soon as possible. I was absolutely stunned as although there had been rumours around for probably a couple of years about the creation of an Operations Branch, similar to most railways throughout the world, I personally had no idea that the changes were being worked on and were so close to happening. Ian Hodges told me that a task force made up of the Heads elect of the new Branches and an outside consultant would be set up, with support staff, to fine tune the proposal and get it implemented as soon as possible. There was to be no departure from the strict guidelines which would be set and a time limit would also be set for completion of the task. The new Branches would be: Operations, Workshops and Transportation. The Traffic Branch would disappear and the Rolling Stock Branch would have greatly reduced responsibilities and staff numbers. Operations staff would consist of all train running grades- Drivers, Guards, Shunters, Signalmen, Train Controllers, Timetable Officers, Support Staff and Administration Staff. It had long been a point of contention that the Driver at the front of the train and the Guard at the back of the train belonged to different Branches and therefore answered to different bosses on our Victorian system which meant that the finalising of correspondence was often delayed and conflicting reports on particular incidents had to be sent back and forth. Further, the rostering of train crews often had an adverse effect on train running. It was not uncommon for the Train Controller to delay a train at a station to change the locomotive crew over so they could return to their home depot and then a station or two along the track, delay the same train again to change the Guard over. With all members of the train crew under the one management it would, in most cases, be possible to roster locomotive crews and guards to changeover with the same train thus eliminating the second delay. There would be other synergies particularly in the administration and accommodation. I was very mindful of the rivalry which had always existed between the Rolling Stock Branch and the Traffic Branch especially in the train running area. I thought one of the toughest challenges I faced was to meld these people into thinking 'Operations Branch' instead of 'Rolling Stock' or 'Traffic Branch', otherwise we would be divided and morale and performance would suffer.

A Man of Principle

From lad porter at Essendon to the first Chief Operations Manager is the story of Ray Barden.

His progress through the ranks is a perfect example of how one who studies and has the determination to succeed can reach top management positions.

Ray started as a 17 year old in 1952 and passed his stationmaster's examination just after his 21st birthday having been awarded the V.R.I. prize for Station Accounts and Management studies the previous year.

For the next four years he relieved throughout Victoria before becoming a train controller in 1960.

During the five years he spent at Head Office, Ray also increased his educational qualifications, obtaining passes at school Leaving and Matriculation level. His studies culminated in 1968 with the transport administration course conducted by the Royal Melbourne Institute of Technology.

After five years at train control, he "crossed the viaduct" to Flinders Street as a traffic inspector in the Metropolitan Superintendent's office.

In 1967 he returned to Head Office on relieving duties and in 1969 was appointed Superintendent of Country Train Running.

After further spells relieving in senior management positions, Ray became Manager, Passenger Operations in January 1973.

In July the following year he was appointed Assistant Chief Traffic Manager. In February 1977 the title was changed to Deputy Chief Traffic Manager and Assistant Chief Traffic Manager (Districts).

His family background is railways. His father was a repairer and later a yard porter at Nyora. His wife's grandfather was a stationmaster and her father a goods guard. His younger brother David is an Engineman at South Dynon.

20

RAILWAYS MARCH 1980

Cutting from 'RAILWAYS' March 1980 re my appointment to head of the Operations Branch.

In the other two Branches, "Workshops" was headed by Graeme Swift and "Transportation" headed by Jack Draper. It was really only a change of name and a big reduction in staff numbers. For instance, the approximate number of two thousand people in the Transportation Branch would all be from the old Traffic Branch and at the smaller stations, their duties in most cases would be the same. Likewise, all personnel in the Workshops Branch would be from the old Rolling Stock Branch and their duties and supervision would not alter. The number of staff in Operations exceeded those in the other two branches put together. In addition to this, I would now have to deal with and win the respect of an additional large union which represented the Drivers and the second man (formerly fireman) on the locomotives, the Australian Federated Union of Locomotive Enginemen (AFULE). There was no doubt that this was the toughest assignment of my railway career and I would have to dig in and rise to the occasion.

As news of this proposed re-structure became common knowledge it was apparent that some officials from the three unions I would now have to deal with, the ARU, the ATOF (Australian Transport Officers Federation) and the AFULE, were hostile to the departure from what had been the traditional structure in our system and a surprising number of everyday rank and file railway people also were very suspicious of the motives behind the change. Many of the ex-Rolling Stock Branch staff, including some Drivers did not like the idea of being responsible to an ex-Traffic Branch official. I guess the majority of people do not like change and therefore this was a perfectly natural reaction to what had been announced.

The Taskforce work was hard going but in terms of what lay ahead, long hours and continuous pressure, it was more like the calm before the storm. The first major activity was to draw up a chart of the proposed organisation of the new Branch.

This was not easy as it included not only Head Office Administration, but a review of the organisation of the Electric Running Depot and yard at Flinders Street, the South Dynon Locomotive Depot, Melbourne and Dynon Yards and their environs, requirements at provincial cities such as Geelong, Ballarat and Bendigo and other locations throughout the state where the establishment of Operation Depots was justified.

Unfortunately, in the latter cases, senior Stationmasters at bigger country locations throughout the state lost a major part of their responsibilities. They had lost their goods sheds and staff only two years earlier and now they were about to lose their yard staff, signalmen, and guards. At this early stage I realised that the guidelines set by the General Manager posed many problems, the biggest one of which when the "dust settled" was likely to be a severe lowering of staff morale.

Some of these locations were left with just a handful of staff to handle passenger bookings, parcels and station cleaning. "Tribalism" and its consequences had long been a problem in the railways in my opinion, and we would now be making it worse by increasing the number of Branches, all with the exception of the Operations Branch, with relatively small numbers of staff.

I thought that while having train running staff, particularly drivers and guards, in the same Branch was a big plus, it would be in part offset, due to only specialist signalling staff (appointed Signalmen), being in the Operations Branch. Part time signalling staff comprising many Stationmasters, assistant Stationmasters and Signal Assistants at both suburban and country locations would go to the new Transportation Branch and while my staff would have to examine them in signalling and safeworking duties and re- examine them as required, they would not answer directly to Operations Branch Staff. We were therefore creating a situation where standards demanded of the staff would vary as would discipline meted out to staff for similar offences.

This matter occupied my mind for many days but there was no way I could solve the problem which I considered to be a reasonably serious flaw in the guidelines provided. In my opinion, in correcting one problem in management we had introduced another. The only satisfactory way of eliminating this problem that I could see was to not proceed with the creation of a Transportation Branch and place those people in the Operations Branch. Although outside my area of experience I was unable to see the benefits of separating the Workshops from the Rolling Stock Branch and thought considerable costs could be avoided if they were left as one but had the internal administration structures reviewed and upgraded.

The major objection to what I was thinking would probably be that the Operations Branch would then have close to eight thousand staff members. I did not see that in itself to be a major problem as it was not so long ago that the larger Branches numbers were something similar.

I marked time on these matters for a few days knowing it was extremely unlikely that the Board would change its decision on the restructure, especially keeping in mind the comments of the General Manager that there was to be no departure from the guidelines set.

Another likely response, at least from some people, would be that I was empire building. Of course, nothing could be further from the truth. My only motivation was to have a Branch with clear lines of authority and responsibility which the whole railway would benefit from. Signalling, safeworking, train running and boards of enquiry were clearly Operations Branch responsibilities and all staff performing these duties should belong to this Branch. I spoke to the consultant whose job it was in part, to guide us on principles of management.

He admitted I had a point but shifted ground saying the number of staff would be too great and in any event, he felt that the General Manager who he reported to regularly, would not agree. He said we should talk to Jack Draper to get his opinion. I said the result would be a foregone conclusion as Jack was not going to do himself out of a job.

He then said he would mention my concerns to the General Manager at their next meeting. A few days later he told me that Ian Hodges was adamant there would be no changes to the guidelines set.

I then accepted that no change would occur and got on with the task of identifying where operations depots should be located, what grades and staff numbers would be required in the administration of each depot and the writing of job descriptions so that the Manager's positions could be advertised and eventually filled.

Another task was to visit each location and see firsthand what accommodation and facilities were available or could be made available. Once the depot locations were settled it was necessary to divide country Victoria into sections with a manager operating from Head Office responsible for each section.

Simultaneously we were working on the Metropolitan area and Head Office position so that a complete organisational chart of the Branch could be drawn up for approval.

There was no doubt that the proposed changes were causing concern and considerable controversy with many staff members, particularly in the country. It was much better for these people to hear details of the changes from the Heads of Branches elect direct and then ask questions, rather than be baffled by rumour or gossip, or perhaps incomplete information from union representatives.

Jack Draper and myself decided to visit as many locations as possible for informal meetings with the Officers in Charge and other staff who might be available at the time. We had tried to keep Union officials informed as we progressed but unfortunately information can get distorted as it passes along the line.

Time did not allow us to visit every location but we certainly visited each place that was earmarked for an Operations Depot (and many places in between), as these were where the greatest dislocation of staff would occur.

I think these trips were well worthwhile despite the demands on our time, as they eased many of the uncertainties and worries about the future that many of our staff had. The next task we were confronted with was to advertise the new and changed positions, short list contenders and conduct interviews.

Obviously, I was aiming to get the very best manager for each depot and other positions advertised, but I was also hoping for a good mix of applicants from the old Rolling Stock Branch and Traffic Branch otherwise staff morale could be adversely affected.

21

New Branch - New Policy

THE OPERATIONS BRANCH and the rest of the re-organisation took effect on the tenth of February 1980, when the Traffic Branch was abolished. The "bedding down" of this new branch was an extremely difficult task still ahead of me, but in a strange way perhaps, I was looking forward to the challenge. My management style had for some years been the subject of conjecture and some criticism. The General Manager of Vic-Rail once told me I had a "very low level of tolerance". His view was supported several years later when the Managing Director of the State Transport Authority said I had "a very short fuse". I was well aware that some people saw me as very direct and quite blunt when dealing with staff, but that was my natural style and it had served me well over time with the exception of my relationship with the former Chief Traffic Manager. I had difficulty tolerating fools or those who handled the truth carelessly.

I HAD BEEN SUPERVISING staff since I was eighteen years of age, albeit at that time only one Lad Porter at North Port and I had learnt early on that we are all individuals and everyone is different. Some you have to push, some you have to pull, some you have to swear at occasionally and other you have to tread softly with to get the best out of them. The secret to staff management I believed was to be firm, fair and consistent. To be honest with them and while obviously with a few exceptions, not to talk down to them. It was much more productive to talk to them at their own level. I think the same principles apply in most cases when talking to Union officials, but it is much more difficult because of pre-conceived ideas, politics and ideologies.

As the Head of a new Branch, I thought it essential to let everyone know quite quickly what I stood for, what my "modus operandi" was and what I expected to achieve. I had been critical of management style, not only in the Traffic Branch, but also in other branches and at the very top level, so now I had to "put my money where my mouth had been" so to speak. I had no intention of trying to change my forthright, no nonsense style in my endeavours to vastly improve the operational and financial performance in my area of responsibility. I saw these two functions as absolutely critical to the very future of freight train services on our railway.

I don't deny that some people would find fault with my tactics and that they would possibly be right depending on your point of view, but I was not in a popular man contest and I wanted results. The following examples fall into this category. They are only a few of many successful direct interviews.

TRADITIONALLY THE RAILWAYS had sent memorandums or "blisters" to staff concerning misdemeanours or oversights which needed to be explained and sometimes led to disciplinary action. I accepted that it was a necessary method but it was often ineffective because of the lapse of time and the number of people handling the correspondence before it was finalised.

Although time consuming, I preferred to settle such matters verbally, whenever possible, instead of entering into correspondence. I found it much more effective.

I usually arrived at work early to get a good start before the events of the day took over and first went through the control rooms to see what had happened overnight and how the morning peak suburban and country was shaping up. On one occasion a train guard who was notorious for being uncooperative and a bit of a "bush lawyer" had refused to work as directed.

The Train Controller had instructed him to change over from the 6:45am up Kyneton commuter train to a goods train which had been side tracked at Woodend, the Guard of which had been on duty for in excess of ten hours. This was in keeping with the traditional practice of first on first off unless there were some special circumstances.

The Guard refused to comply with the instruction and argued with the station staff then the Train Controller, delaying the train seven minutes. A further delay of three minutes occurred in the suburban area due to the lost pathway. He claimed that the ARU had recently told guards that if they did not wish to changeover off their roster they did not have to do so.

On learning of this I decided to confront the Guard. I walked up to Spencer Street Station for the arrival of the train, opened the door of his van and stepped in. I introduced myself and told him I needed to talk to him about the delay to the train and its passengers, all of whom would now be late for work.

He immediately said "I don't think I should talk to you unless I have a union official present". I glared at him, looking him straight in the eyes and snarled, "You can have Jesus Christ present if you wish, but it will make no difference to what is going to happen to you if I don't get certain undertakings concerning your future behaviour".

He looked quite startled and asked what undertakings did I want and what would happen if he didn't comply. I told him I would reduce him from his guard's position to a labourer immediately and his next shift would be hosing out cattle and sheep vans at the Brooklyn wash dock, but I put it a little more crudely than that. The first thing he should realise was that the railways provided his pay on payday, not the union. If Union policy had changed in such situations they had not notified management. He had let a fellow worker down who would also be a union member and now would finish up with a shift of over twelve hours.

If in the future he felt an instruction given to him was wrong, provided it was safe and legal he should not argue and cause delays, but comply stating he was doing it under protest. If he then felt inclined to do so he should complain in writing to his OIC and send a copy to his Union so that the matter could be sorted out in a proper and responsible manner. He then surprised me by stating he had applied for promotion to Yard Foreman and asked if this incident would rule him out. I told him that this incident alone would not rule him out but his reputation and attitude towards authority certainly would, if it did not change.

He then said that he would not have enough seniority for a year or two to be offered promotion and asked that if he had a clear record during that time, would he be given consideration. I left him saying that would be the only hope he had of getting promotion but he would have to prove that his attitude had changed over a period of time. I kept checking on him over the next year or so and found he had kept out of trouble. The train controllers were really surprised at the change and a couple of them said he had actually become co-operative.

He did not come up for promotion before I was shifted upstairs but he did maintain his changed attitude. All the "blisters" he had been given in the past had not changed him but a few minutes counselling, talking to him at his level and using language he clearly understood did the trick.

A SHORT TIME later I received a call from the senior clerk at the Melbourne Terminal regarding another guard who had a bad record for going AWL (Absent Without Leave) and had in fact been disciplined for it and had again offended. The clerk in charge said that the last time he did it he had told him he was on his last chance and should he offend again he could expect to be reduced in grade or even worse.

It was known that he had a drinking problem and that from time to time he would go to the country with his brother who had a truck and would make trips away to buy scrap metal. I had worked with this clerk at Dynon back in 1967 and had every faith in his judgement and competence. I told him if he wanted me to back him up I would certainly do so, but we were short of guards at the time and provided he did not object, it might be prudent to give him one more chance on the basis that he had to get past me in an interview before he could return to work and if he offended again after that, he would be terminated or reduced in grade.

Ken the senior clerk, said he was perfectly happy with such an arrangement so when the guard reported in that he wanted to return to work he explained what was required, but we made him "stew" for a couple of days before I saw him.

He was well groomed and well dressed when he came into my office but was obviously nervous. I probably made him worse by dressing him down and telling him he had no future in the railways if he once again offended. I spoke to him about his family and the affect it would have on his wife and children and then played my trump card.

I said you are in a railway house if my information is correct. He confirmed that he was. I then said "Do you realise that if you lose your job in the railways you will also lose the house with the subsidised rent?" I could see that he was uncomfortable and he suddenly blurted out that the drink was his problem and since he had been off it for a fortnight, he would now stay off it.

I then gave him some words of encouragement to do so and told him I would give him one more chance but he had better keep his word. I got up from my desk and walked around to shake his hand. As I did so I smelt a strong smell of liquor on his breath. I said to him in a firm voice "You lying bastard".

He was unsure what had caused my outburst and nervously asked what was wrong. I said, "You have just told me that you have not had a drink for a fortnight but you smell like a brewer's horse."

He then claimed that he had got ready to come to the interview early and went out to his backyard when his neighbour put his head over the fence and asked him why he was all dressed up. He told him, another railway man, that he had to go for an interview with me. He alleged the neighbour said that in that case you will need something to fortify you, went into his house and brought out a bottle of brandy and a glass for him to have a drink.

I told him I did not believe him but if it was true he should have shown some strength and gumption and knocked it back. I told him he had better leave the office before I changed my mind. He then scurried out and I never ever heard from him again. Reports from his supervisor over a period of time was that the absenteeism had ended and his work performance was quite satisfactory. I would have thought that the workover I gave him could have caused him to dislike me intensely, but such was apparently not the case.

My locomotive driver brother told me sometime after I had retired, that he travelled home from Warragul one night in the guard's van when this fellow asked him if he was my brother. When he replied in the affirmative he allegedly said

"Ray was not only a good railway man, but he also understood people. I had to go for an interview with him on one occasion and it turned my life around for the better." Despite criticism from some areas and of course a few failures, the many good outcomes proved my blunt and direct methods of dealing with people instead of sending them "blisters" was effective. I realise that now days people would label me a bully but in these two incidents and many others, their attitudes changed as did their work life and no doubt family life. I often wonder if many of society's problems today are in part at least, the result of us becoming so "soft" in many aspects of life.

I CAN HONESTLY SAY that I did not realise at the time the affect my management style was having on different groups or grades of people in the Branch.

One example was the train controllers located in Head office. I found it quite amusing several years after I had retired, when I was invited to a retirement function for a Senior Train Controller. I had always got on well with the train controllers I believed because of my train running knowledge and my understanding of the many problems they encountered daily. That did not stop me of course from taking individuals to task when I considered they had not handled a situation as they should have.

During the reminiscing and story telling, some of the speakers obviously felt that it was in order to reveal some situations involving me since I had long been retired. A standing practice was that the Senior Train Controller on duty of a Saturday morning was to ring me at home at around ten o'clock to fill me in on incidents which had occurred statewide through the night and so far that day. It was claimed by this speaker and supported by the other Seniors present, that despite the fact that they had put in much time and effort to comprehensively report to me, never did any of them ever escape a question they could not immediately answer, concerning incidents in the report. He claimed this made them very nervous when ringing me.

A more amusing story concerned a train controller on the Bendigo board who had allowed a goods train to proceed from Woodend ahead of the 6:45am 'up' and Kyneton passenger train which was subsequently delayed some eight minutes. He of course realised his mistake and appealed to the other controllers to try and come up with an excuse which might be accepted by me when I visited the rooms shortly after. They noted there was one van of cattle on the goods train and it was decided he would tell me he had given it priority in case it arrived too late for the market. When I entered the control room the other country controllers apparently left their rooms and unbeknown to me, had wedged the soundproof door open about a centimetre to hear the discussion.

When he gave me his excuse I allegedly asked him how many cattle were in the van. He said he did not know. I apparently said "I will tell you. If they are fat cattle there will be about ten. If they are store stock there might be about fourteen. Now, how many passengers are on the following train which you delayed?" He checked his departure total and his "offs and ons" at intermediate stations and said "about 150". I then allegedly said, "How can I tell the passengers who complain they were late for work or missed their connecting transport, that the controller gave priority to perhaps, fourteen head of cattle?"

I had long forgotten this incident but the train controllers had not and it again emphasised the fact that my methods of dealing with staff were often more effective than the traditional methods of sending them "blisters".

22

Restrictive Work Practices

THE FREIGHT SIDE of the service to our customers and the utilisation of rolling stock was severeley impeded by the abominable restrictive work practices of the Metropolitan Shunters Section of the Australian Railways Union. Most of the restrictions were imposed under the guise of safety, but they went way beyond that. Traditionally each section of Melbourne Yard was allocated a pilot locomotive and shunting crew, some operated for twenty four hours a day, others for varying times depending on the nature and volume of the work to be performed. The number of shunters on each pilot varied according to its classification.

For example, 'Transfer' pilots had two men, 'Dock' pilots' had three men, 'Yard Section' pilots had four men and 'Special Class' pilots had five men. When their full training was completed, shunters were qualified to work on any of these pilots. Wastage in the shunting grade was heavy and absenteeism was rife, particularly in school holiday periods when it was suspected that with both parents working, if the mother was unreliable in attendance, she was much more likely to lose her job than was the father, because we were always struggling to fill the roster, on the early shift especially, and to a degree went easy on absenteeism.

Container traffic was booming at the time. Not only import and export, but also interstate and local. There were three dock pilots rostered each morning at 6.10am, Swanson Dock, Appleton Dock and Victoria Dock. If absenteeism meant that we could not staff all three, usually the Victoria Dock Pilot would be the first cancelled giving preference to the container traffic, but this meant that under the restrictive work practices of the shunters, the other dock pilots could not enter the Victoria Dock area or other sidings that this pilot normally serviced, for the full shift. The same situation applied at the start of the afternoon shift at 2.10pm. The problem was complicated due to the fact that some container companies with private sidings might be serviced on the early shift by one pilot, but on the afternoon shift by another, thus in theory, balancing out the workload.

This sometimes resulted in a container company siding not getting serviced for two shifts, although whenever possible, we tried to avoid such situations by juggling the cancellations. Freight train services to country Victoria were also frequently delayed or cancelled when sections in the yard could not be manned, thus destroying the service to our customers and the turn around of rolling stock, creating an artificial shortage of wagons. The staff in the Freight Operations Division at Head Office responsible for expediting loads and filling orders for the supply of empty wagons and vans were regularly subjected to stress due to abuse and threats from customers whose services were seriously delayed or cancelled. The frustration of one regular client whose action would have been humorous had it not been so serious, was expressed by him walking into the office of the Manager Freight Operations, sitting on a spare chair near his desk and stating he would not move until his vans of butter had been placed for delivery. He could see them in the yard but could not get to them to unload.

Our freight services were in some cases profitable, and had

the potential to be more so if we improved the services. The Railway hierarchy was aware of the situation and so was the Transport Minister, but they seemed to have entirely different attitudes if there was industrial action affecting passenger services, as against freight services.

I guess the media played a big part in this as stoppages to passenger services made headlines but rarely did they have much interest in freight services. The squeaky wheel got the grease. I decided very early in the life of the Operations Branch to tackle this Melbourne Yard restrictive work practices problem head on. Although there were many problems to be solved, this one, if eradicated or even substantially eased, would easily "bear the most fruit". I arranged a series of meetings with the Shunters Section ARU, where I explained in detail the reasons I wanted the restrictions removed and guaranteed that if they were prepared to cooperate, each and every alteration to their practices would be made in consultation with them, with as always, safety in their workspace being the number one consideration. There was a lot of "froth and bubble" but absolutely nothing of any substance came out of these meetings. It was obvious that the shunters had no intentions of altering their policy even though it was made clear that we were losing traffic and if the trend was not reversed, eventually not only shunters jobs would be lost, but also those of staff in country Victoria.

Staff in rural areas were generally much closer to our customers as they shopped, socialised and schooled their kids together. They were constantly complaining about the quality of service with late running and cancellations and failure to supply empty wagons when ordered.

There was of course generally a marked difference in attitude between Melbourne Yard shunters and career railway people. This had not always applied but it seemed that a hardcore of aggressive, militant unionists had taken control in Melbourne Yard despite the fact that there were still some good loyal, solid citizen types there, but they were very much in the minority. The other problem was the recruiting of shunters off the street. They had no railway background going straight into the Shunters' school and being "brain washed".

Union representatives had demanded and been granted access to the class long ago and I believe abused the privilege. On completion of their training, a lot of the graduates had a very blinkered, narrow minded outlook of railways, having no experience or knowledge outside the confines of Melbourne Yard. I decided that instead of wringing my hands and putting the problem in the "too hard" box, as had been the custom for years, I would take the initiative.

Management was always on the back foot with the all-conquering Shunters Section Union officials, so I thought I should reverse this situation and see if it could be a more successful tactic. I had long thought it quite strange that way back in March 1948 the shunters had been granted a seventy-six hour fortnight under their Award. I don't know the background to this, but it meant that since they were rostered eight hour shifts they would be paid penalty rates daily after working seven hours and thirty-six minutes. This did not seem much but it was a nice little bonus at the end of each fortnightly pay period.

The restrictive work practices imposed by the shunters were far too numerous to be detailed here, but I will mention some that caused the biggest problems. If a pilot could not be fully manned it could not operate, even if the work could be done quite safely by taking more time for certain moves.

An example would be to push and pull instead of loose shunting which was possibly much less likely to cause a safety incident than the normal work practice. Phone calls would be made to see if the staff member who had not come to work had maybe just slept in and might yet report, but in the meantime, the remaining members of that shunting crew would be idle. Sometimes it was possible to cancel a less important on the day pilot, to create a mini pool of shunters from which a shortage on a more important pilot could be filled. This enabled the pilot to operate albeit after a late start. Once a pilot had been cancelled, other pilots were not permitted to enter that area for the shift.

This applied even for a siding such as Wooldumpers on the lead to Swanson Dock, serviced by different pilots on different shifts. If the pilot rostered to service the siding could not be fully staffed and had to be cancelled, a minimum delay of eight hours would occur. The Swanson Dock pilot could have been utilised to place their wagons of wool as it passed enroute to Swanson Dock and this would have only taken a few minutes to do so, but the prevailing restrictions prevented this, which I thought was outrageous. When a section of the yard was closed for the shift because a pilot could not be fully staffed, a train assembled on the previous shift could not depart if the Train Examiner "red carded" a wagon for repairs, or the train had not been pushed together for coupling. Only a few minutes' work would have been involved to remedy either of these situations in complete safety with a two man pilot, but because of the policy of the shunters of not entering a closed section for the shift, a minimum delay of eight hours would be once again destroying the service to our customers and the utilisation of rolling stock.

Even when a pilot was fully manned, if during the course of the shift a shunter took ill, suffered a foreign body in the eye, or had to knock off because of a problem at home, or for any other reason, if he could not be replaced, the pilot was cancelled for the remainder of the shift.

In the circumstances I have outlined, I thought it was plainly wrong that shunters for whom there was no work for either their full shift, or part of their shift, should be paid not only for eight hours, but also penalty rates on a daily basis, as had been the custom since most of the restrictions were imposed in 1973. I was getting absolutely nowhere trying to negotiate a satisfactory solution to the problems with the Union representatives so I decided to write to each individual shunter. The letter gave statistics showing the alarming decline in the number of vehicles being handled in Melbourne Yard over recent years despite an increase in shunting staff strength of approximately fifty percent.

I pointed out that efforts had been made to have restrictive work practices eased so that better use could be obtained from pilots and staff, but to no avail. I therefore felt that where staff become surplus on a daily basis due to circumstances beyond the control of Management, i.e.: restrictive work practices of the union, the payment of eight hours, plus daily overtime penalties, could no longer be justified. It was therefore intended, starting the following month, to discontinue this practice and instead pay staff in accordance with the minimum allowance clause of their Award.

If nothing else, the letter let everyone know that I was deadly serious about obtaining reform in the working of Melbourne Yard and its environs, and would not be fobbed off. The Shunters' Section of the ARU were quick to respond in writing to their members, not unexpectedly claiming that I was provocative and insensitive, I was telling half truths and making false accusations, that I was being divisive and that in fact the real reason for my letter was to cover up my ineptitude and my inability to manage the State's Rail Operations.

They had yet again resorted to a personal attack on me which I thought indicated that they were perhaps a little unsure of their strategy for dealing with the matter. They had a long history of calling stop work meetings for sometimes even trivial matters and I thought it quite significant that they had not done so on this important occasion.

Instead, the ARU went to the Conciliation and Arbitration Commission notifying that body of a dispute. This was a pleasing interim result for me as it represented a major departure from their usual tactics and I was of the opinion that an independent person directing discussions would surely see how unreasonable the work practices were.

My optimism however was misplaced as although there were several meetings and a lot of talk over the next couple of weeks, no real progress was being made. In order to move things along a bit I decided to suggest at the next meeting at the Conciliation and Arbitration Commission, to put up a proposal for a "period of adjustment" to take place where by a senior member of management accompanied by two union representatives nominated by the Union and on full pay, would oversee and assess the effects which result when restrictive work practices were suspended.

During this period I would not implement the minimum award provisions but the shunters would have to agree to work as and where required at anytime during the currency of their shift, on duties which they were competent to perform.

In addition to informing the Union of my intentions, I decided to again write to each individual shunter, so there could be no misunderstanding about what I was actually proposing.

The reply the very next day from the Shunters' Section Committee did not mention the proposal for a period of adjustment but instead continued the personal attack on me. They raised matters which clearly were not in my area of responsibility, e.g. the alleged shortage of staff in No. 4 shed and the alleged lack of planning in locomotive maintenance.

These were red herrings. The routing of block trains avoiding Melbourne Yard when it was more efficient to do so had been happening for many years prior to the introduction of the restrictive work practices in 1973, e.g. briquettes for the Powerhouse, Paisley and Western Victoria; but had increased since then, as a direct result of the shunters' actions in closing sections of the yard and causing delays. It had become more expedient to assemble rakes of empties elsewhere and run them direct to the wheat growing areas or the Phosphate Siding at Geelong.

They brought up other problems which certainly had an adverse affect on efficiency and productivity in the yard, but were completely irrelevant to the matter in dispute, i.e. the restrictive work practices of the shunters. Many meetings followed over many weeks which were extremely time consuming but finally a temporary compromise was reached. I undertook to keep the shunting staff numbers at 227 and not to invoke the minimum allowance clause of their award. In return, the Union would not close sections of the yard and would allow other pilots to place or clear loading or empties, subject to all safety rules applying. This was a significant breakthrough for management but unfortunately, did not include the dock areas which were the subject of ongoing negotiation. We were however able to improve the service considerably in the dock areas with the restrictions being lifted in the yard. Once the new working got underway we received many commendations, both verbal and in writing, for the improved service.

We never did reach a final agreement on the dock areas but because of the improved service, the pressure and complaints reduced over the period of about nine months that the compromise operated and management kept statistics of vehicles placed or cleared from sections which previously would have been closed, thus involving delays of between eight and twenty four hours. This amounted to over two thousand vehicles for that period, a vast improvement. Because of the loss situation the railway operated in, we were forever being urged to cut costs and improve productivity.

Toward the end of each financial year, we were instructed in recent years to reduce overtime payments but maintain services, to delay payment of accounts wherever possible until the new financial year and conversely, to make contact with clients in an endeavour to get as many outstanding accounts paid before the financial year ended. Recruiting of new staff was to cease until the start of the new financial year. This was a "rob Peter to pay Paul" situation, politically inspired no doubt. It was a desperate attempt to improve the current year's financial result at the expense of next year's.

I had an obligation to keep the shunting staff strength at 227 as one part of the compromise agreement. In keeping with that, application was made to the Personnel Branch to recruit a further ten shunters as their numbers were dwindling. The reply was that they could not do this until the new financial year. I spoke to the Director of Personnel, trying to impress upon him the importance of maintaining the interim agreement to the whole of the railways, not only the Operations Branch, and suggested that if necessary, he speak to a higher authority to get an exemption on this occasion.

He stated he had already done this as a result of a request from the AFULE to recruit firemen (that was news to me), but had been knocked back. It would be absolutely industrial relations suicide to now recruit potential ARU members. I agreed that normally that would be the case but these were very special circumstances and there was an enormous penalty to pay if the agreement was broken.

I got on very well with most AFULE officials and would explain the position to them. I was confident if we did this they would not object to waiting another few weeks for new staff, but the shunters certainly would. I told him I would speak to the General Manager. Unfortunately he sided with the Director of Personnel and I had lost this one to bureaucracy.

It was the greatest disappointment of my whole railway career up to that time as some of my staff and I had worked diligently over many months to obtain the agreement and monitor it. If the number of shunters dropped below the agreed figure it would clearly break the agreement and the restrictive practices would resume.

I could not believe senior management would risk this simply to reduce the deficit by the cost of wages for ten shunters for three or four weeks. To me it was sheer lunacy.

I thought it would be prudent to meet with the ARU and explain the situation to them. If the numbers did fall below the authorised staffing it would only be for a very short period of time as we would schedule a Shunters class for the start of the new financial year, and would continue recruiting thereafter as required. I don't think they could believe their luck. So much work and effort had been put into arriving at our compromise agreement and now, I was about to break it. The fact I had personally fought hard to obtain an exemption from the temporary recruitment ban but failed, appeared to be music to their ears.

Despite false allegations to the contrary, I had never once gone back on my word or broke an agreement with the Union, but now they had me dead to rights in their view, and I would pay the penalty for it for the rest of my railway career.

I felt that senior management had let me down badly, not only on the decision not to recruit shunters in a timely fashion to maintain the agreement for which I now had to take the blame, but also during the hearings over several months in the Commission. Normally the Personnel Branch would supply a senior person, usually the Industrial Advocate, to prepare the case. On this occasion they supplied their most junior Industrial Officer who had been transferred from my branch a short time beforehand. I therefore ran the case myself.

I was absolutely devastated as now the Union (ARU) could spread it far and wide that I broke agreements and could not be trusted. Of course they had done this before, but now it maybe had some credence. Needless to say when the numbers fell breaking the agreement the restrictive work practices were resumed. This action made a complete mockery of the paragraph on page two of their letter dated the 27th June 1980, in which they stated, "We have always been prepared to work in a spirit of cooperation to achieve efficient operations and service to clients. It is up to Mr Barden to display the same good faith which we have, to solve the current problems".

My letter on 27th May, 1980, to each individual shunter evoked a quick reply from the shunters section of the ARU.

VICTORIAN RAILWAYS

Operations Branch,
Room G.14. RTB:BM.
27th May, 1980.

Memorandum:-

MELBOURNE YARD OPERATIONS

Have you given any thought lately to your job and its future?

Did you know that Melbourne Yard handled equal to 80,382 vehicles in four weeks during January, 1974, but only equal to 55,037 vehicles in four weeks during January, 1980. For 18 weeks to date in 1980, the total is equal to 256,762; in the same period in 1974 equal to 385,076 vehicles were handled.

Although the workload of pilots has decreased since 1974, the numerical strength of shunting staff in Melbourne Yard has increased from 154 to 227. The smaller number of vehicles handled in Melbourne Yard is of great concern to me and I am sure must be a worry to you. You must realise that less work eventually means less jobs.

Efforts have been made to re-organise your work to make better use of pilots and staff and provide our customers with a more reliable service, but these efforts have met with continued opposition. Delays to traffic in the yard are a major reason for our loss of business.

Despite cancellation of pilots due to a variety of reasons staff have been paid 8 hours per day plus penalties when they are surplus to operational requirements, although the guaranteed fortnight provisions of the Railway Traffic and Permanent Way Award now applies to all Leading Shunters and Shunters.

The Executive Officers of the Metropolitan Shunters' Section, A.R.U., have recently reminded me of our mutual obligations under the Traffic and Permanent Way Award.

The payment of 8 hours, plus daily overtime penalty, cannot be justified for staff who report for rostered duties which cannot be performed due to circumstances beyond the control of the Operations Branch.

It is therefore intended to arrange as follows as from 1. 6.80:-

(1) Staff reporting for duty who are not required due to cancellation of pilots and/or for whom alternative duties cannot be found, will be paid in accordance with the minimum allowance clause of the Award.

(11) When it is necessary to cancel pilots during the currency of a rostered shift, for reasons beyond the control of management, payment will be made for hours worked, subject to the Award.

Unless we can give our customers the quality and type of service they require on a regular basis, the alarming decline in the traffic handled in the Melbourne Yard area will continue and place our livelihoods in jeopardy.

Your Union has been told of this decision and I am taking the opportunity to tell each of you in person so that you may be aware of my intentions.

R.T. Barden,
Chief Operations Manager.

MELBOURNE YARD.

Australian Railways Union
(Victorian Branch)

114 King Street,
Melbourne, 3000
1st & 4th Floors.
Telephone: 62 1176 (4 lines)

Railway Address:
C/o S.M., Spencer Street,
Auto. Phone: 2378, 1619

28 MAY 1980

SHUNTER'S REPLY TO BARDEN'S ATTACK ON JOBS

Barden's provocative letter to Melbourne Yard Shunters has been discussed by the A.R.U. Chief Executive Officers and Shunters Section Officials.

An urgent discussion with the Assistant General Manager and Personnel has been organised.

Barden's insensitivity to his own employes comes out again in his latest push to cut shunters livelihood and smash the Shunters Section.

It boils down to a full scale attack on your rosters, on your pay and on your jobs.

BARDEN WANTS:

1. A permanent pool of casual shunters, who will be on call when it suits VicRail;

2. To smash the A.R.U. Two weeks ago he tried us on with the Guards over their brake vans;

3. To weaken the Shunters so that key operational changes can go ahead.

   These include closing the Melbourne Freight Terminal and reducing VicRail to a line haul operation of single commodity block trains.

If Barden and VicRail win it means the end of many railworkers' jobs. Not only Shunters will be affected but also Guards, freight workers and train examiners.

Barden's letter makes a lot of false accusations and tells many half truths.

It is designed to be devisive and to confuse Shunters because this weakens our ability to withstand his plans.

For a start, pilots have not been cancelled because of any fall in business.

In fact, it is arguable that tonneages have not dropped and that changes in the routing of trains around Melbourne yard has been conveniently ignored.

The real reasons behind Barden's move is to cover up his own ineptitude and inability to manage this State's rail operation.

Pilots are being cancelled because of management's blunders, including:
- their deliberate policy to take out of running 4 wheel wagons and create an artificial wagon scarcity;
- their inability to effectively plan locomotive maintenance requirements and shortages of staff in key operating grades, for example, locomotive crews.

WE MUST STICK TOGETHER - WE MUST NOT BE STAMPEDED INTO STRIKE ACTION, AS THIS WILL ONLY PLAY INTO BARDEN'S HANDS.

Ian COOPER   Frank LACEY
CHAIRMAN   SECRETARY

THE PREVIOUS TWO pages show my letter of May 27 1980 to the individual shunters and the quick reply which it evoked from the prompt response from the ARU Shunters section.

It attacks me personally and makes several incorrect assumptions on the reason for my letter.

The increase in the number of trains by-passing Melbourne yard was forced upon us due to the restrictive work practices. Sections of the yard were closed for varying periods daily and this meant that empties going to wheat areas or the phosphate sidings could be delayed for hours or perhaps a day.

Operationally, it became far better to assemble them elsewhere and run them direct to their destinations.

Other matters of locomotive maintenance and wagon maintentance are really "red herrings" as I had no responsibility or control over them.

Australian Railways Union
(Victorian Branch)

636 Bourke Street,
Melbourne, Vic., 3000
Telephone: 60 1561, 60 1562

Railway Address:
C/o S.M., Spencer Street.
Auto. Phone: 2378, 1619

Our Ref.:

3rd June, 1980

MEANINGFULL NEGOTIATIONS

Negotiations between the Operations Branch and the Shunters Section over Barden's letter are now underway.

Deputy President McKenzie recommended a two weeks cooling off period last Friday, so the parties could negotiate.

Earlier VicRail had refused Union approaches to negotiate but D.P. McKenzie said it was normal practice for the status quo to remain in these sort of situations, until the matter had been negotiated.

He also said there was room for negotiations because the Union and the Shunters Section were prepared to be constructive.

On Monday the Shunters Section asked to see Barden and a discussion was held on Tuesday, 3rd June at 9 a.m.

The Section and Union officials requested the following information and Barden agreed to provide as much of it as possible at the next meeting scheduled for tomorrow -Thursday.

1: A detailed list of the specific practices and changes Barden wants to negotiate on.

2: Annual tonneage figures for the Melbourne Yard, particularly Melbourne Freight Terminal since January 1974.

3: Numbers of wagons requested by the Freight Branch for Melbourne Freight Terminal and the number actually supplied by the Traffic or Operations branch over a similar period.

Deputy President McKenzie has asked the Union and VicRail to report back to him on Friday at 2.15 p.m. on progress.

Jim FRAZER
BRANCH SECRETARY
A.R.U.

Frank LACEY
Secretary,
SHUNTERS SECTION

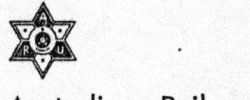

Australian Railways Union
(Victorian Branch)

114 King Street,
Melbourne, 3000
1st & 4th Floors.
Telephone: 62 1176 (4 lines)

Railway Address:
C/o S.M., Spencer Street,
Auto. Phone: 2378, 1619

Our Ref.:

REPORT ON ARBITRATION PROCEEDINGS BEFORE JUSTICE MCKENZIE -6.6.80

Last Thursday we met the Department again. We asked for the information we had requested and they had agreed to give. We also asked for the specific areas of work practices that they wished to see changed.

Between Tuesday and Thursday they had changed their minds and said they could not see what the statistics about cancellation of pilots and supply of wagons had to do with the matter in hand.

They also produced a letter that said in part "you thought our interpretation of the term more flexible use of staff" and further "we mean that shunting staff should be employed as and where required at any time during the currency of their rostered shift on duties which they are competent to perform".

After further discussion they promised to review again their decision about the statistics and on Friday we received some that clearly showed the major reason for inefficiency was the shortage of crews and pilots.

We appeared on Friday at 2.15 p.m. before Deputy President McKenzie and after both parties agreed discussions had been meaningfull, Deputy President McKenzie then put some ideas forward.

He said, in part, that he did not expect workers to be penalised for management inefficiencies and that people who had nothing to do soon became bored.

After a short adjournment we put forward a "package deal" that available section executive members had agreed upon on the day before.

1. We would take repairs off trains made up in closed sections to allow them to depart.
2. Push a train together to allow it to depart.
3. Place empties in the Freight Terminal in closed sections.

We also asked that the special class school be started immediately.

In return for this, we demanded Barden's letter be withdrawn for at least 3 months to allow further negotiations.

The Department said the three points raised were not appropriate to meet requirements and added that VicRail would withdraw Barden's letter while negotiations on work practices took place, with the following provisos:

1. No closed sections or sidings in the yard.
2. Any loading or empties to be placed or cleared as directed by any available pilot.
3. Available pilots to service any area as required by Management (Melbourne Yard).
4. Pilots shall continue to operate provided their numbers are not reduced below two men. It being understood that a reduced workload may result.
5. Work priorities be determined by yard management.

P.T.O

6. Principles of safety and safe-working will continue to apply.

They added that these points were covered by work practices and Rules and Regulations.

We told them that this was totally unacceptable and our package was not negotiable.

Deputy President McKenzie added he felt the Department should supply the list of work practices they wish to alter.

This is the reason for calling the meeting today, and we ask for the continued support and ideas from all section members.

        J. POULTNEY.   J.F. FRAZER.
    BRANCH PRESIDENT   BRANCH SECRETARY

The Union's report to shunters on proceedings in the court appear on the previous two pages. The following two pages show my second letter to individual shunters dated June 26, 1980, and the Union's responseAgain, it avoided comment on the shunters' work practices, which was the subject we were trying to discuss, and introduced other inefficienceis in the yard, some of which I had no control over anyway. The first two concessions they made were very welcome, but the much bigger practice of closed sections was not addressed.

G. 25 L

VICTORIAN RAILWAYS

Operations Branch,
Room G.14, RTB:BM.
26th June, 1980.

Memorandum:-

WORK PRACTICES - MELBOURNE YARD AREA

Since I wrote you on 27. 5.80, there has been a series of discussions between VicRail and Union Officers, both privately and under the Chairmanship of Deputy President McKenzie of the Australian Conciliation & Arbitration Commission and which related to the restrictive work practices at Melbourne Yard and the associated areas.

Because this matter is most important to your continued livelihood and to your fellow employees, I am taking the step of writing to you again.

In order for VicRail to retain its business and to regain lost business (especially that which is related to Melbourne Yard), its operations have to be made as flexible as possible so that we can react to the varying needs of our customers.

It is for this reason that management wishes to change the operating practices and to remove restrictive work practices that have built up in the past.

Rest assured that management is aware that current work practices in the Melbourne Yard area are not the only constraints or problems which prevent adequate service to clients, nor have the Shunters been singled out in management's efforts to improve our performance. Indeed we are taking steps to obviate our shortcomings in other areas.

While the initial discussions with your representatives appeared to be meaningful, it would now appear (as we have been informed) that the Melbourne Yard Shunters are not prepared to consider in any real sense the removal of these restrictive practices.

The reason we have been told is that Shunters are concerned over their continuing livelihood.

Management does not believe that your livelihood will be affected and has offered to implement a "period of adjustment" to safeguard your interests.

During this period, management would not implement the minimum award provisions (and does not expect to, anyway) and the opportunity will be given for two of your representatives to assess, at VicRail's expense, with a senior manager, the effects that result from the removal of the restrictive work practices.

Remember that you enjoy the guarantee provisions of the award and your livelihood is therefore protected.

Further, in line with the comments of the Deputy President "that we should bring ourselves into the 1980's", and the responsibility of Management to determine work priorities, no alternatives are left other than, subject always to safeworking conditions being paramount, to insist, that in order to achieve more flexible yard operations, shunting staff will be employed as and where required, at any time during the currency of their rostered shift, on duties which they are competent to perform.

Please regard this as an approach for realistic negotiation and be assured that no action will be taken until the Australian Conciliation & Arbitration Commission has been advised of the current situation at the conference arranged for Monday, 30th June, 1980.

Let us work together in a spirit of co-operation to achieve our goal of efficient operation and service to clients and thus ensure not only the livelihood of Shunters but all railworkers.

I therefore ask you again to consider your attitude to the proposal to increase the flexibility of operations within the Melbourne Yard and associated areas.

R.T. Barden,
Chief Operations Manager.

Australian Railways Union
(Victorian Branch)

Unity Hall,
636 Bourke Street,
Melbourne, Vic., 3000
Telephone: 60 1561, 60 1562

Railway Address:
C/o S.M., Spencer Street,
Auto. Phone: 2378, 1619

Our Ref.:

SHUNTERS' REPLY TO BARDEN'S LETTER

→ Not Operations
Branch responsibility.
Freight Branch area.

27th of June, 1980

Today, we all received another letter from the Chief Operations Manager, Mr. R.T. Barden.

In it he claims that he is concerned about the future of Shunters and all railway men. If this is true, then he shows his concern in a very strange way.

On Tuesday, of this week, we approached the Department with a view to overcoming the problem of inward perishables into 4 Shed. Each day for the past few week there has been a large backlog of perishables because of the shortage of Freight Terminal workers.

When we expressed concern about this situation and asked for a deputation, we were told they were not interested in discussing the problem. This shows real concern for VicRail's customers.

Another point Mr. Barden raises is the fact that he has been informed that we are not prepared to negotiate meaningfully. At every stage of discussions we have indicated our willingness to negotiate. As all members are aware, our "package deal" ensures further negotiations and we have not changed our attitude. *?* *where*

He also says that he has no intention of affecting our livelihood. His two proposals would clearly affect our livelihood, conditions and safe-working.

Mr. Barden's comment about what Deputy President McKenzie said, is very selective and taken out of context. In our reports back to the Section we have indicated everything the Deputy President has said.

action in court to restrain it sent to country operations depots by Barden —

→ He also states that "management is aware that current work practices in the Melbourne Yard are not the only constraints or problems which prevent adequate service to our clients, nor have Shunters been singled out in management's efforts to improve our performance."

We have asked that other matters, shortage of staff in other areas, and locomotives, etc., be discussed and that information be supplied regarding these areas. Mr. Barden has consistently stated that these things are irrelevant to the working of the Yard. Clearly, this is not so.

If Mr. Barden is really concerned about realistic negotiations, then why does he keep rejecting all the proposals we have put, by saying they do not go far enough?

Have only agreed to push a train together for coupling purposes and to remove a red card so trains already made up can depart from a "closed section" of the yard

They are irrelevant to the subject of restrictive work practices of Melbourne yard shunters which is what we are negotiating on.

P.T.O.

We have always been prepared to work in a spirit of co-operation to achieve efficient operations and service to clients. It is up to Mr. Barden to display the same good faith which we have, to solve the current problems.

To help overcome any confusion members may have, we urge all members who can, to attend the hearings in the Arbitration Commission. The next one is at 10-30 a.m., next Monday, 30/6/80, at Nauru House - 80 Collins St., Melbourne.

HELP US TO DEFEND OUR JOBS BY YOUR CONTINUED SUPPORT!

SHUNTERS' SECTION
COMMITTEE

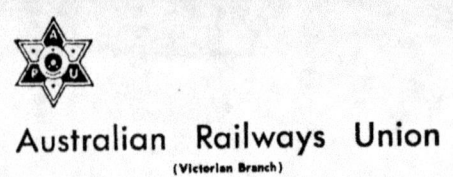 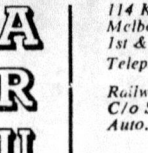

114 King Street,
Melbourne, 3000
1st & 4th Floors.
Telephone: 62 1176 (4 lines)

Railway Address:
C/o S.M., Spencer Street,
Auto. Phone: 2378, 1619

Our Ref.: FL/ca

METROPOLITAN SHUNTERS' SECTION

STAND ASIDES AND SUSPENSIONS IN THE MELBOURNE YARD

Over the last couple of days the Metropolitan Shunters Section has been taking action in support of Shunters at Geelong.

This arose out of another of Barden's broken promises. A threat has been made against two Leading Shunters and the Secretary has been suspended.

A meeting of the Section's Executive has been held and a course of action has been decided upon.

The whole of the A.R.U. is behind our decided course of action. You will be kept informed of all developments but, it is important, at this stage, that whatever we decide is well considered.

We must not allow Barden's attempts to intimidate individuals and split the Section and Union. It is at moments like these that disciplined unity will win out.

This is a struggle to save our jobs and to let the vandals like Hamer, Maclellan, Lonie and Barden etc., know that we will resist their attempts to destroy our industry.

J. Poultney - Branch President,   J.F. Frazer - Branch Secretary

I. Cooper - Chairman   F. Lacey - Secretary

9th of September, 1980

23

Unsolicited Publicity

ON THE LIGHTER side of things, I had some years back when Manager of Passenger Operations, given rise to a cartoon appearing in the Melbourne press depicting a special train at Spencer Street Station bound for Sydney. Some of my staff made some minor alterations to the cartoon and presented it to me. At the time radar technicians at Sydney Airport were taking industrial action causing many aircraft to be diverted to Melbourne. Qantas in particular, but also other airlines, were keen to send diverted passengers to Sydney by train. We were able to increase capacity on the daylight train to Sydney, but as the situation worsened, the number of diverted passengers demanded special trains. We had no standard gauge carriages spare so I had to borrow old wooden, non airconditioned cars from N.S.W. This action attracted a lot of criticism as it was thought by some to be bad publicity for our railway using such old rolling stock, but it did bring in extra revenue and the airline people were very pleased with our responses to their requests.

"Passengers on BARDEN'S SPECIAL to London via Albury, Wagga, Sydney, please board at Platform 3 . . . !"

Jeff Hook cartoon, Sun News Pictorial. Used with kind permission from Pauline Hook.

"THANK goodness — a commercial break!"

Jeff Hook cartoon, Sun News Pictorial. Used with kind permission from Pauline Hook.

TVs, trannies get the shunt

VICRAIL has cracked down on rail workers who take radios and TV sets into their signal boxes.

By WAYNE GREGSON

A recent VicRail circular warns rail workers that they face severe discipline if they are found with TV sets in the signal box while on duty.

They could get a written reprimand, fines up to $10, or a demotion.

The circular claims that rail workers have been seen walking around on the job with transistors pressed to their ears, and over recent months a small number of workers have been punished for using TV sets at work.

"I have even heard cheerios over certain radio stations to shift signalmen and drivers and guards on early shift," the circular said.

The Australian Railways Union said the offences were rare.

But, like the VicRail and Train Travellers' Association, the union frowned on the practice, which it said could not benefit rail safety.

The circular said the use of radio and TV at work led to "unavoidable" train delays because of distraction or inattention.

ARU secretary Mr Jim Frazer said: "Reports give the impression that this is an epidemic. If that was the case, we would not have the good safety record we now have.

"This has been hopelessly exaggerated."

The ARU checked the claims yesterday and found that one employee had been disciplined recently for having a TV in his signal box, and a "couple of others" were caught a few months ago.

Fast forward a few years to 1981 and another cartoon I thought really funny appeared in the Sun News Pictorial, following an article in the same paper the day before. The newspaper response indicated that the secretary of the Train Travellers Association had come into possession of a copy of my internal staff bulletin and passed it on to the media. He agreed that having TV sets and radios in the workplace was a safety issue and that rail management should "crack down" on the practice. The Sun News Pictorial then contacted the ARU Secretary who agreed that the practice "could not benefit rail safety" but claimed that the situation had been "hopelessly exaggerated" and offences were rare. The Union Secretary then contacted me and severely criticised me for putting such matters in writing. I was amazed at the attitude and told him so. It was an internal document and an effective way of communicating to staff.

If an accident occurred allegedly due to this practice, he would no doubt also criticise me for not having alerted staff to the danger. He was also ignoring the fact that avoidable delays were occurring which inconvenienced our passengers and adversely affected our timekeeping performance. He certainly didn't appreciate it when I said that he had already agreed that the practice "could not benefit rail safety" and perhaps he should consider putting out a circular in support of my bulletin as such action would surely reinforce the need to stamp out the practice before it did become an "epidemic".

A Man of Principle

TV in signals box: VicRail clamp

By MICHAEL VENUS, Herald Transport Reporter

VicRail has severely disciplined several suburban signalmen for watching TV in their signal boxes while on duty.

It has also warned "appropriate action" will be taken if future offences are detected.

An internal VicRail document strongly criticises, on safety grounds, criticises, on safety grounds, operations staff who watch TV or listen to radios.

It says they also cause many "unavoidable" delays because of distraction or inattention.

A VicRail spokesman said this afternoon that each of the signalmen involved had been fined $10 — the maximum fine allowable. They also were threatened with demotion.

"We have that power under the Railways Act," he said.

VicRail's chief operations manager, Mr Ray Barden, issued the "Staff Bulletin 2 (Suburban)" recently.

In it, Mr Barden said he had seen:

* Radio sets in signal boxes and shunters' cabins.
* Radios on ledges behind the windscreen in the drivers' cabs of trains.
* Guards and drivers holding radio sets to their ears when "proceeding between the depot and yard or platforms and when changing ends at terminals."
* Shunters holding radio sets to their ears when moving about the yard.

"I have also heard cheerios over certain radio stations to shift signalmen and drivers and guards on early shift," he said.

"On some occasions, the location has been announced and on two occasions the actual names of the staff have been announced.

WRONG PLACE

"I have not personally noticed any television sets, but several signalmen have been severely disciplined recently for operating or allowing television sets in their signal boxes."

Earlier, Mr Barden told staff in the bulletin: "Our duty hours are certainly the wrong time, and the train running scene certainly the wrong place, to operate radios or television sets.

"Safe working and train handling are very vital and serious matters and one moment's lost concentration can have disastrous results to members of the public, staff equipment, or all three."

Mr Barden said he believed "many unavoidable delays are caused through distraction or inattention as a result of the operation of radios and-or television sets on the job . . ."

He said the case against their use at work — whether connected to departmental power or not — had now been clearly put.

"It will be quite futile for any operating staff so detected in future to claim ignorance, or pinpricking, when appropriate action is taken," he said.

A copy of the document was released to The Herald by the Train Travellers' Association today.

Association secretary Mr Ken McIntyre, said: "Signalmen, drivers and guards are handling, and are responsible for, hundreds of lives of rail passengers.

"The rail management should crack down on this unsafe practice and the staff and rail unions must co-operate in the interests of safe working of trains."

24

Politically Inspired Industrial Action

THE SHADOW MINISTER OF TRANSPORT had formed a "Transport Committee" which comprised officials of the three major rail unions. Sometimes accompanied by the shadow Minister, many meetings were held at country locations where they highlighted the proposed closure of branch line passengers services, (not instigated by me) and many other inadequacies, as they saw them in the railway services. This action was no doubt part of a campaign leading up to the State Election in 1982. Because of my efforts to rationalise country depots which were really relics of the steam age where locomotives had to be serviced about every fifty or sixty miles, and also my efforts to stamp out restrictive works practices, I became a prime target for the ARU in particular. I actually got along quite well with the AFULE even though they certainly were against the proposed closure of depots. My relationship with the ARU had deteriorated to such an extent that at almost every meeting I had with them, I would be told by one officer or another, from the President Joe Poultney down to section officials, that there will be an election next year when the government will certainly change. We have compiled a "hit list" of unwanted railway managers and guess who is number one on it. I had no doubt that they had done this but I did not place a great deal of significance on it at the time. After all, I was a career railway man and had never been a member of a political party. I thought my experience and knowledge of railway operations, plus my proven ability to handle an extremely heavy workload, would be useful no matter what political party was in government. I had absolutely no motives whatsoever, other than to improve the performance of the railway and the service to our customers. I understood that my refusal to compromise when I knew that from the railway operations aspect I was right, frustrated them enormously, as did my resilience, stubbornness if you like, and determination. I don't think this group of ARU officials had experienced this from a Head of Branch previously. Quite clearly, the ARU had become even more militant and had given authority for Sub Branch officials throughout the State to impose "black bans" where they saw fit, as Melbourne Yard shunters had been doing for years, and not to wait until they could contact state officials. Sometimes a train would be "black banned" said to be in protest at the railways policy of cutting out jobs and reducing staff numbers. Other times it would be an alleged safety breach. To try and counter this I advised the Unions I was introducing a policy of "no work, no pay". That meant if a "black ban" was applied to a siding or train, details would be conveyed to me at any time of the day or night, when I would assess the situation and if I thought the safety matter was frivolous, I would direct that staff member involved be informed the ban was not accepted and that they resume their duties immediately. If they refused to do so, payment of wages would stop immediately and not resume until they indicated they were prepared to work as instructed. If it was a general protest "no work, no pay" was "effective" immediately. I informed top union officials that to ensure absolute consistency I was the only one who would make these decisions. On some occasions the ban would be lifted with very little delay. Other times, particularly if the train was in the yard, it could last for days. I shall detail a couple of the more interesting instances.

ONE SATURDAY NIGHT I had just gone to bed when I was informed that an Adelaide bound express goods train which had stopped at the platform to change crews at Ararat, had been banned, as a protest against management policies. An off duty Yard Foreman who was a local ARU official had applied the ban stating he would allow the train to be shunted to the yard to clear the main line for the passage of *The Overland* (overnight passenger train to Adelaide) and then it would remain in the yard until further notice. I immediately rang Ararat and spoke at first to the OIC and then to the union official. This case was a little bit different as it was not the Guard of the train or the Signalman who had applied the ban, but an off duty employee. I told each of them that in no circumstances was the train to be shunted to the yard. It should remain where it was until the ban was lifted. Both men quickly pointed out that *The Overland* was approaching Buangor, the next station in the rear, and it would be delayed indefinitely. I made it abundantly clear to the union official that he would wear the full responsibility for any delay to *The Overland* and if we had to terminate it and transfer the passengers into buses, we would make sure all passengers knew the reason, so if it come to that, he would be wise to keep out of the way. I then asked him to put the OIC on the phone again and suggested to him that he alert the bus companies as to the possibility we could need buses. I hung up but a few minutes later the phone rang and the OIC said the ban had been lifted so he was going to put the train into the yard to allow the *The Overland* to precede it as it had already been delayed eight minutes at Buangor. I told him if he did that we risked the probability that the ban would be re-imposed on the train in the yard, which was what they wanted in the first place. I told him to depart the goods train immediately. I spoke to the Train Controller and instructed him to keep the goods going ahead of *The Overland* right to the South Australian border and endorse his graph accordingly. I would take responsibility for any further delays to the passenger train which subsequently arrived at Serviceton twenty five minutes late.

ANOTHER INCIDENT OCCURRED at about 4.00am one morning when I was informed that a Union official had entered the signal box at Sunshine and instructed the signalman not to operate the signals for the passage of the 'up' Mildura *Fruit Flyer*. He would not say how long the ban would remain. I immediately rang one of my Block and Signal Inspectors who incidentally lived at Sunshine and asked if he would be prepared in the circumstances to signal the train through, assuring him that I would not hold it against him if his conscience told him he should not. He said he was sick and tired of the actions of the union and he had no qualms about operating the signals. He would be in attendance at the signal box in a short time. Quite frankly, I was getting sick of being pulled out of bed so often and my family being disturbed, but I had to stick with it. I decided there and then if I was getting pulled out of bed at all hours, so should some of the more senior Union officials. I rang the then Assistant Secretary of the ARU and told him I had decided that if I was woken up in future, I would ring a member of their executive on each occasion to ensure they knew what was going on and approved of it. He said he did not know what was happening at Sunshine but what I had done was futile, as his man would simply move up the line and put a ban on at the next signal box. I said I am out of bed now so I will stay up and come down to the City as an extra man to work signal boxes. About twenty minutes later

I received a call from Control to say that the ban at Sunshine had been lifted. There were no further incidents that morning.

ONE AFTERNOON I was about to leave the office and come home when the Yardmaster at the West Tower at Melbourne Yard reported that the shunters had placed a "black ban" on Contrans siding alleging a breach of safety whilst placing their wagons. Siding holders were well aware of the safety rules which applied while the warning bells and lights were operating indicating that a shunting move is taking place. They must keep clear and not climb on a vehicle or otherwise touch it until the warning devices stop operating, indicating it is then safe to do so. I immediately rang the operator at the siding to get his version of what had happened. He said he had gone outside and stood close enough to the siding to lift envelopes containing paperwork out of the clips on the wagon as they slowly passed him. He had done this for a long period of time and had not been queried previously. I informed him that he had technically contravened the safety rules and now we had the problem of getting the ban lifted. He assured me he would not do this again and would make sure that others at the siding were made well aware of the requirement. I told him that I would write to his management and again reiterate the requirements. I passed this information on to the Yardmaster and asked him to speak to the Leading Shunter and explain the action I had taken and request him to lift the ban. However, the shunters would not cooperate. I thought it over again and come to the conclusion that the safety code had definitely been broken, but it was a rather minor breach and from the point of view of the offender, he had done the same thing many times before and had not been challenged. It was a low range breach and action had been taken to prevent a repeat. I therefore decided to request the ban be lifted once more and if they refused, I would put the Leading Shunter, who was a very active member of the Metropolitan Shunters section of the ARU, on a "no work, no pay" situation. He got quite upset about my decision and actually rang me to put his case, but I would not change course. The ban was lifted about an hour later so he went back to full pay. There were other incidents where Leading Shunters were placed on "no work, no pay" situations for brief periods.

25

New Deal Passenger Services

A STUDY of Victorian Transport (Lonie Report) recommended to the State Government that all rail passenger services on country lines be withdrawn. VicRail presented a counter proposal which abandoned branch line passenger services, but upgraded and improved the services on all trunk lines. It was a two year plan involving expenditure of over fifty million dollars on rebuilding the fleet of 'B' class locomotives, building fifty-four new airconditioned carriages, providing a computerised seat booking system and altered signalling and trackwork layouts at some country terminals. The government of the day opted for the VicRail proposal. I had nothing to do with the planning of the proposed new services other than to maintain the supply of a senior experienced operations officer to strengthen the planning group. Their aim was to vastly improve the utilisation of rolling stock, reduce terminal times, improve the frequency of services and to speed up the transit times. In order to achieve this, one factor was to simply run the locomotive around the train at terminals and not "reverse" the guards van (shunting move to take the van from one end of the train to the other). As the Chief Operations Manager I supported this proposal. Difficult as it was to believe, the Guards Section of the ARU, supported by the Executive, opposed this plan as it meant that the van would not be at the rear of the train in one direction. Traditionally, in general operations, the van had been at the rear, but there were numerous exceptions to this which had operated safely and successfully for many years. The Union claimed that the proposal was unsafe. I was requested by the leader of the planning group to accompany union representatives to the Newport workshops for an inspection of the almost completed new guards van. I was also requested to make myself available for a further meeting with the union a few days later. Quite clearly the new services which were to be introduced progressively over a two years period, could not be introduced unless the Union changed its attitude.

DURING THE INSPECTION at Newport Workshops, union members repeatedly made it clear to me that they would ban the new services until arrangements were made for the Guard to be positioned at the rear of the train in both directions of travel. They confirmed this at the following meeting when Planning and Personnel Branch people were present. This was a ridiculous situation, not only in my view but in the view of all others present, except the Union representatives. I would have thought that the union would strongly support the project because it not only virtually guaranteed the guards jobs on passenger trains for the foreseeable future, but also those of others involved in providing the service, and it also created work at the workshops and other places during the construction period. I was convinced that many guards, particularly those at country depots would not be in agreement with union policy on this matter. I therefore thought that it might be productive for me to write to every individual guard throughout the state, suburban train guards excepted, to inform them of the full details of the plan, the advantages of it to our customers, to them as individuals and to the railways as a whole. It was also important that they clearly understood that neither I nor the Safeworking Superintendent had any concerns whatsoever about the safety of the proposed changed working. I have no idea if my letter had some influence on union decision making or not, but they did lift their ban a short time later. An interesting side issue was that soon after the Suburban Guards Section of the ARU asked me to receive a deputation from them concerning the future of their positions. I assured them that although I would not have the final say when and if that question arose, my recommendation would be that we must retain suburban guards until such time as at least these following requirements were met. Power signalling on all lines where suburban trains operated with signals fitted with train stops. (A mechanism which trips the trains brakes if the train passes the signal when at the stop position). All stations with curved platforms be equipped with closed circuit TV so the driver can see the full length of his train before closing and locking the doors. All trains operating on the system must have push button closing doors and locking which the driver can operate before starting. They seemed pretty happy with my response and I never heard from them again on this subject.

A Man of Principle

VICRAIL

Office of Chief Operations Manager,
Room G.14, RTB:BM. 14/83.
23rd September, 1981.

Mr. ....
Passenger/Goods Guard,
....

UPGRADED COUNTRY PASSENGER SERVICES - DO YOU KNOW THE FACTS?

The Victorian Transport Study (Lonie Report), recommended to the Victorian Government, among other things, that <u>all</u> rail passenger services on country lines be withdrawn.

The Victorian Government accepted this recommendation in so far as a few poorly patronised passenger services, mainly on Branch lines, were concerned, but opted for a counter proposal, presented by VicRail, to not only retain, but in fact dramatically upgrade, country passenger services on all the main trunk routes.

The successful VicRail proposal is essentially a two year plan involving investment of over 50 million dollars on 54 No. new airconditioned carriages, provision of on train refreshments on all longer distance trains, the complete rebuilding of all B class locomotives which will be dedicated to the new passenger running, the installation of a modern computerised seat booking system and altered signalling and trackwork layouts at some passenger terminals.

Although the upgraded services will not be fully operative until 1983 when the last of the new carriages will be constructed making all wooden bodied carriages redundant, new timetables incorporating progressive introduction of the new airconditioned carriages, greater utilization of existing airconditioned stock, additional and more frequent services, reduced transit times, reduced terminal times, much improved power to weight ratios, computerised booking facilities and improved operating methods are planned for introduction on 4.10.81.

The proposed upgraded services are, I believe, a major break through for all Railway people and their families. After years of operation with antiquated and unreliable equipment, which in no small way adversely affected our patronage levels, and just as importantly our level of staff morale, by the progressive infusion of much needed capital for new equipment over the next two years, we have at last reached the point where we can reverse the trend away from rail and really show the Government and the public, what we can do.

It is therefore a matter of grave concern to me, and I am sure to every responsible and clear thinking Railway person, that this carefully thought out and positive plan, which without doubt is the most exciting, significant and worthwhile country passenger services project embarked upon during my 29 years of service with VicRail, has now been placed in jeopardy, and may even completely founder, because Guards object to the new operating methods, involving travel in other than the rear vehicle, in one direction.

.../2.

Let us all clearly understand that the very future of the country passenger train service and the job security and opportunities which go with it are at stake if we cannot produce as we are committed to on 4.10.81. It would be a very simple matter to reverse the decision to reject part of the Lonie recommendations and to infuse the capital needed to provide the new and upgraded equipment over the next two years, if we continue to procrastinate and discredit ourselves with the Government and the public.

The plain facts are that in order to achieve the greater utilization of equipment, hence more frequent services, plus reduced terminal and transit times, it is essential that the operating plan as presented to your Union Representatives on numerous occasions over the last four months, be adhered to. I, along with our Superintendent of Safeworking Staff and all senior Management, am completely satisfied that there is no reduction of safety standards in the proposed method of operation.

Under the proposed method of operation there would not be more than four vehicles trailing behind the Guard. Whilst traditionally the Guard has generally travelled in the last vehicle there is a whole range of exceptions to this practice, which have operated safety and successfully for many years.

Probably the best example is the Vinelander to and from Mildura where the brake van is marshalled on the front and up to twelve vehicles trail behind. It has been argued that the Conductor signals the Guard from the trailing vehicle when starting from stations and whilst this is correct, having started the train, it is not compulsory for the Conductor to remain in the trailing vehicle. Indeed his normal duties often require him to leave his carriage between stations. In the event of the Vinelander becoming disabled it is the Guard's responsibility, not the Conductor's, to protect in the rear, negotiating up to twelve vehicles, en route.

A similar situation previously obtained on the Gippslander for many years between Sale and Bairnsdale and on the Albury Passenger between Seymour and Albury after the Goulburn Valley section had been detached. Other examples of the Guard not being located in the rear vehicle or having to look forward and back as the train cleared the platform are on certain Rail Motors or Rail Motors and Trailers, when the passenger section of a B.C.P.L. car van is trailing, when louvre vans are trailed behind passenger stock or when up to five louvre vans were trailed behind a News Goods Train.

It has also been argued that if the Guard travels behind the locomotive on up journeys he would not be able to keep signals in view and look back at the same time whilst his train cleared the platform. This is true but Guards have never been held responsible for signals if they cannot view them and this situation is quite common now particularly at island platforms where the signal is at one side of the train, and the platform on the other side. In such instances Guards observe that the fixed signal is at proceed for the train to depart but Regulation 195, Clause (a), states that the Engineman after receiving the Guard's hand signal must satisfy himself before starting, that the line ahead is clear by observing the fixed signal. The Guard must keep a good look out along the platform until his train is clear.

.../3.

A Man of Principle

- 3 -

Many of you would be aware of practices on other Railway Systems where the Guard is located in other than the rear vehicle. Sydney suburban operations are a good example of this. Enquiries reveal that their safety record is equal to ours.

I am extremely disappointed that an offer I made to your Union Representatives six weeks ago has not been taken up. This involved trial runs for one week which I believe would have clarified the position. The request was that one up train per day from Seymour, Kyneton, Traralgon and Bacchus Marsh operate without a brake van in the rear simulating the new service. This would have allowed Guards and the Union to assess the situation under actual working conditions. There was no objection to rostering Guards nominated by the Union on these particular runs or alternatively Union Officials accompanying the Guard, but there has been a negative response. I fail to see how anyone had anything to lose from such an exercise.

It has been stated by some people that the reluctance on the part of Guards to accept the new operating proposal stems not so much from the safety aspect, but from a fear that the changed positioning of the Guard in one direction could lead to the eventual withdrawal of the Guard from passenger train operation. Ask yourself if this were so would we have provided such a lavish (by world standards) Guard's area, incorporating an expensive adjustable seat, airconditioning, two way periscopes, windscreen wipers and water jets. Even if the abolition of Guards' positions was under consideration, and I can assure you it is not, the provision of a minimum facility small Guard's compartment at the other end of the train as has been suggested, would not alter the situation. It would however destroy the operating plan and create great difficulties with the handling of parcels - a traffic which we hope will increase with the introduction of faster more frequent services.

Your Union Officials have been informed that although the duties of Guards may alter from time to time, and none of us have a "crystal ball", there is absolutely no intention to abolish Guards' positions in the foreseeable future. This statement is, I believe, of paramount importance to each and everyone of you.

There is an old saying that opportunity only knocks once and most of us in our private lives regretfully have experienced lost opportunities which never return. Let us all ensure that this is not the case with the proposed upgraded country passenger service. I am therefore appealing to you and every individual Guard to reconsider the situation, before it is too late, and to voice your opinion where it can influence others. I believe you owe it to yourself, your family and fellow workers in the Railway Industry as quite clearly, the new services cannot commence unless your Union attitude changes.

Yours sincerely,

R.T. Barden,
Chief Operations Manager.

Copy of my letter to every guard (suburban guards excepted) re the ARU Ban on the upgraded passenger services.

26

Relief From The Grind

WHILE A VERY DISPROPORTIONATE amount of my time was taken up dealing with industrial relations matters, correspondence and routine management matters were also extremely time consuming. Rarely did I go home of a night without taking a case full of files to be read and signed after the evening meal. There were of course many other duties and responsibilities which sometimes provided a welcome relief from the daily humdrum of the aforementioned. For instance I was summoned to the Chairman's office one day when he told me that the State Carriage was to be refurbished and the Board members felt that the Governor, Sir Brian Murray and Lady Janette should be given the opportunity to have some input, by inspecting it a couple of times, during the process. This meant that the carriage would need to be brought from Newport Workshops to a platform at Spencer Street to allow them access. Since I would have to arrange this it had been decided that I should be their contact and accompany them on their visits, passing on any requests they may have about décor and so on to the workshops people. They inspected the carriage twice as I recall, but were obviously reluctant to request any changes.

Sir Brian Murray, Governor of Victoria and Lady Janette at Spencer Street Station. Me, Len Cotter, Senior conductor, and Angus McMillan shift stationmaster.

They indicated they were more than happy with the work as listed. A reasonably regular break from routine was the General Manager's inspection tours of country lines throughout the system. The train consisted of the Goulburn Car, (staff quarters) for the train crew, a sleeping car for the General Manager and his support staff, and the Norman Car which had a kitchen, dining area, bar and office area. Notification of the proposed tour would be sent to each Shire Council and the local media inviting deputations from organisations and individuals. Each tour was usually of four day's duration.

My secretary would send me a case of correspondence most days which I would deal with each night. I would also ring in to her each day. My responsibilities included the safeworking of the train and keeping it on time (not always easy) and sitting in on the deputations to assist the General Manager with suggestions or complaints that fell into my area of responsibility.

I was qualified and experienced in all aspects of train operations except driving. The tour train Driver originally came from Wonthaggi and spent most of his firing days operating steam engines between State Mine and Nyora, so he knew me and my family. Whenever the opportunity arose I would ride on the loco with Bill and he would let me drive. The General Manager and other Branch Heads would be aware of this when I went missing. There was a speedometer mounted in the Norman Car and a telephone connection to the locomotive. One day I went up to the loco at Gheringhap and took over the controls with Bill standing behind me. When approaching Warrenheip I slipped out of the driver's seat and said to Bill he can take it down the bank (steep grade). He said "no stay there". I replied that I wouldn't because I had a goods train get away from the driver one night when I was a Train Controller and I had a healthy respect for this bank.

Bill took over the driving saying something like there's nothing to it so long as you have got hold of it at the bowling club bridge. All drivers have their landmarks. He "stoked" it up a bit making it "rock and roll" a little. Next thing the phone rang and Archie the Guard said "Get that bastard out of the seat", to which of course I answered "I am not in the seat". No one said anything to me when I went back to the Norman Car at Ballarat but Archie told us that night when I went down to the Goulburn Car, which was my custom after the evening meal, that the General Manager and others were quite scared with the riding of the train, thinking I was still driving. We all had a good laugh about that but I think Archie might have been a bit scared too.

A couple of other diversions which gave me short respites from the daily grind were firstly, Carmel and I received an invitation in May 1980 to be present at Museum Station (now

Melbourne Central) during a visit by Her Majesty the Queen and His Royal Highness The Duke of Edinburgh, where Her Majesty unveiled a plaque naming the Queen Elizabeth Plaza.

> *The Chairman and Members of the*
> *Melbourne Underground Rail Loop Authority*
> *invite*
>
> MR. & MRS. R. BARDEN
>
> *to be present at Museum Station during a visit by*
> *Her Majesty The Queen and*
> *His Royal Highness The Duke of Edinburgh*
> *on*
> *Wednesday, 28 May, 1980*
> *when Her Majesty will unveil a plaque naming*
> *the Queen Elizabeth Plaza*
>
> R.S.V.P. BY RESPONSE CARD ENCLOSED   ENTER 2.25 P.M. TO 2.45 P.M.

Revenue trains were not operating on the underground at that time. Another little sojourn was for the first train into the underground in 1980. I had arranged for the suburban electric train drivers' Union representative to drive it as an insurance against industrial problems, not that we were expecting any.

Carmel brought Danny (then five years old) down and we sat in the driver's compartment for the breaking of the blue ribbon. Jim the driver invited Danny to sit on his knee and "drive". He held his hand over Danny's to operate the controller and exert pressure to ensure no penalty applications of the brake.

Danny and driver Jim Patterson prior to the first train entering the Loop.

Danny had been on steam locomotives before, but not in the cab of an electric train. At the same time, he was quite excited about that.

In 1983 I was directed to accompany the Royal Train conveying Prince Charles and Princess Diana from Spencer Street to Ballarat. This was another insurance situation as I was instructed that should there be a failure of equipment, or some other incident, I was to take charge of all railway matters. Fortunately it was an uneventful trip and I was only a passenger.

Bill, the driver originally from Wonthaggi whom I mentioned previously, met the Prince and Princess after arrival at Ballarat which I think was one of the highlights of Bill's career.

ROYAL TRAIN 1983

T.R.H.
THE PRINCE AND PRINCESS
OF WALES

TRAVEL AUTHORITY

VICTORIAN RAILWAYS

Royal Train — 1983

TRAVEL AUTHORITY No. 07

Issued to Mr R. T. Barden

Available for travel by the Royal Train between Melbourne and Ballarat on Friday, 15th April, 1983.

H. C. Brown
Secretary for Railways

27

Shunter Invasion

EARLY ONE AFTERNOON SHUNTERS, about thirty in number, marched down Spencer Street carrying placards and chanting. They stopped outside Head Office and continued the chanting for a while. My office which was quite big, was on the ground floor just inside the north door of the building. Suddenly the group walked in to the corridor and continued the chanting, mostly aimed at me, at my door. The noise could be heard apparently over a fair bit of the building. The General Manager, on the first floor, rang and told me to either get out of my office, or lock the two doors. I refused to do so saying such action would only encourage them further. A few minutes later I decided to go out into the corridor to speak to their leaders. They demanded a meeting with me immediately. I said that was alright by me, but it would be impossible to achieve anything with that number of people yelling derisive remarks. I suggested they pick a maximum of five members to represent them and that would make for a more orderly and therefore more productive discussion. They flatly refused my offer saying it had to be all of them. I knew what was likely to happen, but decided to stick to my offer, refused their demands and walked back inside. Within a couple of minutes they all invaded the office. I totally ignored them and went on dealing with a big pile of correspondence I had sitting on my desk. My secretary, my personal clerk, and the Operations Branch Industrial Officer were in the office with me. The noise, the derogatory remarks and the fact that some of them were smoking, dropping ash all over the floor and stomping out their butts in the pots housing Barbara's (Secretary) indoor plants, was "off putting" for her but she remained at her desk. I did not allow myself to comment or retaliate in any way at all. After a while the clerk from the office next door came in and told me I was wanted on his boss's phone. I left the office to take the call. It was the General Manager wanting to know how things were going. He again said I should leave the office but I was determined to see it out. I told him I was completely ignoring them and had plenty of correspondence on my desk to keep me busy. My office was fairly crowded and on threading my way back towards my desk the Secretary of the Shunters Section ARU blocked my way. For the first time I spoke saying "Excuse me Frank, I want to get back to my desk". He did not move but put a silly grin on his face. At last there was a silence. I again asked him to let me through but again, he ignored me and stood fast. I did not speak again but stuck my chest out a bit and nudged him twice in his chest area as I walked around him to regain my desk. About fifteen minutes later the Assistant Secretary of the ARU Joe Sibberas arrived, accompanied by two Railway Investigation Officers. I don't know who called them but suspect it was someone directed to do so by the General Manager. Joe spoke to me first saying he would need to arrange a meeting with me and the shunters in the next few days. He then turned to his members and suggested they disperse as nothing was going to be achieved by hanging around any longer today. They followed his advice but were still trying to bait me as they left. The strange thing was I never did hear from Joe concerning the meeting he said he wanted.

A Man of Principle

A FEW DAYS later the Director of Personnel entered my office carrying a piece of correspondence. He said "You have gone too far this time". I asked what he meant and he handed me a letter. It was from the ARU addressed to the Minister of Transport and the Chairman of the Railway Board, Alan Reiher. It alleged that the previous week when a group of shunters were in my office I assaulted the Secretary of the Shunters Section of the Union by kneeing him in the groin. The letter demanded my immediate removal from the position of Chief Operations Manager. It further stated that should this not happen within one week, they would commence legal action against me. I told him what had happened when I re-entered my office after taking a phone call next door. Shortly after I saw Alan Reiher in his office and discussed all aspects of the "invasion" with him. There was absolutely no way that I had kneed him in the groin. Alan said that I should write the reply to this letter as I was the only one from senior management who was present and therefore was the only one who had an intimate knowledge of what actually happened. I explained in the letter of reply that I had spoken to the protestors demanding to meet with me saying I would accept a deputation of up to five of their members as it would not be possible to conduct an orderly meeting with all of them. They did not accept the offer and a short time later all of them, about thirty in number, entered my office. I did not acknowledge them or reply to the continuous insults and accusations they were making, but instead sat at my desk reading and signing correspondence. I was called out to take a phone call in the next office and on my return, the Secretary of the Shunters Section, ARU, had blocked my path to my desk. I then spoke for the first time, asking him to let me through to my desk. When he didn't move I asked him a second time, but he didn't budge. I then pushed my chest out and nudged him lightly to his chest area as I walked around him. He immediately stepped aside. I categorically deny that I lifted my knee or in any way at all, made contact with him with my knee. I further said I would welcome the legal action if they were to proceed with it, as I was certain I would be cleared. Whilst I accepted that some of the shunters may be prepared to perjure themselves it was unlikely that the majority of them would. Furthermore my Secretary, Clerk and Industrial Officer were present and could testify I did not knee him in the groin. I have only a a limited knowledge of the law but believe that these people were not only guilty of defamation, but also of libel, since they had made this accusation in writing, and any legal action may well bring this out. I heard nothing more about this matter. Perhaps the Minister had suggested they back off. There was no doubt in my mind that this incident was planned to set me up. A strange thing occurred however when I retired in December 1985 when my personal files and property were sent to my home. The copy of the letter from the Union to the Transport Minister and the Chairman of the VicRail Board, and my reply thereto, were missing.

28

Rationalisation of Depots

DURING 1981 I had stepped up my program to rationalise the number of country depots. I believed that the demise of the steam engine should have caused it to happen about twenty years earlier, but now the changed requirements for goods train operations, i.e. much longer block trains for bulk products, the introduction of freight centres which greatly reduced the need to operate roadside goods trains, and the closure of some branch lines, to my mind, demanded change not only to reduce costs, but to vastly improve the running performance of through trains. I thought some depots should close completely, and others should have reductions in train running staff leaving only enough crews if applicable, to cover local schedules, both passenger and goods. A long standing agreement with the AFULE was that crews could operate up to two hundred miles if on a goods train only, up to two hundred and twenty miles if on a passenger train (one way), then on a goods train after changeover, and two hundred and forty miles if on a passenger train each way. The same mileages applied if driving right through, then going to rest. On through and rest rosters they were always short of the maximum allowable miles but not much on some, e.g. Melbourne-Wodonga or Donald-

Mildura. I believed that on through trains between Melbourne and Traralgon (97 miles) or Ararat and Portland (120 miles) for example, crews should be rostered through or depending on the timetables, to changeover, but not with crews located at intermediate locations which could be a very unproductive practice. This showed out at places like Warragul and Hamilton. I guess the main justification for Hamilton as a depot originally, apart from servicing steam engines, was the number of branch lines which were serviced from there. Hamilton to Balmoral, Hamilton to Koroit, Hamilton to Coleraine and Branxholme to Casterton. Some of these had closed officially, others were about to close. Realistically, this made Hamilton just another roadside station, albeit servicing a large area. It was obvious to me that Hamilton crew positions should be relocated to Portland. Crew time was often wasted, particularly in the wheat seasons with trains running up to three or four hours late. Crews would sign on at the rostered time at Hamilton and then either sit in their meal room until their train arrived, or go per a train or taxi, to meet it. These wasteful practices would be eliminated if Ararat crews changed over with Portland crews wherever their trains crossed on the single line. In the old days crews would be booked back when it was known their train was running late, sometimes woken up in the middle of the night to be told they did not have to start work until later. This inhumane practice had been abolished some years previously and rightly so. The answer of course was to run the trains on time but this is extremely difficult on single lines where one delay "snowballs" to others. Hamilton certainly should be abolished as a locomotive fuelling point. Warragul had not had steam trains since the mid fifties when the line to Traralgon was electrified. The branch line to Noojee had closed at about the same time. Whilst there were block trains of timber from East Gippsland, paper products from Maryvale and briquettes from Morwell Briquette Siding and block trains of empties in the 'down' direction, far too many other goods trains were shunting at Warragul and being delayed as a result. Warragul had a yard pilot 24 hours a day which had been a traditional arrangement. With a re-organised timetable the number of trains shunting at Warragul could be minimised and the yard pilots abolished.

I THOUGHT the abolition of these two locations as depots and indeed the changed operations and staff reductions at other depots should be introduced progressively over a period of years, mainly by attrition. Railway staff at that time could retire voluntarily at sixty years of age with a slightly reduced superannuation payout or go through to sixty five. Staff seeking promotion usually, but not always, had to transfer to another location where a vacancy existed. Others often sought transfers to suit their personal or family requirements. I arranged meetings with staff at Warragul, Hamilton and Seymour encouraging them to bring their spouses along so they could hear first hand what the proposals were and the reasons for them. I thought the Hamilton and Warragul meetings went over quite well although there were interruptions at the latter location from one particular antagonist. Seymour, which I envisaged would have a small reduction in staff only was not so successful as a union official had brought along a political candidate who had been endorsed by his party to represent them in that electorate at the forthcoming State Elections. I thought this was out of order as the meeting was for staff and their spouses, and this fellow tried to hold the floor asking more questions and making more statements than all the other attendees put together. He was clearly seeking publicity for his shot at politics ahead of the welfare of railway people. I did not hear much more from Seymour but I certainly did from Hamilton and Warragul. It must be kept in mind that the railways even at that time were still short of staff, particularly trained and qualified operating staff. I did not envisage any compulsory transfers in the foreseeable future, at least five years and perhaps even longer, and no-one would lose their job unless they chose to. The situation was entirely different to most other industries or factories closing down where employment could not be offered at alternative locations as was the case with the railways. It was my intention not to replace staff who retired, resigned or transferred. In the case of locomotive crews I would roster two drivers together rather than replace second men who qualified as drivers and took transfers elsewhere to obtain promotions. It was inevitable that numbers of operations staff would increase at some locations. Portland certainly would. I encouraged employees to keep a close watch on vacancies advertised and suggested if one became available at a location that suited them, they should transfer then, rather than leaving it until later. Some of them took this advice and obviously felt more secure and in some cases that I know of, much happier for having done so. I suppose it was also inevitable, with state elections scheduled for the following year, for sitting politicians to take an interest in what I was proposing, but even worse for "would-be" politicians to highlight what they saw as the negative side of the proposal and agitate relentlessly against it. This happened at both Hamilton and Warragul.

THE SITTING politician for Narracan contacted me through the General Manager saying some of his constituents were requesting a public meeting in Warragul with me in attendance. The same thing happened at Hamilton where both the upper house member and the lower house member said they wanted me to attend a meeting they were organising in the Civic Centre at Hamilton.

A Man of Principle

SAVE!

THE WARRAGUL RAILWAY INDUSTRY

Warragul and district railway workers, their wives, families and friends

SEEK YOUR SUPPORT

TO STOP THE STATE GOVERNMENT AND VICRAIL

WIPING OUT WARRAGUL AS A RAILWAY OPERATIONS CENTRE

We believe pressure should be brought to bear on all Local Members of Parliament, and all political parties to support our cause to:

(1) SAVE THE JOBS OF AT LEAST 100 RAILWAY WORKERS NOW EMPLOYED IN WARRAGUL

(2) MAINTAIN WARRAGUL AS A RAIL OPERATIONS CENTRE

(3) IMPRESS UPON THE STATE GOVERNMENT AND VICRAIL THE NEED TO MAINTAIN EMPLOYMENT IN COUNTRY AREAS, IN LINE WITH THE POLICY OF ALL POLITICAL PARTIES TO MAINTAIN A BALANCED DEVELOPMENT THROUGHOUT VICTORIA

THESE ARE SOME OF THE PEOPLE WHO HAVE SUPPORTED OUR PETITION

This advertisement was placed by railway workers and concerned citizens of Warragul. Authorised by Kevin Burke, 2 Lillies Rd, Warragul

Politicians ignore us — railwaymen

June 9 1981

Copies of a full-page advertisement in last week's edition of The Gazette will be sent to a number of Government and Opposition MPs.

The advertisement was inserted by local people upset at the effects of the winding down of VicRail operations in Warragul.

Apart from causing a considerable amount of local comment, there has been little reaction to the advertisement outside of Warragul.

Local railwaymen are critical of local MPs for failing to take up the railway closure issue.

They are also upset that the State branch of the Labor Party has not come to their aid.

"Apart from the Member for McMillan, Mr Cunningham, and the candidate for Narracan, Mr Gubbins showing an interest in the issue, we haven't heard anything from the Labor Party in Melbourne. It seems they want us to do all the pushing for them. We thought it would be them coming down here to help us. They are just as unconcerned as the Liberals," one union official told The Gazette last week.

VICRAIL CHIEF IN CITY TODAY

VicRail's chief of operations, Mr. Ray Barden is due to meet members of Hamilton's industrial promotion committee tonight to discuss the future of the city's operations depot.

Mr. Barden said yesterday the meeting was in response to approaches made by Mr. Don McKellar (Lib, Portland) on behalf of the committee.

Mr. McKellar and Mr. Bruce Chamberlain (Lib., Western) are expected the attend the meeting.

Mr. Barden said there appeared to be some confusion surrounding the future of the Hamilton operations depot.

The committee was apparently seeking more detailed information about how the move will be handled.

Mr. Barden specified the meeting would not be open to the public, although other interested groups could attend by invitation.

He would be giving a short address and throw the meeting open for questions.

Hopefully, the meeting would resolve any confusion, he said.

The meeting will be at Hamilton Town Hall.

I attended both these meetings and was given the opportunity to explain in detail the reasons for the policy and the advantages the railways would get in improved train operations and therefore service to the public and reduced costs.

VICRAIL MAN'S VISIT PROMISES NO JOY!

This week's meeting in Hamilton with VicRail's chief of operations, Mr. Ray Barden, gave those fighting to retain rail jobs in the city little cause for joy.

Mr. Barden and local operations manager, Mr. Ken Henskel, met with members of Hamilton Industrial Promotion Committee and the joint railway committee, representing the Save Hamilton's Employment Group.

Mr. Bruce Chamberlain (Lib., Western) and Mr. Don McKellar (Lib., Portland) also attended the meeting.

Yesterday HIPC chairman, Cr. Arthur Wiles, said the efforts of the local MPs in arranging the meeting, and the frank exchange which took place, were appreciated.

He said what was difficult to appreciate were hard facts such as:
- That VicRail did not intend to deviate from its determination to wind down at least 50 rail positions in Hamilton over the next five to 10 years by way of natural attrition.
- That VicRail was prepared to write off the railway centre at Hamilton as having little more than scrap value.

Cr. Wiles said it was also made clear by VicRail that the Hamilton freight centre was at risk if there was no increase in patronage by Hamilton's business houses.

"It is pleasing to note that the council is seeking the response of the shadow minister for transport to the VicRail proposals," he said.

"The joint railway committee must continue the fight not to have Hamilton's rail assets and rail personnel stripped from us.

"The Transport Regulation Board hearings are still before us, and the petition with its 5000 signatories is yet to be presented.

"The fight is far from over so long as the joint railway committee continues to receive significant community support and community encouragement."

I realised that the reduced staff numbers, particularly at Warragul where there were many more employees involved would have an impact in each case, but it was my responsibility to run the railway operations more efficiently and that was what I was trying to do.

In each case the local media reported on the proposal and were hostile to it, but much more so at Warragul.

It seemed I was some kind of tyrant reducing the railway payroll in each town and therefore the turnover of traders, reducing the number of students at schools and possibly the numbers of teachers required in the future, reducing the demand generally for services in the area and even affecting junior sporting competitions, with reduced numbers of children available.

At Warragul a committee was formed and a local union representative formed a relationship with the editor of the local press. There were ongoing reports, always hostile to the policy and to me personally. I thought it was "bad form" by the editor that he never once contacted me to check out the accuracy of what he was being told.

The Transport Committee of the Shadow Transport Minister also got involved holding meetings at both locations from which I was personally banned.

So much for democracy.

At Hamilton it was claimed guards were working excessive overtime as a result of me not replacing some who had transferred and the Shadow Minister allegedly promised he would correct this if his party was elected. I thought if this was true, it was a flawed discussion as it was made without any consultation with management.

I arranged for statistics to be provided of other depots, Dimboola, Ararat and Maryborough which like Hamilton, were involved in seasonal wheat traffic and also Traralgon. In each case the amount of overtime worked over several pay periods exceeded that worked by guards at Hamilton.

It seemed that no-one was interested in facts and I was instructed after the election by the new Transport Minister to increase the number of guards at Hamilton by two. During the union campaign against the "run down" of the railways we had trains black banned at both Hamilton and Warragul.

I gained some measure of satisfaction when I was shifted to a new position in 1983, that under my watch as Chief Operations Manager, the number of operating staff at Warragul had reduced from ninety-five to forty-eight and this did not involve any compulsory transfers. Locomotive crews numbered twenty two when I took over in February 1980 but several of the drivers were approaching retirement age and this, together with the non replacement of second men who transferred for promotion, certainly assisted the outcome.

Whilst staff and their families generally opposed the rationalisation of depots, in many cases their thinking was inspired by industrial and political propaganda which was often not accurate.

I RECALL BEING APPROACHED by a lady when having a coffee after one of the several meetings at Warragul. She said she worked locally, her husband was a train driver and the kids were at local schools. They were reluctant to shift, but wanted to do what was best in the long run.

I said it was not for me to say what she and her family should do but she should keep in mind social changes generally and technology which had, and would continue, to change operating procedures and the very role of the railway.

It was possible I was a bit ahead of my time, but it was inevitable in my opinion, for what it was worth, that Warragul could not survive in the longer term as an operations depot.

I therefore thought that if I and my family was in their position, I would make the move earlier while we still had a little time and more importantly, a choice of locations to move to.

The latter could in time disappear. Some years later, I saw her husband at Spencer Street Station and he said that taking my advice was the best thing they had ever done.

Incidentally, after the change of government a consultant from Transmark, the consulting arm of British Rail, was engaged to review the situation at Warragul. His findings were exactly the same as mine. In fact one member of my senior staff claimed he was guilty of plagiarism in some sections of his report.

Next page: Copy of a letter from the sub-branch secretary of the ARU at Warragul to his members after a meeting held on Sunday 12/12/1982.

A Man of Principle

WARRAGUL SUB. BRANCH OF THE AUSTRALIAN RAILWAYS UNION
SUNDAY 12th DECEMBER 1982

The Warragul Sub. branch of the A.R.U. view with grave concern the deliberate run-down of the Warragul Operations Depot which was the policy of the former Liberal Government and is now the policy of the State Labor Government until the Minister for Transport Mr Steve Crabb makes up his mind.

We have repeatedly ask our A.R.U. Executives since the State elections to contact the State Minister for Transport to stop the run-down and now nine months later the answer is still the same Mr Steve Crabb is obtaining more information.

A resolution was passed at Warragul on the 13th of September 1982 at a meeting with the Minister for Transport Mr Steve Crabb, the Federal Labor Member for McMillan Mr Barry Cunningham, the President of the A.R.U. Mr Frank Lacey, the Secretary of the A.F.U.L.E. Mr Jim Patterson and members of the Warragul Operations Depot that a firm directive be issued to Vic.Rail that there be no further run-down of the Warragul Operations Depot until a full study had been carried out and discussed with the Union Executives and the members of the Warragul Operations Depot.

We are now into January 1983 - 5 months later and the Warragul Operations Depot has been escalated into a further decline by Vic.Rail and the State Labor Government.

This Depot has every reason to feel we are being discriminated against as no replacements have been made for retirements, resignations, or transfers in this Depot since the Labor Government took office in April 1982
We have repeatedly ask for a Senior Shunter who has been running full-time Guard at Warragul for over 15 months to be appointed to the position of Guard but Vic.Rail states no replacements or appointments till the Minister for Transport Mr Steve Crabb makes up his mind, but they appoint 2 Shunters running full-time Guard at Hamilton to the position of Guard.
We have repeatedly ask for a 4th signalman to be appointed at Warragul as the Traralgon Signal-Box and the Warragul Signal-Box are manned the same number of hours and the Traralgon Signal-Box has 4 classified signalmen but according to Ray Barden who we believe is still running Vic.Rail under the former Liberal Governments polices the Warragul Signal-Box is only entitled to 3 classified signalmen.

We have 2 Station Officers residing and buying their departmental residence in Warragul, one travels to Morwell every day, the other travels to Bunyip every day and both have applied for the position of a 4th Signalman at Warragul.

With deep regret the Warragul Sub. Branch of the A.R.U, unanimously passed a resolution that from the day the Shunter now classed as a Yard Assistant and relieves in the Warragul Signal-Box goes on leave on the 21st of February 1983 the three Guards who also relieve in the Warragul Signal-Box will stay on their rostered shifts in the Guards Van and the three Signalmen who now work a full amount of overtime are not to be extended more than their normal rostered shift until a 4th Signalman is appointed at Warragul.

Warragul Sub.Branch Secretary

Kevin E. Burke
(signed)

29

Interbranch Problems

TOWARDS THE END of 1981 the passenger services between Numurkah and Cobram were to be discontinued and replaced with buses. I was not directly involved with this. The VicRail Board had made their decision in their alternate proposal to the "Lonie Report". The last passenger train out of Cobram was to be on the Monday morning. The Area Stations Manager (Transportation Branch) had been made aware on the Sunday evening that members of the Shadow Minister's "Transport Committee" were on the train and there was a very strong rumour from his staff at Numurkah that they intended to blockade the train on arrival at Cobram so that it could not depart as scheduled next morning. I had no managerial staff at Numurkah other than a Driver in Charge. I was not informed of this rumour and the subsequent actions of both Transportation Branch management and the unionists until after I had arrived at work on the Monday morning. Otherwise, I can assure you, the result would have been entirely different. The Area Stations Manager had telephoned the Chief Transportation Manager informing him of the situation and suggesting that he terminate the 'down' Cobram train at Numurakh to counter the alleged proposal of the unionists. The Chief Transportation Manager told me he had told his Area Manager to "do as he saw fit" and as he was going to bed shortly, to ring him at seven o'clock the next morning to fully apprise him of the outcome. I simply could not believe what I was being told. The terminating of a train and dealing with the blockading of a train were clearly the responsibility of the Operations Branch. The Area Manager should have phoned me in the first place and failing this, his boss should have contacted me before going to bed and leaving it in the hands of his staff. His actions were entirely different to what mine would have been. I always encouraged my staff to ring me at any time of the day or night, not let them handle it and then ring me the next morning. The result was that they did terminate the train at Numurkah but they certainly did not tie up the loose ends. I had circularised every depot and terminal stations only a week previously after a locomotive reverser key had been lost at Korumburra, that such keys must be locked in the station or depot safe overnight and not left where unauthorised people could gain possession of them, yet the reverser key had been left on the counter just inside the outer door to the office. The Chief Transportation Manager further told me that a Union official had gone to the home of an off duty Assistant Stationmaster and asked for a loan of the station keys, or for him to come to the station and open the outer door. He refused to cooperate but I found it incredible that when he alerted the Area Manager to this, he was not asked whether the reverser had been locked away. I certainly would have as it was patently apparent that something untoward was planned.

I was then told that the outer office door had been forced open, obviously to obtain the key, and that the train had been driven through to Cobram sometime during the night, in fact hijacked. This act represented the most serious violation of rules, regulations and safeworking that I had ever encountered or even heard of, during my railway career. Apart from the forced entry to the outer office which alone, I thought, should have been a police matter, they had departed without the staff for the section, passed a home signal at the stop position, and passed over the level crossing at the 'down' end, where I am told, the warning devices would not have been activated until the locomotive was almost on the crossing, due to the home signal being at the stop. This seriously endangered the general public as well as the people on the train, staff at roadside stations to Cobram had not been notified of it's operation and in certain circumstances, could also have been endangered. The Chief Transportation Manager told me that he did not contact me as he thought my Train Controller would have done so. This was a real fiasco and I thought a "cop out" by people who did not realise the potential of what they were dealing with, and /or had conveniently ignored the fact that their Branch did not have the authority to terminate trains or make other train running decisions. They had acted as if the Traffic Branch still existed and the Operations Branch did not. When I spoke to the Train Controller later in the day he gave a perfectly plausible explanation. The Area Stations Manager had told him there was no need to ring the boss about this as he had already spoken to him and had to ring him again in the morning. The Train Controller naturally thought that I had been advised since it was entirely an Operations Branch matter. My mind went back to the taskforce days where I had requested changes to the then guidelines to avoid situations such as this, but had been knocked back. By my standards there was absolutely no excuse for the Area Stations Manager not contacting me as he well knew he was dealing with an Operations Branch matter which as it turned out, was going to have much greater repercussions than even I would have expected. As I had been doing daily for a considerable amount of time, I reported to the Chairman of the Board to update him on industrial action which involved the black banning of trains and any other developments in the Unions' campaign.

WHEN RELAYING the details of this debacle to him I gave the opinion that we would be able to identify the driver of this train by examining the speed chart and comparing it with previous charts of all drivers at Numurkah. The gossip was that it was a local who drove the train accompanied on the loco by a union official from Melbourne. I made the point that they had gone way too far on this occasion and their actions could not be considered as acceptable or reasonable industrial action. Once the driver was identified beyond doubt, we should set an example by terminating his services. Further, I thought we should refer the matter of the forced entry to the Police for their investigation. He agreed that we must put a stop to this type of action before someone was killed or seriously injured, and that when we clearly identified the driver, we should certainly terminate his services. He did not agree to involving the Police with the forced entry but told me to "go my hardest" to identify the driver. I was not an expert on speed charts myself but some of my staff were and we quickly had a prime suspect. Train drivers operating over the same section of track week after week have their markers and tend to be repetitive with where they brake, where they power up, where they cut off and their use of the vigilance control apparatus, yet each one of them seem to operate just a little differently. I sent a senior officer up to Numurkah to interview the suspect and obtain his statement. However, he flatly refused to make a statement. I directed that he be informed that I considered this to be a refusal of duty and he would be stood aside without pay. If and when he was prepared to answer questions and make a statement his pay would resume. He would not be permitted to drive locomotives in the meantime. Things went quiet for almost two days but on the Thursday afternoon I was called to the Chairman's office where he told me he had been contacted by the Victorian Branch President of the AFULE and the Shadow Transport Minister concerning the incident at Numurkah and the driver I had stood down without pay. They had requested a meeting with him the next day but insisted that nobody else was to be present. The Chairman told me that he had put it to them that I should be present but they would not agree. He said that I should, nevertheless, be in my office and available during the meeting in case he needed to talk to me or call me up.

I IMMEDIATELY THOUGHT this was setting up a sell out. What other reason could there be for banning me in such a situation? I had no other option but to wait and see. I received a call from the Chairman through the afternoon on the next day to say the problem was settled. I was to immediately put the driver back on the payroll and not pursue the matter anymore. In return the Union President would send me a letter to say his union would take no further part in the joint campaign with ARU (they had very little involvement anyhow) or the black banning of trains. The Transport Committee (same people - different hat) would also be backing off. On one hand you could say Alan Reiher had done a good job with settling the dispute that these unionists had started, but so much for the serious safeworking breaches, the forced entry and the stealing of a train endangering people and our equipment. Alan Reiher had, two or three times since the ARU demanded my removal for the false allegation by the shunters that I had assaulted their Section Secretary, confided in me that he was also concerned about his future if the government changed. His concern was based on the fact that he had been terminated and paid out by the Wran Government immediately after it came to power in NSW, from his position of Chairman of the Public Transport Commission, when he still had three years of his five year contract to run. Since he was subsequently appointed by a conservative government in Victoria to replace Bill Gibbs when he retired, he feared that history could repeat itself if the government changed. He never ever mentioned this concern again following this meeting with the Shadow

Minister and union official. As predicted the Government did change in the state election of April 1982 after which VicRail was progressively broken in half during late 1982 and 1983 and business men from outside industry appointed to head the newly created State Transport Authority and Metropolitan Transport Authority. Alan Reiher was appointed to a new position at the Transport Ministry titled "Director General of Transport". I have no proof whatsoever, but I have often wondered whether a "deal" was done at the meeting I have referred to above, a sort of "quid pro quo", a something for something. I guess I shall never know but the Chairman did completely reverse his thinking on how the incident and the transgression should be dealt with. It was obviously a good thing that the media never got hold of the details of the "hijack" and its implications, as it could have been very embarrassing for the railways, but more so for the Shadow Minister.

30

Barnawartha Collision

AFTER MY DISCUSSION with the Chief Transportation Manager following the Numurkah/Cobram debacle, I felt that the responsibilities of his senior staff to respond directly to me on Operations Branch matters and responsibilities in which they became involved, as would be inevitable from time to time, was clearly settled. However, only a short time later there was another episode which to me was equally as blatant. I must say that this problem had only occurred to this stage in the old Seymour district. Situations which had occurred at places in Geelong, Bendigo and Eastern areas for instance had been reported to me in a timely, efficient and ongoing way by the Area Stations Managers concerned. In June 1982 a rear end collision occurred on the standard gauge track opposite the Barnawartha broad gauge station where the *Spirit of Progress* (SOP) express passenger train from Sydney to Melbourne had become disabled due to locomotive failure. In heavy fog an 'up' interstate goods train ran into the rear of the SOP. The Guard of the SOP had jumped clear of the rear van moments before impact. The van was derailed and elevated to the top of the locomotive cab which was crushed. The driver and locomotive assistant were both killed. The time of the collision was 7.54am yet the notification of the fatalities was not given to the standard gauge Train Controller until 8.29am and then only by default. The Driver of the SOP had spoken in regarding the fault on his locomotive. I had arrived in the control room a few minutes before. All the Controller could tell me was that there had been a collision, there were some injuries, and damage to the van of the SOP and the locomotive of the goods train but he did not know if they were actually derailed. When questioned the Driver was able to confirm that both the locomotive of the goods train and the van of the SOP had been derailed and the Driver and Locomotive Assistant had been killed. I was stunned. I could not believe that this information had not been available long before this. Admittedly the Signal Assistant was inexperienced and badly shocked but his Stationmaster was on site within a few minutes and this situation was entirely unsatisfactory. I put a few notes together with the information I had and went back to my office to advise top level officials and get a Board of Enquiry together. I could not believe it when I rang the Chairman and he told me that Jack Draper had given him all the relevant information a few minutes earlier. Subsequent enquiries revealed that the Area Stations Manager had allegedly gone to the broad gauge train control room at Seymour where the Chiltern Stationmaster relayed information to him and he in turn to the Chief Transportation Manager. I acknowledge that Draper probably thought someone else was keeping the standard gauge controller at Spencer Street informed, but I could not understand why he was meddling in Operations Branch matters, particularly after the fairly recent experience at Numurkah. It now seemed that he as the Head of the Transportation Branch was the worst offender.

MY FIRST INCLINATION was to go and ask what the hell was going on but I decided to wait until I made further enquiries. I later examined the transcript of the tape recorded in the Spencer Street control room which was standard procedure and thought that the Train Controller could have, and should have, been more precise when the Signal Assistant spoke in. For instance, the Signal Assistant said at 7.57am, "It looks like the driver has had it" but he did not ask him to elaborate and apparently he did not accept that it might have meant that the driver was dead. Indeed his Senior Train Controller was just as shocked as me when driver, Keith Venville had told us so at about 8.30am. I had always thought that Jack Draper was a pretty good bloke as I believed that most people would. I don't know what his motive was but he should have known better than to tie up people at an accident scene to duplicate information for his personal use. He could have come down to the control room at "Centrol" to see if he could help if his intentions were "honourable" but he tied up telephone lines and staff instead. I noticed that his Stationmaster from Chiltern was reported to be there at Barnawartha at 8.14am but in fact he did not speak to the Spencer Street train controller according to the transcript before I left at about 8.40am. I assume he was talking to the Area Manager at Seymour during this time who would pass the information on to the Chief Transportation Manager. Again, according to the transcript, the relief Signal Assistant spoke to Spencer Street control during this period, not the Stationmaster. I was extremely disappointed that Jack had acted this way, but unlike the Numurkah situation no real harm had been done save for a delay and as he had announced his retirement date, being in his sixties when appointed to the position, I decided not to cause a stir and wait to see if he came to me about it. He never ever did. I spoke to the Chief Train Controller to have his staff stick more to the "ritual" as us older blokes had been required to do and avoid too much familiarity by train controllers which could lead to misunderstandings and misinterpretations. I had always thought that the biggest task I would have in bedding down this new composite operations branch would be getting the drivers to settle in but apart from a couple of minor incidents and one only of their union leaders, they were going really well. I was sorry now that I hadn't pushed harder in the taskforce when I identified a potential problem of safe-working staff other than appointed signalmen answering to two bosses, but I did not anticipate these two senior people in the Transportation Branch to act as they had. Ultimately Draper and his ego were responsible.

31

New State Government

AFTER THE CHANGE of government in April 1982 I was called to the new Transport Minister's office during the first week. He told me he was aware of the tactic I had been using when the union imposed black bans on vehicles, sidings or trains, whereby I directed staff, after telling them I did not accept the ban, to operate as normal or I would place them in a "no work, no pay" situation. If they refused to operate their pay would be stopped until they indicated they were again willing to work as directed in any capacity in which they were qualified and trained. He said the practice was to cease forthwith as the new government would not tolerate such action. I felt gutted and thought this was another indication that my future in the railways was not good. A further announcement made by the Minster the same week reinforced my concerns. He confirmed he would abolish the VicRail Board and create two new authorities, The State Transport Authority (STA) and Metropolitan Transport Authority (MTA) both were to operate under separate management.

Senior management would remain in their positions until the new structures were developed and management positions in each authority could be advertised inside and outside the railway for the selection process to take place. He said selection panels would have a union representative on them which was likely, I thought, to rule me out although I was not sure at what level such an arrangement would apply. The ensuing few months were chaotic. The unions were overjoyed and I kept thinking of the "hit list" which ARU officials had said existed so many times and that I was No.1 on it. Some staff were ambivalent, some were overjoyed and had great expectations, others like me were very apprehensive.

The last major industrial conflict in which I was involved concerned the Signalmens Section of the ARU. I think that probably because I had been a block recorder and some of the older signalmen had actually worked with me, they had some empathy towards me. I doubt that any other ex block recorder had ever become a Branch Head. I got on quite well with their secretary Graeme McNeil who had also been a councillor of the VRI. They made a claim concerning the main western line to the South Australian border which had been upgraded, including the installation of the centralised traffic control system of safeworking, virtually the same as that on the standard gauge line between Melbourne and Albury completed back in 1962, so far as the operation of it was concerned. All points and signals were remotely controlled by a train controller from a control room in Head Office. The signalmen claimed that since about thirty odd signal assistants and signalmen had lost their jobs along the line, a new grade of Area Controller should be created, recruited from signalmen, and they should operate the points and signals leaving the train controllers to perform only their traditional duties. If implemented this effectively would double the number of staff involved and the costs. The standard gauge line to Albury had of course operated quite satisfactorily for the last twenty years with the train controller "pressing the buttons" to operate the signals and points along with his other duties. I had indeed worked in that control room myself on a part time basis back in the sixties and was completely familiar with the requirements. The Union had not complained when the train controllers had become the signalmen also on the Albury line, but I do concede that it being a new track, it did not directly displace signalling staff from the existing broad gauge track running beside it. There is no doubt of course that the reduced number of trains operating on the broad gauge did reduce a few signalling positions and certainly resulted in changed rosters and less overtime being worked. As Chief Operations Manager I had completely rejected their claim for the extra positions. In fact I saw it as a possible impediment to the smooth operation of the system due to the extra unnecessary "link in the chain". Instead of simply pressing his buttons and glancing at his diagram to ensure that the setup was correct, the train controller would have to verbally give his instructions to the signalman and then check the diagram to ensure they had been carried out. Potentially this could cause delays due to misunderstood instructions, the signalman being absent on toilet breaks and "boiling the billy" for meals to mention a few problems. After the change of government the Union stepped up its campaign for the extra positions but now it was being handled by executive members supporting the Signalmens Section of the ARU. I continued to maintain my view that no additional jobs could be justified.

Eventually Alan Reiher informed me that the new Minister was of the opinion that a trial should be conducted with signalmen (Area Controllers) working in the control room with the train controllers, operating the points and signals under their direction, to see if the new positions sought were justified. I told Alan Reiher there was no way the positions could be justified and that history had shown this beyond doubt during the years the CTC had operated on the standard gauge line to Albury. The reasoning behind the Minister's opinion puzzled me as all the displaced people on the western line had been offered alternative employment and they would not be candidates for these proposed new jobs which would go to more senior people from the grade of Special Class signalmen in the metropolitan area. I suspected that there was some ulterior motive, perhaps a pre-election promise in return for support the ARU had given. Train controllers in "Centrol" objected strongly to the proposal. They showed their solidarity when those who were members of the ARU all resigned and joined the Australian Transport Officers Federation (ATOF). This did not bode well for a peaceful and cooperative workplace. I think the ill-conceived proposal probably stemmed from the creation of Area Controllers positions in the new "Metrol" building at Jolimont which had opened with the introduction of the underground loop. Apart from a short section of track between East Malvern and Glen Waverley where CTC was installed in the late fifties, and operated from the signal box at East Malvern, the CTC system had not been operative on the suburban system and suburban train controllers had never been required to operate signals or points, a task which would have been impossible because of the frequency of suburban train services and the short sections. Any comparison therefore was not valid and I believed anyone experienced in train running operations who had thought it out, would come to the same conclusion. I made my thoughts abundantly clear to the Chairman that if implemented the proposal would end in disaster. Despite my contrary opinion, supported as it was by facts, the Chairman informed me that the Minister had instructed him to go ahead without further delay and install three signalmen, one per shift, in the control room. The Minister thought that if I was correct and the jobs could not be justified, the signalmen would soon realise this and withdraw. This was absolute rubbish.

I knew each of the signalmen personally that the ARU had selected and one of them actually confided in me that he knew no job existed, but he felt he had to go along with it in support of the Union. There was unrest from the very first shift although of a minor nature. A train controller complained that his concentration was upset due to the signalman learning with him constantly smoking. I spoke to the Signalman and suggested to him that in the interest of harmony, he go out into the wide corridor when he wanted to smoke. The control rooms were air conditioned, quite small and sound proofed by padding and in the circumstances, I thought the complaint, from a non smoker, was not unreasonable even though I was a heavy smoker myself at the time. The Signalman agreed not to smoke in the room in future so we got out of that one lightly. Further complaints followed including one about a signalman who fell asleep on night shift and snored loudly thus making it difficult for the Train Controller to concentrate and he pointed out that when he depressed the foot pedal to speak on the selector phone, the snoring could be heard at locations right along the track over the top of his conversation. Silly as it may be, I thought the complaint was genuine and it showed me two things. Firstly it confirmed that there was insufficient work to justify the extra jobs proposed and secondly, the relationship between the train controllers and the signalmen was deteriorating to the extent that a demarcation dispute was fast approaching. I could not comprehend why other people could not have foreseen the futility of this exercise and the potential for it to turn into a major dispute. The opportunity for signalmen to become train controllers had always been there although only a few had successfully taken it up. One of the trainee Area Controllers surprised everyone by applying to become a train controller and shifted out to the suburban rooms to do his training. I had known him since the early fifties when he was a signalman at Ingles Street and I was the booking porter at North Port Station. The Union of course demanded that he be replaced by another trainee Area Controller. The train controllers, now all ATOF members, passed a resolution that the signalmen be removed from their work stations as they were finding it difficult to carry out their duties with them present. As you would expect, the ARU opposed such a move. The train controllers then imposed some work restrictions, minor at first refusing to record statistical information, but when the signalmen remained in the room they issued an ultimatum that if they were not removed, they would strike. Efforts were made over the following days to try and solve the problem but to no avail. I did not take part in these discussions as I was seen to be biased by the ARU and some of the senior railway industrial relations "experts".

The whole proposal had surely been proved to be a sham but no-one would admit to this. In what looked like a time buying exercise, the Minister allegedly agreed to the removal of the signalmen for the time being while ongoing discussions took place. In a move obviously designed to buy off the ARU, the signalmen, three in number, would not return to their appointed jobs, but stay at home on full pay. This "deal" included the payment of overtime where rostered if they had been "working" in the control room, shift allowances and weekend penalty rates. In an industry where maintenance was often deferred and urgent capital works delayed due to the shortage of funds, thus making it impossible for people in operations to deliver the advertised services let alone upgrade the services, I thought this waste of taxpayers' money and was nothing short of an absolute disgrace. As if it had not already been proved beyond doubt, the fact that the signalmen had been removed and the operation of the system by the train controller alone as it had been previously went on with no problems whatsoever, surely proved that no extra jobs existed. While this was going on Alan Reiher took up his new appointment as Director General of Transport at the Ministry and Keith Fitzmaurice from outside industry, was installed as Chairman and Managing Director of the State Transport Authority. The chaos I have previously mentioned reigned supreme.

However human nature being what it is, the attitude of many staff members changed overnight. The creation of the STA and MTA to replace the old VicRail meant that scores of positions from the top level right down through middle and junior management would be duplicated and while the top management jobs went mainly to outside people, there was considerable competition for line manager positions. The railways had to continue to operate but the minds of a large number of staff were occupied on where they might be in the near future and what positions they should apply for, rather than the day to day operations of the railway. There was no doubt that many of them believed that the new government was creating some kind of paradise for railway workers. Personally, I was well credentialed by experience and I thought performance, for a level 2 position in either new Authority. As the Chief Operations Manager, in VicRail, I was responsible for all train operations, passenger, freight, metropolitan, country and interstate but I guess my heart has always been in the country and therefore I applied for three positions at level two in the STA, Chief General Manager Transport Operations, General Manager Passenger Services and General Manager Freight Services. I applied for one position in the MTA, General Manager MetRail.

Shortly after John Hearsch, a railway enthusiast of considerable renown was moved from the planning division to the position of Assistant General Manager (Operations), I was moved into a temporary position of Director of Operations. John said he wanted me, among other things to coordinate the work of the Operations Branch, the Freight Branch and the Transportation Branch. I thought this was a strange move as it was not all that long ago that all the functions in these three branches and all the staff with the exception of train drivers, were the responsibility of the Traffic Branch which was abolished in the major restructure of February 1980. (The Freight Branch had been hived off the Traffic Branch in 1977). John was a university graduate and was in the Traffic Branch initially, before transferring to the Marketing Branch where he specialised in costing and setting rates for various traffics which we carried. He then moved into planning and research where he later headed the group which was responsible for the upgraded country passenger services introduced progressively, between 1981 and 1983. The fact that John had been chosen to act as Assistant General Manager Operations ahead of me was ominous. It seemed to rule me out of one of the four level two positions I had applied for in the new Authorities, that of Chief General Manager Transport Operations. It was a difficult time for me as all the indications as I saw them told me that being No.1 on the ARU "hit list", side tracking or worse could become a reality. I was located on the first floor and Fred Blencowe my assistant, was acting as Chief Operations Manager. Not long after I moved to this new position I received a call from the Operations Branch and was told that all signalmen at Flinders Street would stop work for two hours in the afternoon if an injustice to one of their members was not quickly corrected. The central figure in this threat was going on annual leave shortly and had applied for an interstate leave pass to Queensland. Signalmen Special were entitled to such a pass provided they had twenty years unbroken service. This employee had well over twenty years service but unfortunately his service had been broken some years back when he suffered from tuberculosis and was superannuated due to ill health. He had been re-employed when he was able to pass the doctor after about two years.

Whilst the branches issued leave passes for travel within Victoria, interstate passes were the prerogative of the Pass Officer in the Personnel Branch who had refused the request quoting the rule about broken service. I first rang the ARU and they confirmed they intended to stop work between three o'clock and five o'clock if an undertaking was not given to issue the pass. They pointed out that bookings for accommodation there had already been made. On this occasion I was on the Union's side. I thought that the rule about broken service had been intended to apply to people who voluntarily resigned from the rail service and then been accepted again for re-employment some time later. I did not believe that it had been designed to penalise people who had been retired due to ill health and then reinstated. I then went to the office of the Pass Officer and pointed out to him that if the stoppage went ahead many thousands of our customers would be seriously inconvenienced and be late home from work as the evening peak train services would be a nightmare with trains and crews out of position when services were supposed to resume. He claimed he realised this but his hands were tied due to the Railways of Australia rule. I asked him if he had checked with his Head of Branch but he stated there was no point in doing so, as rules were rules. I returned to my office determined to have him overruled as I believed the ruling was an injustice to our employee and to the travelling public if the stoppage went ahead. I decided not to speak to the Director of Personnel in case he sided with his Pass Officer and then all would be lost. I knew the staff at the Railways of Australia office in Melbourne reasonably well and had been contacted a couple of times over the last year or so by their officer who handled passes who knew me from attending ROA conferences. On those occasions the federal president of the AFULE, who was located in Melbourne, had requested a pass for his wife to accompany him to Sydney on union business. The rules stated that in such instances he was to contact the Pass Officer in the State concerned to get his agreement. Should the Pass Officer not be available at the time he should contact a Head of Branch in the State to obtain his agreement and endorse his records accordingly. I had not hesitated on those two occasions to agree with the issue of the pass. As a matter of fact, I had suspected that at some time he had probably been knocked back by our Pass Officer and now chose to go around him. I considered going to our Chairman but then thought I would try the ROA first. I explained the situation to my contact there and he immediately agreed that the rule was surely not intended to catch employees who had not resigned, but temporarily retired due to ill health. I really hated doing this as it is against my nature to deceive people and enter into a conspiracy as I had done once before very early in my career at North Port Station, but I guess the end result justifies the means in obtaining it. He said if I could get the Pass Officer to ring him he would tell

A Man of Principle

him there was a precedent at Port Augusta where interstate passes had been issued in similar circumstances and there would be no problem with ROA if he followed suit. I spoke again to our Pass Officer and he reluctantly agreed to ring ROA. A short time later he came to my office and said he had issued the pass. The stoppage was averted and the Signalman got his interstate free pass. This had been a classic example of red tape, inflexibility and bureaucracy at its worst in the dying months of the old VicRail.

32

The New South Wales (NSW) Express Passenger Train (XPT)

FOLLOWING the change of Government in April 1982, the new Transport Minister, Mr Steve Crabb, expressed a wish to VicRail Chairman Alan Rieher that the recently introduced train, then servicing several provincial cities in Northern NSW as well as Albury, be brought to Melbourne so the Victorians could see it first hand and learn of its capabilities. The Chairman told me that the Minister was considering the possibility of Victoria introducing the trains to this system. I was directed to liaise with my counterparts in NSW and see if we could arrange for the train to visit Melbourne.

The NSW timetable at the time had the XPT set arriving in Albury on Saturday evening and standing over until Monday morning, when it returned to Sydney. This provided an opportunity to do a trip to Melbourne, departing on Sunday morning and returning to Albury on Sunday night. The NSW official was unco-operative, giving several reasons why it was not practicable for the train to come across the border at that stage.

The XPT after arrival at Spencer Street. Left to Right Victorian Drivers *Jack Couch, Bill Steedman*, Superintendent Motive Power *Bill Hutcheon*, the NSW Locomotive Inspector, Foreman South Dynon Locomotive Depot *Peter Blackford* and Victorian Drivers *Jim Prentice and Kevin Whelan*.

THE MAJOR OBJECTIONS he put forward were:

- NSW drivers did not know the track and signals in Victoria, and
- Victorian drivers were not qualified to drive the XPT.

He also had concerns with the problems that would be created should the train be involved in an accident or become disabled while in Victoria.

I expressed the opinion that these problems were not insurmountable and if we worked together we could overcome them to his satisfaction. However, after a couple more telephone conversations it became clear to me that I was not getting anywhere and not likely to do so in the future. I relayed this to the Chairman stating that if the trip to Melbourne was to become a reality, it would be necessary for either him or the Minister to liaise with their NSW counterparts. Sometime later I was informed that NSW would agree to the Sunday trip subject to a number of requirements being met.

TWO VICTORIAN DRIVERS were to travel to Harden on the *Intercapital Daylight* on the Saturday, then change onto the Albury bound XPT which would have a NSW Locomotive Inspector on board to instruct them in the operation and driving en route to Albury. The same inspector would rest overnight in Albury and then be in the cab with the Victorian drivers all day Sunday until arrival back at Albury. Another requirement was that a senior VicRail manager must also be in the cab. Alan Rieher said that I should have this role on the trip from Albury to Melbourne.

The last Sunday in November 1982 was selected for the excursion. I accompanied Victorian drivers Jack Couch and Bill Steedman on the *Intercapital Daylight* which was running late so that we picked up the XPT at Cootamundra rather than at Harden as planned. The NSW Inspector was a warm friendly outgoing bloke. He immediately put Jack in the driver's seat. Jack took to driving the XPT like a duck to water. He operated the two T bars, the two-tone whistle and kept his foot planted on the dead man's pedal like a veteran. After a reasonable period of time and distance, Bill took over the controls. He too immediately handled the train as if he had been driving them for years.

Some distance down the track the Inspector asked when I was going to take my turn at driving. I told him I was not a driver and was only on board because I had been directed to be there by our Chairman. He said "That does not matter. Anyone who gets in the cab should be able to drive." Bill vacated the seat and I took over with the advantage of having watched the two drivers and listened to the Inspector. I was a little embarrassed when altering my posture in the seat, I must have released the pressure on the dead man's apparatus and received a penalty brake application. There were no further incidents along the track and the Inspector insisted that I remain in the seat until we arrived at Albury.

That evening, the Minister and some of his Transport Committee, together with some of their wives, travelled to Albury on the *Spirit of Progress*. They had arranged overnight accommodation and would travel back to Melbourne on the XPT in the morning. I met them on arrival to ensure there were no problems and then I went to Lancaster Lodge where Victorian crews rested in Albury, for my overnight accommodation.

Before departure on the Sunday morning, the Minister asked me if it would be possible for him and some of his group to travel in the cab during the journey. I told him I would have to clear it with the NSW official but I believed it would be all right and I would contact him a little later. The Inspector said it would be possible but no more than one at a time. I would have to escort them through the very noisy engine room.

WE DEPARTED Albury on time with the Victorian enginemen in the cab and each one of them to take their turn at driving. When going through the engine room to collect the Minister, I noticed oil on the floor in two places. This was certainly a slipping hazard and I had to warn each excursionist of this when moving through in each direction. I certainly got my morning exercise when going up and down the train, as almost every member of the entourage wanted to go up front.

The trip to Melbourne was uneventful. The XPT remained at the platform for a period, allowing interested people to inspect it. Jack, Bill and I knocked off. Fred Blencowe, my assistant, relieved me but the Inspector remained on duty to instruct and accompany the fresh crew who would operate the train during a trip to Seymour and back and then on the return trip to Albury. Despite the initial opposition from the NSW Chief Operations Manager, the day was an outstanding success but the XPT was never introduced to operate to and from Victoria's regional centres.

33

Vale VicRail

THE PROPOSED NEW AUTHORITIES, the STA and the MTA, were to take effect on the first of July 1983. This was a very demanding and unhappy time for me as several of the new officials from outside the railways were filtering in to take up their positions and it became clear that many of them knew as much about railways as what I would know about space stations. As time passed and I had not been interviewed for any level two positions I had applied for, it became apparent that the best I could hope for was a level three position in either authority and that would in no way be considered a promotion but rather a relegation, as my salary, authority and status would all be reduced. I became quite depressed and I guess, somewhat disaffected. I decided that if I had to leave the railways I was best suited to farming rather than trying to learn a new industry. A look at a couple of properties which could provide us with a reliable income indicated that their value was way beyond what we would be able to raise without going into heavy debt. I spoke to Alan Reiher up at the Transport Ministry concerning the fact that I had not even made it to the interview stage of level two positions. He stated that the new government wanted a fresh start with this massive restructure and reorganisation of the state rail system and as he saw it, that explained why they had engaged people with what they considered proven managerial experience in outside industry or in other rail systems. He said I should not dwell on the fact that I had not been interviewed but apply for level three positions that I would be suited to. When the successful applicants were officially announced I felt even worse. While I had given up hope previously on the position of Chief General Manager Transport Operations due to John Hearsch being chosen to fill in ahead of me in the old position of Assistant General Manager (Operations), I was even more surprised at the appointments made to the other three positions. The General Manager Passenger Services had gone to an ex NSW railways officer who had been in passenger marketing and the General Manager Freight Services went to an ex Myer executive who had become redundant when Myer closed some of their Sydney stores. He had previously worked for a period marketing freight services in the NSW railways. In the MTA the General Manager MetRail went to an ex-Hertz Rent a Car officer who had not been in Australia long and whose command of the English language was shocking. His boss at Hertz Australia had been Lynn Strouse who had earlier been selected as Chairman of MTA. Someone must have been impressed with Hertz management as the position of General Manager of Personnel and Employee Relations in MTA also went to the executive who had held the same position and title in Hertz. As a point of interest the position of General Manager, Personnel and Employee Relations in STA also went to an executive who had held that same position and title in Budget Rent-a-Car. I had long thought that senior management in the railway needed a good shake up but we certainly did not need what we got. I likened it to a farmer shooting his dog because it had fleas rather than treating it for them. I represented a problem to the new bosses because I was relatively young at forty eight years of age and at that time they did not have a redundancy scheme. Most other ex Heads of Branches and Senior Officers were in their sixties or close to it and therefore much easier to "see off".

Testing of the 'train to base' radios between Melbourne and Ballarat. Mentioned in 'Achievements' in the Chandler & Macleod assessment of Ray. There was a dispute between the ARU and the AFULE as to who should be in charge of the radio which was 'new equipment' Standing in front of a C class locomotive Left to Right *Russell Wallace* - Research, *Jack Burke* Train Guard, *Peter Gavin* – Communications Engineer, *Bill Donald* – Fireman, *Noel Murray* – Driver, *Alan Rieher* - Chairman Railways Board and *Ray Barden*

I was however quite busy. John Hearsh had now been appointed to the position of Chief General Manager Transport Operations and I was told to use the title of Assistant General Manager Transport Operations, until the new level three positions were filled. I was told by John Hearsch and Keith Fitzmaurice (Chairman of STA) that I was to concentrate among other things, on two man crewing on locomotive hauled trains. Traditionally these trains operated with a crew of three. It was inevitable that it would shortly come in throughout the ROA and it was essential that Victoria be prepared with a solid plan of how we might achieve this and what changes to equipment and alterations or additions would be required to our rules and regulations and train running instructions to ensure safety. I was not to consult with the unions involved but simply write up a plan which could be presented to them for discussion by the appropriate people at the appropriate time. It was obvious to me that my views and whatever I wrote could not possibly satisfy each of the two major unions involved and once again I would eventually be the target of their dissatisfaction. This in itself did not worry me greatly as I had been through it all before as Chief Operations Manager with my own projects of rationalising the number of country depots and the removal of restrictive work practices by shunters in the Melbourne Yard. Other major projects in which I played a part was the training of staff, drivers, guards, and signalmen for the introduction of train services through the Melbourne Underground Loop and as previously featured, negotiating with the guards and the ARU when they had stated they would not man the trains in the upgraded country passenger train services because their van would not be at the back of the trains in both directions. The introduction of radios on trains both suburban and country and whether the driver (AFULE) or the guard (ARU) should be the operator had also been difficult. Some time after this the Chairman informed me that David Hill who had replaced Alan Reiher as head of the NSW Railways, (he later became Chairman of the Australian Broadcasting Commission) had called a meeting on two man crewing in Sydney and I was to accompany him. Most, but not all rail systems would be represented. While there were occasional exceptions, senior VicRail officials usually travelled by overnight trains to and from interstate meetings, but in this case to avoid being away from home two nights Fitzmaurice said we would fly. The meeting turned out to be a non event. Most of the discussion centred on timing and when each system might be ready to introduce it. I thought this was really futile as ultimately the unions would have a big say in this. There was virtually no discussion on how each system might implement it or what their priorities for two man crewing of trains might be. I thought that an exchange of ideas would have been useful and possibly a help to me but it did not eventuate. We got out to the airport early for our five o'clock flight home but we certainly did not get home early. About twenty minutes out of Sydney the pilot announced that a red warning light had come up and although he thought it was nothing serious, he would have to turn back to Sydney. I must admit I was a bit scared and very relieved when the plane touched down without incident. It was almost an hour later that it was announced that the plane had been knocked out and there would be a further delay while a replacement was flown up from Melbourne. I did not get home that night until about nine thirty.

FOLLOWING my discussion with Alan Reiher about my future and my disappointment that we would be unable to buy a viable farm without going into heavy debt, I applied for two level three positions. Group Manager Operations Coordination in the STA and Group Manager Operations & Maintenance in the MTA. I did not go before a selection panel as such but instead was required to go for a lengthy in depth interview and fill out a heap of questionnaires at Chandler and Macleod Consultants Pty Ltd, Kew. The interviewing officer was qualified as a B Com (Applied Psychology). This surprised me greatly as I know for a fact that many of the other applicants for senior positions did not have to front up to a psychologist, but perhaps there were others who did. Possibly some of the new guard thought I was unstable or plain crazy reacting as I had to being denied an interview for level two positions. There was no doubt I felt insecure as a result of that and also felt that I was being "used", although not wanted in the longer term. An example of this was when Fitzmaurice called me up and told me that from time to time I could get a call from Mr Strouse, the Chairman of the MTA, who might need to discuss a problem which he thought I could help with. When this happened I was to cooperate fully with him. He did call on me two or three times. The results of my visit to Chandler and Macleod Consultants were not made available to me and I feared the worst. However I was in for a pleasant surprise. One afternoon I was busy working on the two man crewing project when a young man whom I had not met previously entered my office. He introduced himself saying he was a recent recruit in the industrial relations section. He was working on some problems in the Melbourne Yard and had been advised to speak with me as I may be able to help. I gave him some background information on the Melbourne Yard problems and was able to answer the questions he put to me. I told him to feel free to come back again if he thought I might be able to help. He asked me where I was likely to finish up in the new organisation and I told him I had no idea. I had missed out on the positions I had originally applied for and fairly recently had applied for two positions on the next rung down, after which I was sent to a psychologist for an interview and tests, but I had not received the result. Perhaps he said I was crazy. He said he would have a look about in the personnel area and see what he could find. He said that by law I was entitled to a copy of the report. About an hour later he returned with a photocopy of the report. I could not believe I had done so well with the interview and tests. I pondered for a while and wondered if I had been given the same opportunity at level two, would the report have been similar. I believed that it would have been. I also wondered who the person was who underlined points in three different sections.

He functions better with people with whom he has already established a rapport as he tends to be a little <u>sensitive</u>. <u>He can take a stand and assert himself where necessary</u> but usually prefers to avoid confrontation. From the point of principle he can be <u>quietly stubborn</u> and is not prepared to compromise on his ideals.

I wondered if the underlining was indicating plusses or minuses.

SHORTLY AFTER THIS Fitzmaurice called me in and said I would shortly hear from Strouse as he was going to offer me the level three position in the MTA. He asked me which operations I preferred, the suburban or the country. I said I preferred the country but I considered I was well qualified by knowledge and experience to do either job. I was quite surprised when he said well go and have a talk to him but let me know if he offers you any incentives over or above the salary and conditions already advertised as it might be that we have to match them. This indicated to me that he was still happy to have me around the place but unfortunately, history now shows that was soon to change. There was no doubt that a lot of the new managers in senior positions saw the old railway managers as incompetent and inbred with tunnel vision. Indeed Fitzmaurice had once asked me when I was showing him over the Melbourne Goods area, "How long have you worked in the rail? When I told him thirty two years he replied, "How on earth can a man stay in the same job for that period of time?" I told him I was not a railway buff as such as I did not have a lot of technical knowledge, nor did I have much knowledge of overseas railways but I nevertheless loved railways operations. I would back myself against anybody with my detailed knowledge of the operation of the Victorian system and I also had a reasonable knowledge of operations on other

Australian systems. While I had been employed in the railways for thirty two years starting as a lad, I had many appointments over this time, each of which presented different challenges. For instance when I was a young relieving stationmaster there was great variety. I might be in the Mallee or Wimmera for a period dealing with mainly grain and woolgrowers, then in East Gippsland for a period dealing with saw millers and sleeper cutters. Then off to the Goulburn Valley dealing with fruit growers, canneries, wineries, dairy products, but also grain and livestock. You might then get a spell in the City dealing mainly with suburban passengers. I was meeting new people on a daily basis and getting to know their likes and dislikes appertaining to railway services. After that I was a train controller, first suburban then country - two vastly different operations. Then I was an Inspector, Superintendent and Manager (Melbourne Freight Terminals, Passenger Operations, Stations Operations and Freight Operations), followed by six years as Assistant Chief Traffic Manager (the longest I had ever been in any one job) and then Chief Operations Manager.

LYNNE STROUSE WAS AN EXTREMELY interesting person. He was born in Germany soon after the end of World War II. His mother was a German lass and his father an American soldier in the Occupation Force. He had spent much of his childhood alternating between Germany and the USA and had attended school in each of these countries. He had worked for Hertz in the two countries and was eventually posted to Australia to head the company here. He claimed he had short listed applicants for the level three position and had discussed them with the Minister who allegedly said I was best suited to it. He further said he was getting married (in his words "to a God damn Miner's daughter from Cessnock, NSW") in three weeks time and he wanted to fill this position before he took a two week break. I asked him about selection panels and whether it could be finalised in that time. He said they could go through those formalities if they want but I am telling you now, if you want the job it is yours. I thanked him for the offer but told him I needed a couple of days to consider the position. I was an applicant for the corresponding job in the STA but had not had any offer from them. I told him I normally would prefer the country train operations because of the greater variety but I would try to keep an open mind. What I did not tell him was that I had some doubts about his number two man, Albrecht Scholer, and his ability to do the job with no knowledge of railways and his very poor English. I found him difficult to understand. Incidentally, he said that Albrecht was going to be his best man at the wedding indicating to me that they must be pretty close. I did not take long to decide that if the STA job was offered to me I would take it. Unfortunately, this decision subsequently proved to be the wrong one. A day or two later Fitzmaurice offered me the level three job in the STA and I took it. Fred Blencowe who had been the Assistant Chief Operations Manager in the old VicRail and was sixty-four years of age was later appointed to the MTA job. I tried very hard to settle down and get on with life and the job but in the atmosphere of great change and bedlam, this was extremely difficult, if not impossible. I almost immediately had a disagreement with Fitzmaurice and his General Manager Personnel and Employee Relations, Dennis Watt, over my salary. Bear in mind the Minister had said "No one will be disadvantaged". The Corporate Group had decided to take the State Executive Service rates of salary rather than the previous Railway Senior Officers Award. This meant that my salary would drop by about fifteen hundred dollars although there was an expense of office allowance of two thousand dollars, which did not apply previously. He argued that I was much better off as the expense of office allowance was tax free and did not necessarily have to be expended. Besides I would get a Ford Falcon car from Hertz Rent A Car fully serviced (petrol, insurance and maintenance-free) and any fully licensed driver, including my wife, could use it. I argued that you would never be certain of the tax free allowance until after you received your tax return each year as you often heard of the ATO clamping down on these "perks". Furthermore the allowance did not attract units of superannuation as did your salary. I recall Fitzmaurice criticising ex railway people for always worrying about superannuation. He said they seemed obsessed with it. I pointed out that for many years I had the use of a departmental vehicle when required and it did not concern me that my wife could not drive it or that it had an identifying red number plate. I liked to travel to and from work by train as often as possible as by doing so, I kept in touch with our customers many of whom knew me, and also with our staff by sometimes riding on the locomotive or in the guards van. At a later meeting with Watt he said if I liked riding on the train so much I ought to save the expense of owning and running a private car and give the rented car to my wife. I told him that such an arrangement would be in my opinion unethical and not practical as in operations I would frequently have to use the car on the job. I further said that if they felt they had to reduce my pay they should reduce the expense of office allowance and not my salary which they finally did.

The following pages detail the Chandler McLeod Report

PERSONAL RESUME

SELECTION SERVICES DIVISION

Strictly Confidential

Report on:	Raymond Thomas BARDEN
For:	Group Manager - Rail Operations and Maintenance (Metropolitan) Group Manager - Operations Co-Ordination
Date:	8th August, 1983
Report to:	Mr. Keith M. Fitzmaurice Chairman and Managing Director State Transport Authority Room 121 67 Spencer Street MELBOURNE 3000.

---

5 Wellington Street, Kew, Vic. 3101   Tel. 861 7023
P.O. Box 96, Kew 3101
    Offices or representatives located in all Australian states and internationally

Chandler & Macleod Consultants Pty. Ltd.

RECOMMENDATIONS

Mr. Barden is recommended for the positions of Group Manager - Rail Operations and Maintenance (Metropolitan) and Group Manager - Operations Co-Ordination. In terms of experience, achievement and personal capacity, he is the pre-eminent candidate for the position.

Mr. Barden has a wealth of experience in the Victorian Rail System rising from a junior position to his current status of equivalence to the position for which he is applying. He has an intimate understanding of the management of the operations activities of the rail system and has been a significant contributor to improvements and enhancements in both country and metropolitan operational techniques. He appears to be a man of conviction, strong character and full commitment to his principles and offers the seasoned management ability that would be expected of a successful performer in this position.

INTERVIEW SUMMARY

Mr. Barden impresses as a down-to-earth and unpretentious individual with the ability to express his point of view in a succinct and telling manner. He appears to be a clear thinking and decisive person with strength of character and firmness of opinion.

He states that he has always felt that the railways have always been run uneconomically and have needed considerable operational improvement to ensure that services are provided in an efficient and cost effective way. He feels that in the last three years he has been in a position to make a significant contribution along these lines and has done so even at the expense of his own personal popularity. In particular, he feels that he has gained a level of unpopularity with various union officials, particularly in relation to his involvement in the rationalisation of country operations. Despite this level of unpopularity, he has attempted to remain true to his convictions and to implement government policy as required.

Throughout his management career, he has attempted to display strong leadership qualities by making water tight and well thought out decisions. He seeks to lead by example and desires to be firm, fair and consistent in supervising others. He believes he has obtained a good rapport with people at all levels and is regarded as a competent "railwayman".

PSYCHOLOGICAL APPRAISAL TESTING indicates that Mr. Barden has the analytical and problem solving ability necessary to operate in a senior management function; further his personality is that of a mature, alert, confident, insightful and well organised individual.

OLEH BUTCHATSKY
B.Com. (Applied Psychology)

 Chandler & Macleod Consultants Pty. Ltd.

PERSONAL INFORMATION

Name: Raymond Thomas BARDEN

Address: Lot 8, Pierce Road, NEW GISBORNE, 3438.

Telephone   Business: 6 1001

Date of Birth: 26th March, 1935

Birthplace: Australia

Marital Status: Married, with four children

Height: 180 cm

Weight: 86 kg

Hobbies & Interests   Farming - 4.2 hectare farmlet, Gardening,
                       Football, Horse Racing - spectator.

Chandler & Macleod Consultants Pty. Ltd.

EDUCATION

INSTITUTION	STANDARD ATTAINED
1940 - 1948 State School, Nyora	Merit
1962 - 1963 University High School	Leaving Certificate (Evening & Correspondence)
1964 - 1965 University High School	Matriculation (Evening & Corespondence)
1964 - 1967 R.M.I.T. Transport	Certificate - Administration Course
1971 University OF N.S.W.	Certificate - Higher Railway Management
1973 University of Melbourne	Certificate - Summer School of Business Administration

QUALIFICATIONS and OTHER COURSES UNDERTAKEN

1952	VicRail - First Aid - Ticket Checking
1953	VicRail - Telegraphy
1955-57	VicRail - All forms of Signaling & Safeworki
1956	VicRail - Stationmaster
1960	VicRail - Train Controller

Current and past memberships of Associations include :

Associate, Australian Grain Institute
Member, Chartered Institute of Transport
Victorian Railways Institute Councillor (11 years)
Senior Vice President, Victorian Railways Institute.

Chandler & Macleod Consultants Pty. Ltd.

EMPLOYMENT HISTORY

Mr. Barden commenced with the Victorian Railways system in 1952 as a **Lad Porter** at Essendon. From there he has been promoted through the ranks to his current position. He was appointed **Station Master** at the age of 22 years and soon after after became a **Train Controller**.

POSITION AND RESPONSIBILITIES

1965 - 1969   Traffic Inspector

In the field supervision of Stationmasters and Train Running. Conduct of Special Traffic (Races, Football, Royal Visit, etc.) Also emergency services, disruptions, etc. Acted as Superintendent Metropolitan Train Running for 10 months and District Superintendent, Eastern, for 6 months.

1969 - 1971   Superintendent - Country Train Running

Monitor the performance of country and interstate passenger train operations. Implement necessary alterations and improvements to services. Finalise public complaints. Represent Traffic Branch on various committees.

1971 - 1974   Manager - Passenger Operations

Responsible for the operation of passenger and parcels traffic throughout the system. Also responsible for the Central Reservation Bureau, Package Tours and timetabling of suburban, country and interstate passenger and freight services.

1974 - 1977   Assistant Chief Traffic Manager

Responsible for wagon distribution and freight operations throughout the system. Also responsible for safeworking systems, signalling and trackwork alterations, etc.

1977 - 1980   Deputy Chief Traffic Manager & A.C.T.M.(Districts)

Responsible for operations in all six country districts and marshalling yards in the Metropolitan Area. Also responsible for the operation of passenger and parcels terminals at Spencer Street.

Chandler & Macleod Consultants Pty. Ltd.

EMPLOYMENT HISTORY(cont'd)

POSITION AND RESPONSIBILITIES

1980 - 1982   **Chief Operations Manager**

Responsible for the safe and efficient operation of all trains throughout the system. Responsible for timetabling, train control signalling, yard operations, freight vehicle distribution, locomotive rostering and running staff rostering. Responsible for the welfare and motivation of all Branch personnel (approximately 5,000 on staff).

1982 - 1983   **Director of Operations**

Direct the activities of the Operations, Freight and Transportation Branches towards achieving performance and productivity results consistent with Management policies and objectives.

Ensure proper co-ordination where joint activities of those Branches were deemed necessary in order to obtain overall efficiency, economy and safety of operation. Oversee the participation of the Branches when project and business developments required their involvement in corporate planning.

July 1st 1983   **Assistant General Manager - Operations - STA**

In this position, he carries the same responsibilities as Director of Operations and in addition is responsible for the operations of the trading and catering division. He reports to the Chief General Manager, Transport Operations, though also has responsibility for the metropolitan running of the railway system.

His current salary is $52,300 per annum, and he receives an allowance of $500 per annum to compensate for his responsibilities in his present position.

EMPLOYMENT HISTORY(cont'd)

CLAIMED ACHIEVEMENTS IN THE TRANSPORT FIELD

Mr. Barden claims that his most significant contributions to the Victorian Railway system are as follows :

1. Member of the full time Task Force, which included outside Consultants, set up in late 1979, to effect major alterations to the VicRail structure and organisation.

   The Task Force was responsible for structuring the new Operations, Transportation and Workshops Branches of VicRail from the old Traffic and Rolling Stock Branches.

   The task was particularly difficult and demanding, as the guidelines set by the VicRail Board represented a major departure from the traditional VicRail organisation and authority structures and were viewed with not only genuine concern, but considerable suspicion, by Industrial Organisations, Senior Key Personnel in the various Branches and Operating Staff alike.

2. As Chief Operations Manager, was responsible to the VicRail Board, for the implementation, staffing and administration of the new Metropolitan Control Centre (Metrol). New technology embracing revolutionary changes in safeworking, signalling and communications were the key issues.

3. Implementation of train services in the Caulfield and Burnley Loops of the Melbourne Underground Railway. Operating conditions and training of Drivers, Guards, Signalmen, Train Controllers and other support and supervising staff were the key issues.

4. Overall responsibility for the training of staff in the operation of the new Comeng trains and for the provision of replacements services when, from day to day, the new trains proved unreliable.

5. Responsible for the field arrangements for the introduction of on train radio communications on suburban trains and extension of radio on country train services.

6. Responsible over the last two years for the consolidation of country freight train services, the rationalisation of several country Operations Depots and the considerable increased productivity of freight train services. This was achieved, to the extent that it has been so far implemented, with considerable opposition from Industrial Organisations and Community Pressure Groups.

EMPLOYMENT HISTORY (cont'd)

7. Participated in the planning and scheduling of the upgraded country passenger train services which took effect from October, 1981. Responsible for the improved locomotive rostering throughout the state to provide the locomotives required for the additional passenger services. Responsible for the recommendations altering the regulations concerning the location of brake vans on country passenger trains, the brake testing of country passenger trains, and the tail signals carried. These recommendations were essential to the operation of the new services but met with substantial reaction from one Industrial Organisation. Implementation was only achieved after prolonged industrial negotiations with which at all times he was was personally involved.

8. Has given close oversight to the planning and implemenation of the new computerised system of wagon control (VELAS). Implementation up to stage 2 has resulted in improved supply and utilization of wagons and vastly improved quality of service to customers.

9. Has played a major role in the planning and part implementation of through working of locomotives between Melbourne and Adelaide and Melbourne and Sydney. Modifications to the locomotives of all systems have been required before they were acceptable and has proved a major, time consuming task.

Chandler & Macleod Consultants Pty. Ltd.

CRITICAL THINKING

This untimed test series assesses MR. BARDEN'S performance in the following areas, as compared to Australian managers.

- the ability to define a problem
- the ability to select pertinent information for the solution of a problem
- the ability to formulate and select relevant and promising hypotheses
- the ability to recognize stated and unstated assumptions
- the ability to draw conclusions correctly and to judge the validity of inferences.

```
             |xxxxxxxxxxxxxxxxxxxxxxxxxxxxxxxxxxxxxx|
             |...|....|......|..........|..........|..........|.......|.....|...|
Stanines      1    2     3         4           5          6        7      8    9
             Low                             Average                           High
```

Mr. Barden achieved a reasonable but not outstanding score on this test, in the sense that his results are consistent with the average for the Australian management group and thus are sufficient for this position.

Chandler & Macleod Consultants Pty. Ltd.

TEMPERAMENT (characteristic behaviour)

He possesses the following temperament traits:

Good self-mastery and is consistent, ethical, sincere, alert to opportunities, confident, insightful, non-aggressive though firm when necessary and well organised.

Although he is subject to some occasionally recurring negative emotions, he is essentially a stable and predictable individual who is able to remain objective and mature in outlook. He is prepared to work in harmony with others as a member of a team and to abide by accepted practices and procedures. He handles pressure without noticeable upset.

He is an honest and sincere individual. He is not overly ambitious in the normal accepted sense of the term, but he does aspire to remain in an environment that provides challenge and excitement. He will show loyalty and a high level of integrity in his negotiations.

He has a preference for work which offers variety and change and he has little difficulty in switching his attention from one task to another; by the same token, however, he is able to keep his end objectives in mind and he can pay attention to detail as necessary. He makes decisions with due confidence being neither impulsive on the one hand nor over-cautious on the other. He likes to be kept busy.

As has been indicated, there are occasions when his usual quiet optimism is replaced by less positive emotions, but despite this, he still remains confident of his abilities; however, he will become a little more quiet and reserved in his inter-personal relationships on these occasions. He functions better when interacting with people with whom he has already established a rapport as he tends to be a little sensitive. However, this sensitivity provides him with insight into the feelings of others plus the capacity for tact and empathy. He can take a stand and assert himself where necessary but usually he prefers to avoid confrontation and is generally effective in achieving his results through other people without having to exercise authority.

He is basically open-minded and prepared to consider all points of view. He will make a decision, and state his own beliefs when appropriate but he could not be described as a particularly aggressive or authoritarian individual. From the point of principle, however, he can be quietly stubborn and he is not prepared to compromise on his ideals.

34

Record Wheat Season

THE 1983 WHEAT season was predicted to be a record harvest for Victoria at that time, in excess of three million tonnes. This coincided with the new Minister's early retirement plan whereby anyone over fifty years of age could voluntarily retire with adjustments to their superannuation entitlements. It also coincided with the introduction of a revolutionary change in our handing of the grain which was advantageous to the railway but also to the Grain Elevators Board (GEB). As previously mentioned the overflow (tonnage anticipated in excess of the silo capacity in its catchment area) was always a challenge as it required the rail to clear the grain progressively from silos through the grain growing areas to ensure continuous uninterrupted receivals throughout the period of harvest. Commencing this year a network of "Central Receival Points" would be set up geographically with ample storages allowing smaller capacity intermediate silos to be closed when they were full. Farmers would then be required to take their grain to the central receival point instead and provided it was in the 'up' direction, closer to the ports or inland storages, would receive a one dollar per tonne discount on freight charges. The closing of silos when full saved the GEB staffing costs for the remainder of the harvest period. It saved the railway the cost of servicing these silos, which often had limited siding capacity, on a daily basis so that the silo did not fill up which was the traditional practice. The productivity of locomotives, wagons and train crews would be considerably improved with greatly reduced shunting requirements at branch line locations and smaller roadside locations, and the running of block trains between the central receival points and ports. I was instructed to personally oversee the wheat shift on a daily basis and ensure a smooth operation. I was quite concerned - the early retirement plan commenced in November as did the early part of the grain harvest. As I saw it we could lose operating staff (drivers and guards particularly) just when we needed more for the peak operation. I informed my superiors of my concern and was eventually told that the Minister would agree for a deferment of up to a year if the operating staff member had elected to retire, but management required his services for a period to maintain seasonal services. It had been the custom in the old railway to call for volunteers from the ranks of drivers, guards and qualified signalling staff to take temporary transfers to the wheat growing areas to cover the extra train running. I was told that since I would be responsible for the wheat shift, arrangements would be made for all applications for early retirement from operating grades to be forwarded to my office for me to determine whether they could be released or deferred until a later date. I thought this was a bit discriminating as those involved in the wheat shift would be delayed but if in Gippsland or the metropolitan area they may well be let go.

I thought the Minister would be seen as a good bloke affording staff early retirement. The new senior management had washed their hands of it but if a staff member went to the Union having been deferred because of his location, the union would again attack me personally.

Central Silos 'Greatest innovation,' meeting told

NYMPEA MAIL-TIMES 21/09/1983

A State Transport Authority official believes Victoria's new central receival point system of grain delivery will be the greatest innovation since delivery went from bag to bulk.

STA and Grain Elevators Board officials explained the new system to 213 farmers at Warracknabeal Town Hall yesterday.

Marma Lake Receival Zone called the special meeting.

STA assistant general manager, operations, Mr Ray Barden, told the meeting that under the new system the railways would be able to shift a far greater amount of grain than under the old system.

"I believe the introduction of central receival points will be the greatest innovation since we went from bag to bulk," he said.

He said that bulk transport of grain had not fully realised its potential yet but would do so with the new system.

The hopper fleet servicing central receival points would be tightly disciplined and would have priority over all fast freight trains throughout the harvest.

Turn-around time at Geelong would be 2½ hours.

The meeting at the Warracknabeal Town Hall was to explain the new system of handling grain by rail. Unfortunately, the farmers were more interested in the recent rises in grain rates and handling charges at that time and the fact that the Transport Minister did not attend.

As it turned out it was not too bad. I interviewed most of the operating staff who elected to retire early and who we wished to retain until after the harvest, and found that the vast majority of them were quite happy to stay on. The few who did not want to stay, I let go.

RAY BARDEN

THE WIMMERA MAIL-TIMES 21/09/1983

FARMERS WILL MARCH IN CITY

Mass protest on freight

Wimmera-Mallee farmers and the Victorian Farmers and Graziers Association will organise a mass protest march in Melbourne.

They hope to be joined by farmers from the Mallee and north-eastern Victoria.

The rally will protest against a 15 percent rise in grain freight charges and 8.5 percent rise in grain handling charges.

More than 400 farmers met at Warracknabeal Town Hall yesterday to protest against the increases.

It was the first of three such meetings; the other two are at Ouyen and in north-eastern Victoria.

The angry Warracknabeal meeting passed five resolutions:

★ That we emphatically reject the 15 percent rail freight increase as directed by the State Government.

★ That we emphatically reject the 8.5 percent GEB handling charge increase as directed by the State Government.

★ That the VFGA executive organise a mass protest meeting of all grain-growers and affected rural people, to expose the rip-off in freight charges imposed by the Cain government upon rural people as a tax.

★ We demand that the State Government deregulates the movement of grain by rail as support for private enterprise to compete with an inefficient rail system.

★ That a protest march be organised in Melbourne as soon as possible.

Yesterday's meeting was attended by farmers from as far as Yaapeet, Salisbury near Nhill, Gymbowen and Noradjuha.

Main guests and speakers included VFGA grains chairman **Mr Michael Cock**, VFGA executive officer **Mr Peter Cook**, Grain Elevators Board chairman **Mr Cliff Semmler**, GEB executive officer **Mr Peter Seletto**, State Transport Authority general manager, freight services division, **Mr Stan Beevor**, STA assistant general manager, operations, **Mr Ray Barden**, and National Party MPs **Mr Bernie Dunn** and **Mr Bill McGrath**.

The meeting was angry that Transport Minister Mr Crabb failed to attend.

Mr Stoney was to have attended on behalf of Mr Crabb.

'STATE OF WAR'

The tone of the meeting was set by posters inside Warracknabeal Town Hall.

Some of them were: We are in a state of war until we obtain justice for our industry, graingrowers unite. Declaration of war authorised by VFGA.

"War was declared September 13 when Mr Crabb announced a 15 percent freight increase.

"The enemy: V-Line, Victorian Cabinet, Minister for (?) Transport and Minister Against Agriculture."

The chairman, president of Wimmera District Council of the VFGA **Mr Don Kent** of Warracknabeal, opened the meeting by saying that floods, drought and stripe-rust had hit farmers.

NEW DISEASE

"And now a new disease has erupted. State Government take-all."

The hall erupted with cheers.

Mr Michael Cock told the meeting that the increases were not a result of negotiation but were a directive from Cabinet and Treasury.

He urged growers to make every endeavor to use other means to move their grain to terminals.

35

Freight Gates

THE 1983/84 wheat shift was handled reasonably well despite the record harvest. I had issued an instruction that no wheat train was to be cancelled without control or freight operations staff first contacting me, no matter what time of the day or night. This way we were able to alter priorities on occasions particularly with locomotives, to avoid as far as practicable cancellation of block trains of wheat or empties.

We had already cancelled some less important trains for the duration of the harvest, including the Freight Centre Train to Horsham, to make extra staff and locomotives available.

It was an extremely busy time for me as the new General Manager Freight Services had been making trips to the grain growing areas to try and market the Central Receival Points to growers and had insisted I accompany him. As with most changes to long established practices there was some opposition to it mainly, but not entirely, to the growers belief, and I agreed with them, that they were not getting a fair share of the economies being made. The situation was compounded shortly after, when grain rates were increased.

Meanwhile the Minister had established a task force to look into and make recommendations on how less than car load (LCL) traffic should be handled in the future and how many Freight Centres (later called Freight Gates) should be established. This was a very similar task to that which Jack Emmins and I were given when we went overseas in 1975.

We had recommended revolutionary changes including the establishment of no more than ten to twelve Freight Centres and the closure of goods sheds at smaller intermediate locations, which would be serviced by road from the Freight Centres. Our proposal was knocked back, the General Manager of the day informing us that it was politically unacceptable.

Instead, at great expense, thirty-five Freight Centres were established. The new task force was made up of several union officials, the General Manager Freight Services, freight marketing staff and people from the Personnel and Employee Relations sections. They toured country Victoria meeting with Shire Councils, community groups and railway staff.

The Minister chaired the monthly meetings held in the railway head office where progress, ideas and problems were discussed. I had been instructed to attend these meetings to report among other things, the progress of the wheat shift.

I got a bit of a shock when Jim Frazer, the Secretary to the ARU, reported on their trip to Horsham claiming that I had sabotaged their project by cancelling the Freight Centre Train in favour of wheat trains and had not made adequate replacement services. Instead of freight being available for delivery at 7.00am it was now almost lunchtime and sometimes later and staff and customers at Horsham and surrounding areas were most unhappy.

The Minister asked me to comment. I said I was at a complete loss to understand how this could be. Only the day before I had personally telephoned the Freight Centre Manager at Horsham to check before this meeting, on how the temporary arrangements were going. He stated all was well. There had been an occasional complaint from clients about the later delivery times but overall our clients seemed quite happy.

Experience had shown me that in situations such as this, some staff members could be unhappy as their routine had been upset, their peak working time had shifted from the morning to the afternoon and they could not get away at knock off time strictly on time or perhaps even a little earlier, if some special circumstances prevailed.

We had arranged for the marketing people to canvass the business community explaining the situation prior to implementing the arrangement and reports were that it was accepted quite well. These people understood the importance of a successful wheat shift to the local economy and seemed happy to make adjustments where necessary to suit their needs.

For instance the brewery (CUB) had been contacted and arrangements made for publicans to order their beer a day earlier so it was actually arriving half a day earlier, not later. Jim Frazer then asserted that all of this would have been unnecessary if I had arranged for the Horsham loading to be placed on the 9.30pm "Jet" as a trailing block which could be quickly detached at Horsham and then placed for delivery with the rail tractor.

Obviously he did not get this information from management at Horsham who knew the situation with this proposal but probably from his union representative who obviously did not know.

I have mentioned earlier how the views and policies of railway people in the county often differed from those of the shunters in the Melbourne Yard. I was surprised that Jim Frazer had not done a bit more "homework" before raising it. I said I would arrange for his suggestion to be implemented immediately if he could authorise it but the facts were that the restrictive work practices of the Melbourne Yard shunters made it impossible. He looked bewildered and perhaps embarrassed. I further explained that several weeks previously I had personally had a meeting with the Metropolitan Shunters Section of his union and asked them to give an exemption from their policy for one movement only each week day, to transfer the Horsham loading from the Melbourne Goods area to the Canal area, to be attached to the 9.30pm "Jet" which had been made up earlier predominately with loading from the bogie exchange.

I fully explained to them the importance of shifting the record grain harvest but they flatly refused even though there were no safety issues involved in a simple transfer of a relatively small "rake" of loading to the "closed" area. At that stage we were not operating an afternoon shift Canal pilot and were not likely to be in the near future. The canal area was therefore "closed" in accordance with shunters' work practices. A short time later before the cancellation of the Horsham freight centre train, the Manager Melbourne Freight Terminal had a further meeting with them and asked them to reconsider but to no avail. Notes of these meetings were available if he wished to see them. He turned to the Minister and said that we should have come to him in the first place and he would look into it further. Despite this nothing changed, so the Melbourne Yard shunters had won again.

LATER ON IN the meeting there was another example of Frazer not having checked out a situation before raising it. He claimed we were short supplying Melbourne Goods with empty wagons because we had put some wagons in storage.

He said there were about forty wagons stored at Wallan which could ease the situation if we released them.

Again I was asked to comment. I pointed out that they were not in storage by design but in fact could not be moved due to a black ban that had been imposed on the siding by the Metropolitan Guards Section of the ARU some months back. I had not been particularly worried about it as no bogie vehicles or GY wheat wagons were involved and Jim himself had said earlier in this meeting, that they had to have bogie vehicles for freight centre traffic.

A short time after the meeting finished the General Manager Personnel and Employee Relations called me into his office. He criticised me for embarrassing the Secretary of the ARU in front of the Minister. I did not understand and asked him what he meant.

He said "Me and my team are trying to build a good relationship with the ARU and you are undoing it by speaking as you did today." I asked him did he want me to "cop" inaccurate and misleading information which made the railways and me personally look incompetent, rather than correct him by telling him and the meeting the true and accurate position.

There was no doubt that Frazer had been trying to show me in a bad light and I was entitled to reveal the truth when asked to comment by the Minister. It was clear that Denis Watt was trying to impress the ARU and perhaps the Minister by sweeping these matters under the carpet and allowing management to take the blame for the problems created in these two examples by sections of the union which it appeared couldn't be controlled by the executive, or perhaps, they did not want to control them.

I offered to make a bet with him that neither the ban on entering a so called "closed" section of Melbourne Yard or the ban on the siding at Wallan would be lifted anytime soon. He declined and was clearly unhappy with me.

A couple of weeks later he telephoned saying he had spoken with the Chairman, Keith Fitzmaurice, and I was not now required to attend future Freight Gate taskforce meetings. Instead I was to send a more junior officer who could supply statistics of the wheat shift and bring back to me for actioning any queries the task force had on either the wheat shift or the freight centres.

It seemed that ignorance was bliss. It also confirmed to me that my standing in the new authority was slipping badly and again I pondered my future as I clearly had difficulty in working with these new people.

I knew that if I changed my attitude and pretended to be

something that I was not, I could possibly improve the situation but I just could not do it.

I had long believed that you must follow your conscience and if you tried to fool yourself, then you are also trying to fool everyone.

I still had plenty of work on my desk, not the least of which was the two man crewing. Sometime later it was announced that the freight centre taskforce had completed its examination of the freight situation and twelve number "Freight Gates" would be created to replace the thirty-five old centres.

This was in line with what Jack Emmins and I had recommended about eight years ago. I thought procrastination was the thief of time and in this case, several million dollars.

A Man of Principle

THE CHARTERED INSTITUTE OF TRANSPORT

Founded 1919   Incorporated by Royal Charter 1926

This is to Certify that

Raymond Thomas Barden

has this day been elected a

FELLOW

of

The Chartered Institute of Transport

established to promote the study and advancement of the science and art of transport in all its branches

Witness our hands and seal

this *19th* day of *September* 1984

.... *President*

.... *Director-General*

THIS DIPLOMA IS NOT ISSUED UNDER, IN PURSUANCE, OR BY VIRTUE OF ANY STATUTORY OR GOVERNMENT SANCTION, BUT BY THE AUTHORITY OF THE INSTITUTE ONLY, AND SHALL REMAIN THE PROPERTY OF AND, ON DEMAND, BE RETURNED TO THE INSTITUTE.

Certificate of Ray's election as a Fellow of the Chartered Institute of Transport

THE AUSTRALIAN GRAIN INSTITUTE INC.

This is to Certify that

Raymond Thomas Barden

having satisfied the examination requirements has this day been elected a

MEMBER

of

The Australian Grain Institute Inc.

established to promote the study and advancement of the standards and practices appertaining to the Australian grain industry in all its branches

Witness our hands and seal

this 1st *day of* March *19* 84

_____ Chairman

_____ Secretary

THIS DIPLOMA IS NOT ISSUED UNDER, IN PURSUANCE, OR BY VIRTUE OF ANY STATUTORY OR GOVERNMENT SANCTION, BUT BY THE AUTHORITY OF THE INSTITUTE ONLY, AND SHALL REMAIN THE PROPERTY OF AND, ON DEMAND, BE RETURNED TO THE INSTITUTE

Certificate of Ray's Membership to the Grain Institute.

36

Area Controllers, Main Western Zone

I WAS TRYING to finish my "two man crewing" recommendations when I was called to the Chairman's office. He stated he had been in Adelaide the day before with Doctor Don Williams who was the Chairman of Australian National Railways (formerly Commonwealth Railway and South Australian Railways). During their discussions the stalemate on the staffing of the control room for the main western line came up. Fitzmaurice claimed Williams had asked him where I had fitted into the new organisation and when told, allegedly stated he was surprised the matter had not been settled as he considered me to be somewhat of an authority on CTC working. He told Fitzmaurice how he had sent two of his senior officers to Melbourne on a couple of occasions to discuss with me problems they had encountered with the installation and staffing of CTC on their system, and that I had been most helpful. Fitzmaurice then went on to say he found it most unsatisfactory that after several months nobody on our system had come up with a solution. It was his experience in life that there was always a solution to problems, no matter how unpalatable they might be. I replied that I had told the then Chairman, Alan Reiher, on many occasions and the Minister on at least two occasions that the area controllers' positions on the main Western Line could never be justified and if they put signalmen in the room they would never get them out. They ignored my advice and opted for a so called trial, the Minister saying if there was no job there, the signalmen would realise it and return to their appointed positions. Had my view been accepted the problem would never have arisen. As if there was not enough evidence to prove there was no extra positions justified, before the trial began, surely now that the train controller had been working alone for some months since the signalmen were withdrawn, shows beyond doubt that no extra job exists. At no time did the train controllers say their workload was too heavy or ask for assistance, and at no time did management think that train running or operations in general would be improved with extra staff. In fact I felt that the move would be detrimental to train running. I felt that the only realistic and satisfactory solution was for the Minister to meet with the Union Officials and tell them that the trial had proved that the extra positions were not necessary and return the signalmen to work in their appointed jobs. After all he had directed that they be given the trial in the first place and he had also directed that they stay at home on full pay when the train controllers, out of sheer frustration, threatened for the first time ever, to strike.

Fitzmaurice was clearly angry with me. He said, "You can't tell the Minister what he should do." He pointed out to me in no uncertain terms that I only got my job and a place in the corporate group because of my experience and knowledge of railway operations and he was looking to me for a solution. I said if you want to turn the clock back twenty odd years to pre CTC days, you could revert to ATC (Automatic & Track Control). He asked what that involved. I briefly explained the system to him. It was worked under the direction of the train controller but there were signalmen in the field who carried out the train controllers instructions on all train running matters, but should a train become disabled in the section, in certain circumstances, it was the train controller who authorised and issued a "train order", not the signalman. Should a signal protecting the entrance to a section fail (home departure signal) the train controller gave authority for the signalman to issue a caution order to pass it at the stop position by exchanging and repeating back, a written authority with the signalman. Should he see ATC as a solution to the problem I estimated it would be very, very costly.

At least five, perhaps six signalmen would be required to cover the weekend work, annual leave and sick leave. The operating equipment would require to be duplicated and housed in a separate building and there would be additional maintenance costs. He then asked me a strange question… "How long have you known this?" I told him I had been qualified in the system for about twenty five years. He said "No, how long have you been aware this could be a solution?" I told him only since he had challenged me by saying "every problem has a solution no matter how unpalatable it might be". I emphasised I was not recommending it as a solution as I saw it as unnecessary and a waste of taxpayers' money, which would be better spent elsewhere. I would see it as more "feather bedding" and we had far too much of that already. By his attitude and demeanour, if I did not know it before, I certainly did now. I was on the way out.

This was "confirmed" in my mind the following Monday at the Corporate Group meeting when Fitzmaurice announced he had a possible solution to the Area Controllers problem. The STA had very recently employed a lawyer called Bruce Shaw who was said to be an expert in industrial relations. He was to ease the load on Dennis Watt, the General Manager Personnel and Employee Relations. He asked Shaw to give the group a rundown on ATC. Shaw said he had studied it up over the weekend from "Janes Book of Railways". I thought this was an insult not only to me, but also to my immediate superior, John Hearsch, the Chief General Manager, Transport Operations. A short time later the "ATC solution" was adopted and eventually, Area Controllers were appointed. Imagine my feelings a little further down the track after I had retired and Roper had replaced Crabb as Transport Minister, when I read in the daily press a list of economies Roper was making to ease their budget problems. This list included the abolition of the Area Controllers positions on the main Western Line. Once more the Train Controllers were "pushing the buttons" as they should have been all along and my assertions, far too late, had been vindicated.

I finished my report and recommendations on two man crewing and after a time was told that the Unions would be brought in to discuss the matter. The ARU had stated that they would not discuss it if I was present. I will never know whether the ARU had actually banned me or whether management had decided it was best I was not present, but unless there had been a leak the ARU would not know at that time that I did not favour their proposal that the guard should be simply shifted up into the locomotive cab replacing the locomotive assistant and therefore a very important training position. He also would be in charge of the train. An extremely interesting situation developed when I was on sick leave and the Australian Federated Union of Locomotive Enginemen contacted me asking if I would be prepared to give evidence in support of their union at a forthcoming hearing in the Conciliation and Arbitration Commission, as they were in dispute with the State Rail Authority of New South Wales on the matter of crewing. They had read my recommendations for Victoria and thought my views generally would make very useful evidence. I said that although it was crystal clear that my railway career had finished, I thought it might be improper for me to do so as I was still officially employed by the Metropolitan Transport Authority in Victoria. A day or so later they again contacted me and asked how I would respond if they arranged a subpoena for me to attend. I replied that if they did that I would have no option but to attend, and as I would be under oath, I would have to give evidence in accordance with my beliefs on the matter. I subsequently attended and gave evidence. I have included a photocopy of the transcript. The lawyers retained by NSW Railways and the ARU, plus Shaw on behalf of V/Line and the Bench gave me a thorough working over, but I came through alright I thought.

The full records begin on the next page.

CONCILIATION AND ARBITRATION
ACT 1904

C. No. 3932 of 1984
C. No. 1921 of 1984
C. No. 4505 of 1984

IN THE MATTER OF -

THE STATE RAIL AUTHORITY OF NEW SOU[TH]
AUTHORITY

and

AUSTRALIAN FEDERATED UNION OF
LOCOMOTIVE ENGINEMEN

Notification pursuant to Section 25
of the Act of a dispute re manning
proposals

AUSTRALIAN FEDERATED UNION OF
ENGINEMEN

Application under Section 142A of
the Act by the Australian Federated
Union of Locomotive Enginemen for a[n]
order that it shall have the right
to represent the industrial interes[ts]
of any employee of the State Rail
Authority of New South Wales, State
Transport Authority of Victoria and
Australian National Railways who
works upon an operative locomotive
hauling any train, to the exclusion
of any other industrial organizatic[n]
and in particular the Australian
Railways Union

AUSTRALIAN RAILWAYS UNION

Application under Section 142A of
the Act for exclusive representatic[n]
by Australian Railways Union for
employees required to work on trair[s]
or locomotives in the capacity of
second crew member.

SUMMONS TO WITNESS

To: Raymond Thomas Barden
Lot 8 Pierce Road,
NEW GISBORNE   VIC.   3438.

You are hereby summoned to attend before the Australian
Conciliation and Arbitration Commission (Deputy Presidents Williams

and McKenzie and Commissioner Nolan) at 10.15 in the forenoon on Monday 11th February 1985 at Nauru House, 80 Collins Street, Melbourne in the State of Victoria and so from day to day until the hearing of the abovementioned matter is completed or until you are excused from further attendance to give evidence on behalf of the Australian Federated Union of Locomotive Enginemen.

DATED this 8th day of February 1985.

REGISTRAR

but how to categorize them all, As, Bs, Cs - - -

Twenty, at a rough guess?---Near enough to 20, including inter-system locomotives.

If you are dramatically wrong, Mr Dee, when you think about it, I am sure the bench will allow me to correct your first guess.

WILLIAMS J: Yes, Mr Black.

MR BLACK: That is all I had for this witness, sir.

WILLIAMS J: Unless there are any other questions, that is all, thank you, Mr Dee. Thank you for your assistance. You are at liberty to leave now, if you wish?---Thank you.

THE WITNESS WITHDREW

RAYMOND THOMAS BARDEN, sworn:

WILLIAMS J: If you would like to sit down, Mr Barden?

MR BLACK: Mr Barden, is your name Raymond Thomas Barden? ---Yes.

And do you live at Lot A8, Pierce Road, New Gisborne, Victoria?---Yes.

And what is your present - you work with V-Line?---With Metrail, MTA now.

Metrail. I am sorry. I must appreciate the difference? ---I am the group manager, special projects.

Thank you. Until late last year were you the group manager of operations co-ordination of V-Line?---That is correct.

Have you had, to summarize it, a long railway career?---Yes.

Starting at the bottom of the ladder in 1952?---That is correct.

And did you progress up the ladder through the ranks of stationmaster, train controller, traffic inspector, superintendent of country running, acting district superintendent, manager of passenger operations for the whole system?---Correct.

Assistant chief traffic manager?---Yes, sir.

Acting chief traffic manager, and chief operations manager?
---That is so.

You come from a railway family?---Yes, sir.

And you are now in your 33rd year of railway service?---
Correct.

After studying, did you become a member of the Chartered
Institute of Transport?---Yes, I was a student,
current student member of the Chartered Institute
of Transport in 1963.

And last year were you made a Fellow of that institute?---
That is correct.

For 14 years have you been a councillor of the Victorian
Railways Institute?---Yes.

Is that an old and well-known organization in the state?---
Yes, it goes back to about 1911, I believe.

And was it founded to further the educational, social, and
other interests of railway people?---That is so.

And were you a senior vice-president of that organization?
---I served a period as senior vice-president, yes.

Yes. Do you claim to know quite a lot about railway people
and railway operations?---Yes, I think I know quite
a deal about railway people and railway operations.
It has been my whole life, in fact.

Yes. In your former position did you represent VicRail, as
it then was, on various committees that there were?
---Yes, I represented VicRail for many years on
various internal and external committees, and alsp
represented VicRail on operating and train-running
matters with the Railways of Australia committee.

And have you in fact - some years ago did you undertake a
10-week study tour of overseas railways?---Yes, in
1975 I did a 10-week study tour of railways in
England, Europe, and North America.

Yes. Now, I wish to make it clear you are here as a witness
and you are not speaking in an official capacity on
behalf of any - on behalf of V-Line?---That is
correct.

Well, I want to ask your opinions about various matters.
Now, were you, as chief manager of operations, one
of the people who had to consider the proposal for
two-man crewing of trains in the operations at
V-Line?---Yes, I was.

And did you work on that task for a considerable period?
---Yes, I worked on that task, I would believe, for about eight or nine months - along with other things, but yes.

Other people in the operations branch?---Yes.

And during that time did you formulate views as to how - your own views as to how that might be introduced.

MR BUCHANAN: I object to that. Whatever Mr Barden's views were, in my submission, they are not directly relevant to the issue which is at present before the commission: namely, what the operational position will be, or ought to be, in New South Wales. He has not been qualified to translate any views he might have had about the V-Line situation into a New South Wales context.

MR BLACK: We would submit, if the bench pleases, that this witness is emminently qualified by training, study and experience, to express an opinion as to the matter in which, in his view, two man crewing might be introduced. The only other alternative would be to produce a university professor who might have studied a great number of books and written a lot of thesis, but would lack some of the essential attributes that this witness ~~lacks~~ as an expert. And we submit that he is qualified according to all principles applying the strict rules of evidence.

WILLIAMS J: Yes, we think that you can lead the evidence.

MR BLACK: If the bench pleases.

During last year, had you sufficiently formed an opinion on these matters to submit proposals on behalf of V-Line as to how it might go about this?

MR SHAW: I think I must object at that stage. We are going a bit beyond the position of Mr Barden's opinions, which I have no objection to, but - - -

WILLIAMS J: I think he did say on behalf of V-Line. I think you are getting a bit close to the bone there, Mr Black.

MR BLACK: I am then going to ask the witness about his own view of the matter. I appreciate that he is not representing V-Line, and V-Line is not - - -

MR SHAW: V-Line is not a subject of these proceedings at this stage, and I think we may perhaps prejudice the negotiations which the commission has directed us to enter to.

WILLIAMS J: I would have thought that with your skill, Mr Black, you could rephrase the question so that V-Line was not implicated - - -

MR BLACK: Mr Barden, I would want to make it quite clear I am asking you your opinion as a person who studied this problem. Let us hope it is not too much of a problem. Now, in your opinion - let me start again. Have you turned your mind to the question of whether those who ride in the cab as a second person should be people who are drawn from the ranks of enginemen and are undergoing enginemens training - have you turned your mind to that question?---I have, and I believe that these people should be people undergoing enginemens training.

And what are your reasons for that opinion?---My reasons for that opinion are that I believe in any change in the operation of a railway, the magnitude, any change for that matter, but this is of great magnitude. The first consideration must be the safety of the system. You must ensure that you at least maintain the existing safety standards and if possible, of course, improve them. You must not, on any account, reduce your safety standards. And I believe anything short of a person in the cab committed to do his training in becoming a driver, for instance a part time fellow who might be in the cab for a day and then be doing other work for a week or a fortnight and then back in the cab later on, I believe in that way you lose something. I believe you would place a higher degree of stress and responsibility on the driver, and I believe that that is totally unsatisfactory arrangement for two reasons - for two major reasons. One is that it is likely to create some kind of disharmony in the cab. If you create disharmony there I believe you are likely to lose concentration, and if you lose concentration obviously the safety factor comes into it. The other thing is I believe that if the driver is constantly concerned about the fellow who is on the other side of the cab and is constantly checking him and does not have trust and confidence in him, it places an unreasonable and undue stress on that driver.

Do you - - -

WILLIAMS J: On the other hand, might it not be of some comfort to the driver, and perhaps to the authority to have someone in the cab with the driver under those circumstances who had the knowledge and skills say to use an untechnical word - the guard? ---Yes, I believe it would be of some comfort to the driver to have a fellow in the cab with the skills of a guard provided. That fellow had indicated that he wished to become a driver and was pursuing that course of training. He was committed to do that.

WILLIAMS J: I do not mean the dual qualification?---A qualification is one thing. I think experience and an application is another thing, and I would believe that a chappie who is a jack of all trades or a part time man on the engine would not have those other attributes. He may have some attributes but not the necessary ones.

I just ask the question having in mind that the person who was assisting the - the second person in the cab who was, if you like, the person training as a driver, might not have any detailed knowledge about the other end of the train, and therefore he could throw an extra duty or obligation or concern on the driver for that reason?---No, your Honour, that was, if I may refer to the proposal, that was well covered in the training in that you would give that man to overcome whatever the shortcomings might have been in his knowledge of guards duties that were transferred to the . . . .

MR BLACK: The point that his Honour is making, you had at least partly turned your mind to as a real question, is that what you are saying - this point about giving the extra training to the - - -?---I acknowledge that there is additional training required of the engine person before he could confidently carry out all the duties required of the second person, when it becomes a two man crew rather than a three man crew.

And what about the driver himself, in your view would you envisage as a desirable matter, as a matter of opinion, some training for the driver so that he understands more about the rear end of the train? ---Yes, that was proposed, quite clearly proposed, additional training there to pick up the gaps if you like, in his training, to cover the additional duties you would now be responsible for as the person in charge of the train.

WILLIAMS J: Well, if the second person in the cab came from the rear end of the train, would not the driver have some additional confidence by the knowledge that the person who was working with him had a knowledge of that end of the train - from his own experience if you like?---I agree wholeheartedly that that would be the case if that fellow had become a committed trainee for a driver's job. What concerns me is the spare time job, or the part time, the nature of it, where he is here today and gone tomorrow. I do not believe - he may be some comfort in some area, whether the truck sheet is correct, documentation is correct and that sort of thing, but I believe that would be far outweighed by the concern that the driver would have of what is happening up front and what the fellow - - -

Thank you. Yes, Mr Black.

MR BLACK: There are a number of witnesses I am sure I can lead on this point, that have talked about trust that has to be between the two members of the team on the cab of the train, do you agree with that?---I agree wholeheartedly, yes.

And that they ought to work harmoniously together?---It is essential.

And you see that as a safety factor apart from anything else?---I do, indeed.

Now what about people giving orders to other people in the cab, does that happen, does the driver give orders to the locomotive assistant as a matter of practice now?---He certainly does.

And has that always been part of the relationship between the two?---Yes.

Is it important that that capacity to give orders, without resentment, should be maintained?---Yes, it certainly is, and it is important that the ability to accept orders be maintained also.

Are there situations in railway operation where things happen very quickly and one has to act very quickly?---That is correct.

And is that a rare occurrence or something that would happen, not necessarily every day, but with sufficient frequency to make it something that most people would know about?---I believe in train running, in the field activities of train running, it is something that happens quite frequently, yes.

Now you mentioned commitments in your evidence a moment ago. What importance do you ascribe in your opinion to commitment to the duties that an engineman has to perform?---I consider it is of paramount importance that he has a firm commitment to what he is doing.

McKENZIE DP: A commitment to what?---To becoming an efficient train driver.

At what level?---At any level when he is working in the cab of a locomotive.

So is it fair to interpret your view as saying that he needs to have a commitment to become at least - as I understood from the previous witness, a driver, class 2. In other words, a commitment to become an electric train driver, even if he goes no further, that is adequate in your view?---Yes, I believe it is, I say that because I feel if he has not got that commitment, he will have difficulty in his application to his job all day, shift after shift after shift. And I believe that if he has not got that, we lower or run the risk of lowering our safety standard.

So it is fair to say in your view, the commitment is to becoming a driver even at the lowest level, not to the career of engine driving which would take him to the top of the scale?---Even a driver class 2, he needs that commitment, to become a driver class 2 certainly.

Yes, thank you.

MR BLACK: The question of who is in charge of the train, has that exercised your mind?---Yes, it has, for many years.

And have you formed an opinion about it?---Well - - -

MR BUCHANAN: I object to it, on the basis that I outlined to the commission yesterday, that that is not an issue in the proceedings, we submit, and Mr Barden's opinion about it cannot be relevant.

WILLIAMS J: What assistance do we get from it, Mr Black?

MR BLACK: Well, it is an issue, and first of all I might deal with the issue question. As we understand it, one of the matters in dispute are the duties of the second person. Now the second person on the latest SRA proposal, SRA2, is to be in charge of the train, and one of the - that means necessarily, as there are only two people in the train, the driver is not, but therefore, one of the issues to be determined, as a matter of industrial matter, is whether that is right or wrong. And we submit it is an issue, and this witness is qualified to talk about it. All these matters ultimately, even though this is a very calm and polite and clinical atmosphere, they ultimately concern people, and what the people think, and how they react to each other. Now that is the stuff of a lot of industrial disputes, and that is why I want to lead the evidence. And I submit it is relevant.

WILLIAMS J: Yes, our view is that you should proceed Mr Black.

MR BLACK: If your Honour pleases. First of all, can we clear up some possible confusion about what is being in charge of the train actually means. Now as I think we understand it, in some senses a guard is in charge of the train. Now, if that is so, and if it is so, what does it mean? ---Well, he is in charge of the train as I would see it inasmuch as if there is work at the roadside station, and the work is complete, and he has taken his numbers and his continuity test and all the things that he must do, and the station work is finished, for instance he will indicate to the driver that the station work is finished and give the all clear signal to proceed.

He will - at the commencement of the journey he will give the driver the tonnage of the train, the locations, if any, that the train is to shunt at. If they have shunted at a no one in charge station, again at the next most convenient point he will advise - the guard will advise the train controller of the work done at that station and how the time was occupied. So from that sense I guess you could say he is in charge of the train. If he is on a passenger train of course he will put a hamper of parcels in his van or something, he will put them out, that sort of thing. But one could dispute very much just what is meant by being in charge of the train. The fact of the matter is whilst he will indicate to the driver where he wants him to stop in a shunting movement or on a platform when they are pulling in to do van goods or something like that the driver certainly does not wait for the guard to tell him to stop if there is something up front that he sees that the guard cannot possibly see from where he is. Likewise when the guard - - -

WILLIAMS J: Just interrupting you for the moment, you say that you have doubts in seeing how the expression, in charge of the train, could be fully implemented without confusion, if you like, even in shunting operations?---Yes, I would go as far as to say that, your Honour. I firmly believe it has never been clearly defined what is meant by being in charge of the train. It has never been clearly defined to my mind.

MR BLACK: What do drivers think about this in your experience, that the guard is in charge of the train?

MR RYAN: With respect, your Honour, in our submission what this witness thinks about what drivers think about - - -

WILLIAMS: I think you are going the wrong way in that question, Mr Black.

MR BLACK: As the bench pleases.

If the train is disabled according to the regulations who then "in charge of the train" once it is a disabled train?---It depends on the nature of the disablement.

Well, it can become a station, cannot it?---It depends on the nature of the disablement. If it is a stall and divide and the driver and his offsider take the front portion of the train forward and the guard remains in charge of the rear half of the train and protects it. If the total disablement and the guard must go for assistance, the rule book quite clearly says that the guard puts the driver in charge at the point of ,. . . . . so it depends on the circumstances as to who is in charge but I think, you know, the opinion I have formed over many years of railway work is that quite clearly because the driver has the ability and the equipment to start the train and stop the train and more recently when radios were provided in Victoria the base to train radio system goes to the engine not to the guard's van, quite clearly it is my opinion that whilst the regulations certainly in certain circumstances clearly say that the guard is in charge of the train I believe that in fact in the practical situation the driver is in charge of the train.

WILLIAMS J: Could not that lead to complications however in shunting operations?---Yes, it can, but we must bear in mind that a guard is only involved in roadside shunting and that is becoming less and less a factor in railway operations in Victoria - less and less a factor - we hardly run any roadside goods trains now. There are very few run. We are going to bulk trains. Certainly if a vehicle has to be put off en route because of a repair, well it will have a roadside shunt and there still are some roadside shunts but it is declining all the time. The guard does that shunt. If it is a manned station he is usually assisted by the station staff. It is only from unmanned locations that he would do that shunt on his own. Now, in marshalling yards where times are made up and . . . . to go to the majority of marshalling yards the engine-driver and his mate work with a crew of shunters.

In some instances could it not put the award requirement in conflict with the regulations to which you referred earler?---Well, when you are shunting with the train, for instance, you are shunting either in a marshalling yard or within station limits or in a siding and it is not the same situation as if a train becomes totally disabled or blocked out in the section. It is an entirely different situation.

Yes, but in the shunting operation do not the regulations put the guard in control of the train?---Oh, yes. During shunting operations there is no question about it the driver moves forward or moves back or stops when he is signalled to do so by the shunter, whether he be a shunter guard or station staff. There is no question about that.

McKENZIE DP: And on passenger trains, does the driver move forward only when the guard indicates that it is appropriate to do so or does he do it on his own initiative?---No. He does so only when the guard gives him the okay to do so, on passenger trains, yes.

And the same is true on freight trains?---The same would be true on freight trains if he is departing the location or moving forward the vehicle. There are other situations, of course, where the fireman might cut the engine off on a freight train but it is generally correct, he would only move when the guard or the shunter says so.

MR BUCHANAN: Could I register a plaintive protest, if I may. We are here involved in a case which at the direction of the commission as at present constituted is concerned with New South Wales.

WILLIAMS J: Yes.

MR BUCHANAN: And what is happening is Mr Barden and other witnesses have referred, and no doubt other witnesses to come, are giving evidence and making judgment and illustrating their views by reference particularly to what happens in Victoria. And it is very difficult for us to meet that in any sensible way. We do not want to have to explore the operational position in Victoria unduly but the basis for the evidence is the experience of people in the Victorian situation, not the New South Wales situation.

WILLIAMS J: Yes. I think there is some merit in what is being put.

MR BLACK: We of course are doing the best we can with what we have available to us and if the Victorian Railways were different in a significant extent to other parts of this Commonwealth, well, then we would understand the force of the objection, but the evidence is that the railway systems of this of this country and engine-men and work practices and so forth in the country have a very substantial similarity and in my submission the evidence is relevant to the railway problem that exists, as it happens, in New South Wales.

WILLIAMS: I can understand that Mr Barden is giving evidence as a person who has a particular knowledge of the railway industry and operations and that he can express his views about such matters. I can understand that he necessarily draws his comparisons with the regulations in operation in Victoria because they are the ones he is familiar with, but whether he would draw the same conclusions on the regulations and practices in operation in New South Wales I must say I am not quite sure.

MR BLACK: Yes.

WILLIAMS J: And there has been no attempt, I think, to put the New South Wales situation before him to comment so far as the regulations and so forth are concerned.

MR BLACK: Mr Barden, are you familiar with the regulations related to train running in New South Wales to any, and if so, what extent?---I certainly do not have the detailed knowledge of regulations in New South Wales but I would be reasonably familiar with train operations in New South Wales, I believe.

I do not wish to - I want you to be careful about this: are you able to say whether the considerations that have led you to an opinion about the desirability of one person or another being in charge of a train depend upon any particular regulations that might exist elsewhere that you are not familiar with? ---I would have to say, I guess, that that may be so.

Very well?---That may be so.

WILLIAMS J: I am afraid, Mr Black, that I, to some extent, brought into consideration the regulations which are applying and of course naturally the witness referred to the Victorian situation with which he is familiar, but as I said whether those same things apply in New South Wales I am not sure.

MR BLACK: Well, Mr Barden, subject then to that qualification, have you formed a view - your own view - as to how one should work a two-man train when one has to decide who is going to be designated in charge of the train, whatever that means?

MR BUCHANAN: In Victoria, I assume, and if it is not qualified I object to it.

MR BLACK: Well, on the basis of the knowledge that you have, which is primarily Victorian knowledge?---Yes, I - - -

MR B. SHAW: I think if it is qualified I have to object to that. I am not trying to be facetious, your Honour but we are - - -

MR BLACK: 1901 we federated.

MR B. SHAW: - - - we are not reaching - well, I agree with Mr Black's evidence entirely on that point. . . . . is a fact of life. The evidence is not that we are dealing with one homogen ous railway system. We have made assertions, and so has

Mr Buchanan, that the railway systems are different in each state. Mr Black has made an assertion to the contrary, but we are now getting all of the evidence coming from the State of Victoria. Now, it may well be that it does apply everywhere, but it is certainly putting our potential negotiations in a - a great deal of jeopardy, I would have thought.

WILLIAMS J: Well, I do not know, Mr Shaw, because what is being sought is the witness' view in certain circumstances. The circumstances that he is familiar with happen to be the circumstances in Victoria. Now whether those circumstances are similar to those in New South Wales or not, I do not know, and no doubt that will be conveyed to us at some time or other. But I cannot see how the expression of views on particular stipulated circumstances - whether they be Victoria, Western Australia, South Australia, or some other place, would necessarily - or should, in any way - complicate the negotiating situation so far as VicRail is concerned.

McKENZIE DP: Is your worry, Mr Shaw, that Mr Barden is or has been in the past involved in the negotiations and that - although apparently is no longer involved and that has got - that may have some bearing on the use that is made of the information that he puts forward?

MR B. SHAW: Yes.

McKENZIE DP: Is that your worry?

MR B. SHAW: To an extent that is the case, your Honour. I know, and those who have been involved in the Victorian situation, sitting in this room, know that Mr Barden has been involved in those development of policies and attitudes and presumably he is still aware through his own knowledge of and friends within the system of the way those policies and attitudes may be developing and presumably his opinions are not just simply his opinions. They are opinions developed during the course of that development of STA policies and attitudes.

Now it seems inevitable that if the evidence continues in this - or the line of questioning continues in this way that there will be use made of this evidence in those negotiations. It may well be that . . . . resumption of this case if those negotiations are not successful this evidence will be very relevant and the AFULE are perfectly entitled to pursue their case properly at that time, but I cannot see how it can help their case in New South Wales. It can only in some form, perhaps even a remote form, hinder the negotiations in Victoria.

WILLIAMS J: Mr Black - - -

MR BLACK: Yes, your Honour.

WILLIAMS J: Our consideration, our concern is about the point which Mr Shaw has raised, that is that if Mr Barden has been involved in negotiations with the Victorian authority on these issues and if the negotiations are still in train, as we have been told, well then I can understand the embarrassment which Mr Shaw refers to.

MR BLACK: Your Honour, as to that, we - as I understand my instructions - we do not for our part see an embarrassment. Of course that is one side of the coin, but as to the other side of the coin there is documentary material which I had not proposed to introduce that sets out a particular position very clearly and we would have thought that evidence from Mr Barden would do no more than to indicate something that we already know about, the V/Line view and I am going delicately because I do not want to try and get in something that I was not going to try and get in.

WILLIAMS J: Would not Mr Barden's views be more useful to us if they were put to us against the material which is or should be in due course before the commission regarding the situation in New South Wales?

MR BLACK: I would certainly be happy to recall Mr Barden to see if his opinion is still capable of being expressed when the New South Wales situation has been clearly outlined. Of course one does not have pretrial discovery of the thing; this is happily enough, in this jurisdiction.

WILLIAMS J: Would not that be the more useful time?

MR BLACK: Quite happy to do that, if the commission pleases, and then his opinion can be expressed on concrete examples of the specific system.

WILLIAMS J: Yes. Yes, I think that would suit us.

MR BLACK: Very well. If the commission pleases I will pass to a few other matters.

You are not a member of the AFULE?---No, sir.

And the fact that - your railway family have belonged to another organisation, I gather? The whole railway side of your family was not in the AFULE?---I have a brother who is a driver.

You have, I see?---In VicRail, yes, V/Line, I am sorry.

Anyway you are not?---I am not.

You of course had knowledge of the work the AFULE does for its members in the railway system?---I certainly have.

Are you able to express any opinion as to the way in which you have seen it do its work for enginemen?---Yes. I believe that the - it is a very close-knit organisation, the AFULE. I believe that is so because they represent the one grade of people, the enginemen, and the officials of the union are all enginemen or ex-enginemen and therefore they intimately know the environment and the problems that their members work in and encounter. I guess they are able to - because of that they are really specialists and they are able to devote their entire efforts towards the one grade of people, the enginemen, and I have found in the years that I did - was responsible - traffic branch representation and main line inquiry boards and the like - that the AFULE representatives were always on the scene and ready and willing to represent their people and help their people.

And they presumably know what they are talking about, having had the same - - -?---Same background experience.

Yes. If the commission pleases.

WILLIAMS J: Thank you, Mr Black.

MR RYAN: Mr Barden, I suppose in the course of your movements through the various senior management positions which you detailed in answer to my learned friend, that you had a considerable experience in evaluating levels of motivation and application of different employees and officers in the rail service?---Yes, I have.

Would you say that those levels of application and motivation varied from individual to individual?---Yes, I would.

And that is so, I suggest to you, even within a particular class of employee such as enginemen? There are some who are more highly motivated than others?---That is correct.

And I suppose the same applies with guards or stationmasters or almost any group that one can think of?---Yes, it does but I would like to qualify my answer, if I may, in that I think the engineman has a much greater incentive to be motivated because if he makes a mistake and for instance passes a signal at the stop position, he is downgraded and it costs him a lot of money. It hurts his ego but it hits his pocket also. He may find himself labouring for three or six months, whereas the guard on that train would find himself, if he was found also guilty of the offence, he may find himself reduced to a shunter and in fact find himself earning more money over the next six months than he was as a guard, to quote an example.

Yes, well that indicates that there are differing degrees of incentive to be motivated, depending on where one is located in the service?---I believe the difference is one, as I say, hits the pocket and the other hits the ego.

Now you indicated to my learned friend that in your view anything short of a commitment to full time driving on the part of somebody entering the cabin of a locomotive would be detrimental to safety?---I did.

Now why do you say that a commitment to the job in the hand or a commitment to a career in the railway service would not be sufficient to ensure maximum safety considerations?---I believe that traditionally and that it is desirable in the future that people in the cab of a locomotive who have one line of progression, that is to driver, I believe there must be a full commitment there and I believe that that was the reason - that is how you get it, because they only have one career path, to become a driver. They may - an odd few - progress from there to administrative jobs or inspector or something but by far the vast majority of them they have got one course open to them to become a driver, whereas in the area that I come up in, in the railways, you have the opportunity to embark on many different career paths. You might become a signalman, you might become a train controller, you might become a stationmaster, you might become a guard, and on it goes. So if you know that you have one chance and one chance only, that is to become a driver, I believe that you are far more diligent and far more committed to the situation. I have actually observed this over my years of having been responsible for these grades of people.

Would not it follow that a black mark is a black mark in the sense that if, as a second person in the cabin of a locomotive, I made a mistake. Even if I had no ambition to be a driver that could retard or prevent my progress in the service generally?---It could, sir, but my argument is that you are more likely to make that mistake if you are not committed and not on that career path than if you are, because you have that - other opportunities available to you.

You see, what I put to you is that the commitment really should be to doing the job in hand well. Whatever one's ultimate aspirations are, that if one has ultimate aspirations they can best be fulfilled by doing the job in hand well and as safely as possible. Does not that follow?---I would certainly agree that ideally that should be the situation, but in practice my experience in the workplace does not say that that is so.

Yes, well I can understand there may be areas where that degree of motivation might not exist, but if one were promoting somebody to a responsible position presumably steps would be taken whatever the position was to weed out that element, would not they, as a matter of managerial practice?---You are certainly correct there, but I think you have got to weigh up what the risks are. It is too late to weed him out after you have had a collision or a train smash.

Is your view about the need for commitment to the attainment of a full time driving position modified if one supposes for the moment that there might not - there would not be enough full time driving positions for all second persons to be promoted to them?---Could you ask that question - - -

If one's manpower projections were that there would not be enough driving vacancies in the future to provide for promotion for all second persons or trainee enginemen or call them what you will, does that modify your - cause you to modify your view about the need for commitment to a career as a driver? ---No, it would not cause me to modify my view in any way at all.

Do you accept as a possibility that manpower projections might be made which have that consequence?---No. From my knowledge, again on the Victorian system, I could not see that happening at all.

I take it is because you cannot see that happening that you have not contemplated the possibility that I just put?---I have considered it, if only from yesterday when the question was asked of another witness, but I have considered it and I believe that whilst - in fact, I would predict that in the future there will be a much, much longer period before people become drivers than what the situation is at the moment. I could not ever see a situation in Victoria, anyhow, whereby a person could come on as a second person - or into the cab of a loco as a second person and not see his way clear at some time in the future, even be it three or four times longer than at present, becoming a driver eventually.

Now you gave us an illustration of somebody who would not have the necessary commitment to full-time driving, somebody who worked only part-time in the cabin. Is it your understanding that having second persons who are not trainee enginemen involves them working only part-time in that capacity? Is that a necessary consequence of that method of staffing? ---No, not necessarily a consequence of that level of staffing.

It could be, for example, that one has a substantive position as a second person which would be undertaken while it was filled full-time, that would be one way of doing it, would it not?---Are you suggesting permanent second persons who do not go through to drivers.

Well, who may have perhaps a number of promotional opportunities available to them after that, but while they are in it, it is a substantive position in which they work full-time?---I would believe that that situation would be highly undesirable - - -

I understand you believe it to be undesirable, but I am just asking you whether you accept that one way of structuring the thing would be to organise it in that way?---No, I cannot agree with that because I believe it would be tantamount to returning to a situation we had in Victoria some years ago where we had permanent firemen and that was found to be unsatisfactory from several aspects, and I believe it would go back to that situation.

The real reason for that being unsatisfactory, I suggest to you, was that there were no - there were seen for those people to be no promotional opportunities at all, that was the end of the road for them, was it not?---Generally speaking it was, although some did become chargemen, but generally speaking it was the end of the road for them, but it was an unsatisfactory situation from several other aspects other than that.

But at all events, that - whatever the vice in that was, it was not because they were part-time employees; while they were in that position they were full-time?---No, the vice comes from the fact that they were not committed to become drivers, I believe.

Yes, and that is a different matter from being part-time in the position?---Yes.

And you indicated that stress on the driver is accentuated if he does not have complete trust in his colleague in the cabin?---Most certainly is.

And it would be fair to say, would it not, that trust is a thing which is built primarily on personal acquaintance, on the assessment that one makes of ones colleague?---I would agree.

It is not a thing that is generated by - is built on whatever academic qualifications the colleague might have, or where he might have worked before, but primarily I suggest to you on the assessment that you make of him after you have seen him and worked with him for a time?---I agree.

Have you yourself ever worked as a driver?---No, not as a driver.

Have you ever worked as a guard?---Yes.

For how long?---Only one-trippers and that sort of thing, not - I was never an appointed guard.

Did you ever undertake shunting work?---Yes, very much so. That was in my capacity as a station master, assistant station master and what have you.

Then you mentioned that you had - I think in 1971 or 72 - undertaken an overseas study trip?---1975.

1975, was it; in the course of that, did you have an opportunity to form an appreciation of how a change to two-man operations was effected in the United Kingdom?---No, I did not. Whilst - I went overseas primarily to study container traffic and LCL traffic, and whilst I did ride up front on several occasions and ride on trains, my time requirement was freight sheds and container terminals and what have you.

Do you have any understanding from any other source of how that - the basis of that change in the United Kingdom was effected?---I have some understanding of it, some knowledge of it.

And in essence, I suggest to you that that change involved the abolition of the position of fireman and the maintenance of the - in the second person of the duties of a guard, does that accord with your understanding?---No, not entirely, no, it does not. My belief is - and I certainly am not an expert in this area, and I do not claim to be, but my belief is that where the two-man crewing applies - and of course on British Rail they have got one man up front on some trains - but where it applies, I believe it was an amalgam of the two jobs. That is my belief.

No, I have no further questions.

MR BUCHANAN: Mr Barden, I suppose - do not just talk to me, the commission needs to hear - I suppose if a driver feels unable for one reason or another to rely upon the person who is in the cabin with him, then he falls back on his own resources, is that right?---He would during that trip, but my experience is that he very quickly does something about this. If he has no confidence or he feels his off-sider is incompetent or is unlikely to make it, or because of a personality clash or something like that he is undesirable to work together, my experience is that the driver very quickly does something about that.

It follows from that that it happens from time to time, that he finds that the person that he is with unreliable? ---Yes, in my period as chief operations manager we on occasions - not all that frequently, but on occasions had to arrange separation of driver and mate, yes.

And if he finds somebody unreliable he makes his view known and something is done about it?---That is correct.

And you would expect, would you not, that in the event that a second crewman was placed with him who was not a driver in training - if there was any unreliability detected by the driver he would make that plain also? ---Yes, certainly most drivers would but I think as already was brought forward earlier on in my evidence, each person is a little different and some are more hesitant than others to bring to notice a problem that they have, particularly when it might be seen as dobbing a mate in. They will sometimes tolerate it longer than they should, and I believe again if that situation prevails you have got an undue risk situation there that ought not to be.

Well, I suggest to you that that is a situation which is more likely to occur under the current arrangements than under some altered arrangement where the second crewman was taken from the ranks of guards?---No, I would strongly disagree with you on that point.

You think they would be more likely to protect somebody who was taken from the ranks of guards than a trainee engineman?---No, I did not say that.

I rather thought that is what followed from what you were saying?---Well, it was not intended if that was the case.

But in the event that this measure of unreliability is detected, even at the present time, until something is done about it does it follow that the driver falls back on his own resources?---No, I believe at the present time if a fellow is - if the second man or the loco assistant, as he currently is - is not being diligent in his application to this responsibilities, the driver takes him to task, and because of the relationship between the driver and his fireman - and his loco assistant, because of that relationship, on most occasions the driver is able to bring him into line, on most occasions.

How do you know that?---I know that from personal experience, from travelling on locomotives, from having supervised these people are various country depot stations and being responsible for them in various senior administrative positions.

It was suggested that it would result in a greater degree of stress for the driver, this unreliability, make up for the lack of trust?---Yes, it does. If the young fellow is not responding to the efforts of the driver to bring him into shape, again depending on the personality of the driver, you know, we have all got our peculiarities, it most certainly can . . . .

You do not suggest the driver's task - the driver's operational task - becomes more onerous than if he was entirely on his own, do you?---Yes, it can do, I guess, if you do not trust the fellow there. It can in these circumstances - - -

Well, Mr Barden, please do not guess; do you suggest that that happens or not?---I assert very strongly if the driver was on his own he would be in a cab where he got a good view, etcetera. Many of our cabs and certainly cabs on other systems are such that a driver on his own cannot get a view therefore he needs somebody else up front with him, and if he does not have trust in him, his situation I would suggest - the stress situation - is much worse than if he can do it himself from the centre of the cab.

I see. Your concern has been primarily in relation to the safety aspect, is that right?---Yes, safety is the first and foremost duty of every railwayman.

That is every railwayman in every system, not just in Victoria, is it?---I believe it appears in the regulations of most railway systems, yes.

You have addressed yourself, obviously enough, to the particular operating situation in Victoria? ---In particular in Victoria, yes, but I - - -

And you have applied to those considerations the benefit of your years of experience in the Victorian railway system?---And also knowledge gained in the years of travelling on other systems, particularly in Australia.

Yes, it is true, is it not, that people - especially at a senior level - in the various railway systems, come to acquire very often a reasonable degree of familiarity with the systems in other states? ---That is so.

Now, you have applied all that knowledge, both your experience in Victoria and your familiarity with the other systems, to come to the view to which you have come, is that right?---Correct.

You know, do you not, members of the senior operating management in New South Wales?---Some members of the senior operating management, yes, certainly.

Well, for example, you know Mr Gill?---Yes, I know Mr Gill.

Is it right that the view that you have expressed today is not a view universally held?---That is right.

And is it true that people equally well intentioned as yourself, and equally knowledgeable have applied their mind to the situation and come to a different view about it?---Equally knowledgeable - and what was the one? Equally - - -

Equally well intentioned?---Well, I would agree that people equally well intentioned might have come - I cannot answer the question about their knowledge, I do not know.

Right?---Sorry.

But the question of safety to the operation of that particular system, you would agree, is particularly the responsibility of those who operate that system?---Well, it - - -

So that in Victoria it is particularly the responsibility of Victorian management, and in New South Wales it is particularly the responsibility of New South Wales management?---I would agree with that, yes.

Thank you.

WILLIAMS J: Mr Shaw, do you wish to ask any question?

MR SHAW: No, your Honour.

MR BLACK: Mr Barden, the other side of the coin. There are some people who - well intentioned to disagree with you, are there eminent people who agree with you?---There certainly are, sir.

And are they - can you give us a broad indication of where we might find them; are there any in AN as far as you know?---I would believe so, yes.

And Westrail?---Yes, I would believe so.

Very well. I have no re-examination.

WILLIAMS J: That is all, thank you, Mr Barden, you are free to leave. Mr Black - before you leave, do you - did you wish to reserve your right - - -

MR BLACK: Yes, I am most indebted, your Honour. Yes, I did.

WILLIAMS J: Yes.

railon 13.2.85
t368 1 chf

MR BLACK: And if he might be excused for the time being.

WILLIAMS J: Yes. You are free to go, subject to a recall if Mr Black wishes to cross-examine you further, in which case you will receive advice, Mr Barden? ---Thank you, your Honour.

MR BUCHANAN: I wonder if I might just seek some clarification from my learned friend about that. I do not know whether your Honour had it in mind that Mr Barden would be recalled later in my friend's case in chief. I am a little apprehensive that what my learned friend may have in mind is that he will recall him in reply after we have presented the information about New South Wales rather than he.

WILLIAMS J: I would anticipate that he would call him as part of his case - recall him as part of his case.

MR BUCHANAN: Yes. Well, your Honour, that is what we would have suggested, with respect, was the appropriate couse to take, and we would certainly have no objection to that, but if the intention is as I am a little anxious it may be, we might want to address ourselves to that.

WILLIAMS J: Yes. Well, you are right to reserve it in that direction, of course.

MR BUCHANAN: Thank you, your Honour.

MR BLACK: I would seek to reopen the case at an appropriate stage, that was what I understood.

WILLIAMS J: Well we can - I do not think we can debate it at this stage. I think, Mr Black, the course to take is that in view of what has been said by Mr Buchanan that if you do decide that you wish to recall Mr Barden on a future date, well then you should advise Mr Buchanan and us, and if necessary it can be debated.

MR BLACK: May it please your Honour.

MR BUCHANAN: Well, really - I do not wish to - obviously to canvass what your Honour had ruled, but it puts us in this difficulty, if I might say so. If my learned friend simply closes his case without calling Mr Barden and subsequently he makes an application to reopen, we will be placed in a very difficult position of trying to prevent him from getting more evidence in.

WILLIAMS J: .Yes.

MR BUCHANAN: And, in my submission, we will be prejudiced. If that is his intention, he ought to say so now and the question ought to be given some attention prior to him closing his case.

WILLIAMS J: Yes. Well, I do not think you need do it now, Mr Black, but I think probably - I think you should give notice of that before you close your case - - -

MR BLACK: May it please your Honour.

WILLIAMS J: - - - so that Mr Buchanan will know what he has to face.

MR BUCHANAN: Thank you.

MR BLACK: May it please your Honour.

THE WITNESS WITHDREW

MR BLACK: If the bench pleases, I propose to call two witnesses from New South Wales. One will be very short, a very senior engineman now retired; and another a much younger man, actually working in the Hunter Valley. I will call the more senior gentleman first. Mr Reed, would you go into the witness box please.

HENRY REED, sworn:

WILLIAMS J: Would you mind spelling your surname?---R-E-E-D.

Thank you. Yes, if you would like to sit down, Mr Reed?---Yes. Certainly.

MR BLACK: Mr Reed, your name is Henry Reed?---That is so.

You live at Beechwood in New South Wales?---Yes.

You are a retired locomotive inspector - - -?---That is right.

- - - for the state rail authority of New South Wales? You retired some years ago, in 1978?---Yes.

And you had a lifetime of service as an engineman at various grades?---That is right.

Kay,

Thought you might be interested in this.

Kind Regards.

LEGISLATIVE ASSEMBLY OF VICTORIA

With the Compliments of

Tom Reynolds M.P.

THIS LETTER DATED 4/8/1986, eight months after I had been retired, was sent to me by Tom Reynolds the local Member for the Legislative Assembly seat of Gisborne. It is a bit of a 'political' document but it confirms much of what I had said and predicted earlier in this Chapter and it makes interesting reading. The reference to two signalmen staying home on full pay plus penalties is possibly a factual error or perhaps the situation had changed since I left in December 1985. At that time there were definitely three signalmen involved in the stay at home 'arrangement'.

Monday,
August 4th, 1986.

The Parliamentary Liberal Party

<u>UNIONS RAILROAD GOVERNMENT : AGAIN</u>
<u>$1 MILLION WASTED SO FAR</u>

The Cain Government was recklessly squandering money in an absurd attempt to appease unions involved in a demarcation dispute over Metrail signalling operations, the State Opposition said today.

The story is a classic case of how greedy and selfish union bosses tell the Cain Government how things will be done.

Opposition Transport spokesman, Alan Brown, said the Government's spineless approach had already cost more than one million dollars, had seen two signalmen paid for over 12 months to stay at home, and had resulted in the "invention" of several new and unnecessary positions in Metrail.

"The Government has apparently given Metrail a virtual blank cheque to meet outrageous union demands, rather than face its responsibility to resolve the dispute," Mr. Brown said.

"This sick story of unions taking charge began with the revelation several months ago that two signalmen had been paid full pay, plus penalties, to stay at home for over 12 months.

"The reason for this ridiculous situation was a dispute between the Australian Railways Union and the Australian Transport Officers Federation over who would operate the main Western Line Centralised Traffic Control installation.

.../2

Parliament House, Spring St, Melbourne (03) 651 8131
Further Information   EDDIE DEAN

"Following adverse publicity over the two signalmen being paid to stay at home, they were brought back to work - but not as signalmen.

"Despite a shortage of trained signalmen, they were employed on clerical duties, in positions which did not previously exist.

"These two men have over 50 years' combined experience as signalmen, or area controllers, in the Metrail area, but the A.R.U. has refused to allow them to be employed in signals or controller's work.

"This already stupid story has now turned into an expensive farce because Metrail is building a duplicate signal control panel at a cost of more than one million dollars to meet the unions' continuing demands.

"When this new installation in the West Tower in the Melbourne shunting yards is completed, TWO men - one from each union - will do the train control work now done by one man.

"An A.T.O.F. member will operate one board, and an A.R.U. member will operate the other.

"Worse still, SIX new positions will have to be created to man the second panel - to cover annual leave and minimise overtime payments.

"The extra wages bill for these positions will be well in excess of $100,000 a year.

"This pathetic affair makes a complete mockery of Transport Minister Roper's claims that he is increasing efficiency and reducing staffing levels in the railways.

"The Minister, and the Government, have again given-in to the unions - and on this occasion have created a costly, on-going farce."

* * *

37

Compulsory Transfer

THREE DAYS before Christmas in 1984, Fitzmaurice had called me to his office and said things were not working out as he and some members of the Corporate Group had wished. He went on to say that it was clear that I was not happy in my position and he was also unhappy with me. He considered I was too much of a "hands on Manager'. He preferred a manager who could delegate and manage much more from his office. He said he had spoken to the Transport Minister about the unsatisfactory situation as he saw it and it had been agreed that after the Christmas break, I would be transferred to the Metropolitan Transport Authority (MTA). I was to telephone the Minister's Secretary and get a time for an interview with him when he would explain what he had in mind for me. I had felt for a long time that something like this was inevitable, but it still came as a shock, particularly so close to Christmas. I saw the Minister the next day and he said, would you believe, he was sorry things had turned out this way, but when Fitzmaurice told him he did not want me in the STA, he had no option but to move me to the MTA. I would retain all my privileges such as the fully serviced car, the taxi card, my gold pass and my existing salary and allowances. He felt in fact that

I could benefit many more people in the long run, in my new proposed role, than I could in the position I was leaving. He did not mention my problems with the ARU. He stated that the government planned to abolish the centralised suburban trains maintenance facilities, including the Jolimont Workshop and stabling sidings in Flinders Street Yard and replace it over time with a number of smaller facilities strategically located throughout the suburbs. He felt that I was suited by knowledge and experience to head this project and I would be given the title of "Group Manager, Special Projects". I said that my background probably did fit me for such a position but I thought that the problem I had with the ARU would rule me out. It was only recently for instance, that they had allegedly refused to attend meetings on two man crewing of locomotive hauled trains in Victoria if I was present, even though I had written the proposal for the STA. He quickly replied that it was his problem and he had to fix it. It might take a little time, but he would. I certainly did not share his confidence and I immediately thought of the comment from Fitzmaurice not so long ago when we were discussing the ARU which was, "might is right".

DURING 1984 I felt the pressure I was under with a lot of the management group not supporting me was "getting at me". This had not happened to me to such an extent before, even though I had experienced a Head of Branch I could not get along with. During my career I did many jobs which subjected me to considerable pressure, but nothing as bad as what I was experiencing at this time. I was not sleeping properly, waking up many times through the night and not getting back to sleep again on some occasions. Carmel said I was always pre-occupied and was a grumpy old man, even though I was only forty-nine years old. I made an appointment to see our family doctor. He asked me what was causing the problem and what changes, if any, had occurred in my life. I told him how the new government had broken the railway into two new authorities, virtually doubling the number of executives required to run them but although I had been responsible for all operations in the old railway, passenger freight, suburban, country and interstate, I had not been considered for the top operations job in either authority, and had been relegated to the next level down on a slightly lower salary where I thought I was simply being "used'. I felt I had no future whatsoever. He said I should get out as soon as possible otherwise I would be shortening my life. He said he was familiar with this type of situation when companies were taken over, rarely did they retain the old management people in any numbers. He said. "Don't stay on because of superannuation or other entitlements because you won't be happy, and if you're not happy, nor will your family be. You should make the decision and move before you completely ruin your health."

He told me to take time off while considering my future. Soon after I was in a short queue at the Railway Credit Co-op on a pay day. The Welfare Officer, Wes Gordon came up to me and said something like, "what's this I have been hearing about you, I think we should have a talk". We talked in the street. I told him I felt I had to resign after thirty-three years, but I knew nothing but railways, so was concerned about the future for me and my family. I felt I could perhaps be suited to farming and had looked at small properties which could be viable but they were well beyond my price range and I did not want to go into deep debt. He immediately said, "Don't do that or you will lose much of your superannuation entitlements." He then asked if I thought our doctor would be prepared to put what he had said to me in writing. I replied that I really did not know, but he was certainly not the sort of bloke to make reckless comments or say things that he did not mean. Wes said to go and see him again and see if he would be prepared to give you a letter setting out his detailed prognosis. I did not do this immediately as I have to admit, I was scared of taking this step. Instead I went back to work to give it one more go.

FITZMAURICE INTERVIEWED me telling me there was some office space in Marland House in Bourke Street on which the lease had not run out but the rail staff had vacated. I was not to start back in Head Office but to shift up there. He would arrange for a parking spot for my car in the basement of the building. On no account was I to use the parking spot marked off for me on the old southern concourse at Spencer Street Station. I would shortly receive formal notification of my transfer to MTA. I felt like a leper. If I was not depressed before, I certainly was now. I subsequently shifted into an empty office at Marland House. I was 'incommunicado' as the telephone had been disconnected and it took a couple of weeks before it was reconnected. This was before the days of mobile phones. There was still some Rolling Stock Branch staff in the office next door so when necessary, I could use their phone. I was given no work and never ever did receive the formal notice of transfer. Perhaps it was lost on the way to Marland House. I would sometimes go for a walk up the street but then would think someone might be looking for me and would go back and try and relax by reading books. I found it an extremely depressing, degrading place. The Family Court was in this building, above where I was located and it seemed that every time I got into a down lift I was confronted with the saddest of sights; kids, their mother and sometimes I presume, the grandmother, all crying. Apparently a decision in the Court above had brought this on. Whilst I have probably exaggerated a bit here, it was surprising the number of times it did happen. It would have been futile to go to Fitzmaurice again so I decided to try and see the Minister to see what progress might have been made with the Union, but to no avail. On one occasion when I went up to Spring Street I spoke to Alan Reiher, then well ensconced as the Director General of Transport,. He said he was not aware of the Minister having spoken to the Union on the subject of my future as yet but given time, it would happen. I decided, rightly or wrongly, they were trying to wear me down to a position of breaking down completely or resigning, either of which would suit their ends. I had read of such tactics in the USA. In my opinion, Fitzmaurice had never regarded me highly, but for a time had tolerated me. He probably thought I was too direct and blunt with people, unpolished and possibly even uncouth. I had churned it over in my mind trying to decide what had brought him to the tipping point with me. I decided that perhaps it was the demarcation dispute between the ARU and the ATOF. I cannot recall him telling me previously he was looking to me for a solution. I thought it was a matter for his team of experts in industrial relations as they cosied up to the ARU. None of them had requested any help from me. What troubled me was the question he had asked, "How long have you known that?" He may have thought that I had worked out the possible solution months ago but purposely withheld it from him and the industrial people, Nothing could be further from the truth. I would have nothing to gain from such action. I was really surprised when he grabbed the idea and started to run with it immediately but in reality I guess he wanted to please the Minister, irrespective of the cost and the bad example it was setting. All my railway career I had been required to reduce costs, not increase them, and my record would show that I had certainly done this whenever possible. As I said previously, I never did think of this personally as a solution. My answer to him was spontaneous when he challenged me but I did not see it in reality, as a satisfactory solution. While sitting in this Marland House office with no work to do, I used to mull things like this around in my head but all I was doing was upsetting myself further. Some people might think that I was in a good position with absolutely no work coming my way but still receiving full pay and other entitlements, but I can assure them it is not. I have never experienced anything so soul destroying or debilitating. I felt I was a failure and got to the stage where I did not want to meet old workmates. It was a terrible period in my life so I decided to go off sick again. I went back to our doctor and after discussing the deteriorating situation, I received a medical certificate for sick leave and a letter to my employers detailing my health situation and his prognosis. I did not put the letter in immediately but sat on it for a couple of weeks before "biting the bullet".

Telephone 61001 Ext.
Reference
Date 20 December 1984

K. M. FITZMAURICE
CHAIRMAN and
MANAGING DIRECTOR

Mr. R. Barden

Dear Ray

TRANSFER OF EMPLOYMENT

This is to confirm my verbal advice to you on 19 December 1984 concerning your future employment.

In early 1985, you will take up a new position being established by the Ministry of Transport in conjunction with the Metropolitan Transit Authority. I understand that this position will be structured to take advantage of your extensive railway knowledge and operational skills. The Ministry has identified a need for these skills in the new $200 million dollar Jolimont development project scheduled to commence early in 1985.

From the date of your return from leave on 14 January 1985 you will be seconded to duties associated with your transfer.

It is confirmed that you will continue to be employed by the State Transport Authority and that the transfer will not adversely affect any of your entitlements as regards salary, superannuation, motor vehicle, Rail Gold Pass or reimbursement for business expenses such as telephone and incidental travelling costs.

It is understood that discussions with the Minister of Transport should reassure you of the desire to maximise your potential contribution to the rail organisation in Victoria and, at the same time, provide you with a challenging position that will call upon your extensive operational knowledge and skills.

Kind Regards.

K. M. FITZMAURICE

State Transport Authority
67 Spencer Street Melbourne Victoria 3000. Telex-VLine AA33801

38

The End

A SHORT TIME LATER, I was directed to see the railway medical officer. I had not met him previously. He was a pleasant enough fellow and had been well briefed on my situation - I suppose by Wes the Welfare Officer, but I suspect, also by others. His candour actually surprised me somewhat. He stated that it was quite wrong that he had been placed in this situation, as on one hand he clearly had no option but to agree with my doctors prognosis, but on the other, he felt it was a personal matter in that in all probability my health would not be affected as it had been, if I was working elsewhere with different people. He actually stated that if this situation occurred in the USA or in many other places, they would give you half a million dollars or so, and send you on your way, but because the railway had no redundancy provisions, the final decision was forced onto the doctor. His decision was that for health reasons, I should be retired. It is my understanding that very soon after, redundancy provisions or the "golden handshake" were introduced in the railway. Although I knew this decision was right as a few more weeks in this office with no work to occupy me would have sent me "right around the bend", I saw it as a form of solitary confinement. Being off on sick leave helped a bit, but not near enough as my situation weighed heavily on my mind and my health was not improving. I now had to face up to being unemployed and perhaps unemployable, because of the circumstances of my retirement. One thing that has intrigued me ever since and I probably will never have the answer to is how my isolation at Marland House actually came about. Was it a deliberate act to break me down and force my retirement or did the Minister genuinely want me to head his decentralised maintenance program, but was unable to convince the ARU to accept me, as he said he would. On the tenth of December 1985, I was officially retired. There was no farewell function given after almost thirty-four years service but the VRI and the AFULE each gave me a small function which I appreciated very much. A close confidant of mine told me that in an atmosphere of great change and considerable turmoil, when most people knew what had happened to me, the word had gone around, don't be seen to be in the 'Barden Camp' as it could adversely affect your future. This was an inglorious ending to what had been a very successful and more importantly mostly happy and satisfying career, the last three years excepted. I shall forever be grateful to the old railway for the opportunities given to me. Where else could a lad who left school originally at thirteen years of age do so well. Unfortunately, with the new regime after the change of government in early 1982, I had become a sort of "Pauline Hanson" of the railway. Those in power did not want to hear anything I said.

39

New Life

I NOW HAD a period of adjustment ahead of me. I decided not to rush into anything but rather catch up on a few jobs around our property and help out family members now that I had time on my hands. Our three daughters had each been married for some years and I helped each of them out by painting the outside of their homes. In each case the houses were brick veneer so it wasn't as big a job as when I used to paint our weatherboard home at Strathmore. In one case I also painted out the interior. The husband of our eldest daughter worked in his family's trucking business which was expanding and moving to new premises. I worked with them for a short period purely as a labourer, helping to prepare the new premises for the shift, then cleaning up the premises vacated. I quite enjoyed the change of work and the people I was working with. I then took on a casual job at a duck farm at Riddells Creek. Once a week I candled all the eggs in incubators. The infertile ones were delivered the next day by the owner to cake shops in Melbourne. Each Friday I counted and boxed the fresh hatching of ducklings ready for delivery. I stuck at these two little jobs for some years. Although I knew nothing about sheep before shifting to Gisborne, having been

been a dairy man when I first left school, we had acquired a small flock of sheep shortly after. I took advice from an elderly sheep farmer who lived just around the corner from our place and soon learnt how to crutch them, drench them, inoculate them, deliver lambs if the ewe was in trouble (I could already do this with cows calving) and mark the lambs. I also learnt how to kill a lamb and cut up the carcass for the freezer. I killed our own lambs until we sold our beloved hobby farm in 2020. He had a much larger flock than us and I learnt these things by assisting him when each of these tasks were due to be done.

40

Consultancy Work

MEANWHILE, I had been contacted by a firm of consultants who in turn had been retained by the Nunawading Council to report on a proposal by the State Government to acquire twenty five acres of land which was mostly industrial, but also had some housing on it, for the purpose of establishing train stabling sidings and a train repair and maintenance depot. The consultants had contacted the retired General Manager of Vic-Rail who in turn, suggested they contact me. I had long favoured stabling facilities at the extremities of the section of track involved rather than at an intermediate location. This reduced empty running and therefore costs in power consumed and crewing. It also reduced the blocking of road traffic at boom barriers as after the evening peak the trains would be stabled on arrival at their destination instead of running empty cars back to Nunawading. Likewise after the morning peak, trains not required to operate daytime off peak services would be required to run empty cars, from the City to Nunawading. I compiled a report highlighting the undesirability of empty running from the cost and community aspect and the fact that land was available in the North Melbourne area which could be developed for electric suburban train stabling day and night with minimal empty running to access it. Likewise additional stabling sidings could be developed beyond Ringwood on the Belgrave and Lilydale lines. I don't know what influence my report had but the plan to acquire the land was dropped and I noted that additional stabling sidings were provided at North Melbourne.

LATER ON I was approached by another firm of consultants who were acting on behalf of associates in London. The association of East African Railways had disbanded and the countries concerned would henceforth be acting independently. The Kenyan Railways were seeking an experienced rail operations person to assist and advise their General Manager. These consultants knew me as I was involved with them from time to time during the development and construction of the Melbourne Underground. They felt I could fit the bill and after a short time I was offered a two year contract to go to Kenya. I was quite keen at first as such a position would establish me on the international scene and Carmel and our son Dan indicated that if I wanted to accept such an appointment, they would come with me. However, when we got down to some of the details involved in the move, such as Dan would attend an International School in Nairobi, but I would be located mainly in Mombassa, it became obvious that neither of them were then so keen. The local consultants stated that if Dan wanted to remain in Australia they could probably negotiate payment for him to attend a boarding school and perhaps a flight once a year for Carmel to visit home. This did not impress either of them. I think Dan's main objection was that he was playing junior football with Gisborne and he did not want to give that up. Now that there was a considerable doubt about the move in their minds, I decided to withdraw. My family had suffered to some degree in the past by me pursuing a railway career, mainly in their long term interests, but that was no longer valid. There were considerable risks in this proposed move such as how we would handle the culture and the climate. The last thing I wanted to do was to break up the family. Other approaches were made to me over time to take on consultancy tasks, but tempted as I was by the payments involved I was happy with my new life, having gone back to my roots so to speak, and declined. One that I did take on because of the short term nature of it fell through shortly before my scheduled departure. The same consultants who offered me the Kenya job contacted me with an offer to go to Hong Kong for a period estimated to be about three weeks. The London office was dealing with an extension to the Hong Kong rapid transit system. They had engineers there but their only operations man had been called home due to an illness in the family and it was uncertain as to when, or whether he would return. If I was interested I should leave within a week or so. My main task would be to calculate, along with the engineers, the number of extra trains which would be required to operate the proposed timetable. I was happy with the remuneration they offered and had a valid passport, so agreed to go. A few days later they called to say their original man could return straight away. They apologised profusely for the inconvenience caused.

41

Life on the Hobby Farm

DURING A WEEKEND VISIT to friends in Bairnsdale, Carmel and I looked through a shop specialising in wool products. She was particularly interested in this as she had bought a spinning wheel and was spinning her own wool and knitting it up into jumpers and other items of clothing. I was amazed with her skill as she could spin and knit while watching television of a night. I had bought a couple of coloured sheep to keep her supplied with suitable wool. I had also started to tan the skins of the lambs or hoggets I had killed for the table. When they had dried out completely Carmel would finish them off by brushing and combing the wool out. A friend of hers would sell them for her at the monthly Gisborne market. We could have sold many more than we could ever produce. Carmel won first prize over several years at the Sunbury Show for her floor rugs and also for her scones. We were both enjoying the rural life but one of the problems we were experiencing was getting the sheep shorn. Professional shearers did not like travelling and setting up to do a small flock of sheep. They could make much more money working in the bigger sheds. The one we were using would do them on a Saturday morning but he let us down a couple of times by not turning up after we had rounded up the sheep and kept them dry in the shed overnight. I had bought a very old shearing plant to crutch our sheep and thought I should take the next step and learn how to shear them myself. While in the wool shop at Bairnsdale I noticed a poster put out by the Wool Corporation detailing with diagrams, the correct way of shearing sheep. They had no spare posters so on return home I wrote to the Wool Corporation and they sent me a copy which I put up in the shed. From this and also by watching the professional shearers at the elderly chap's farm nearby when "picking up", I learned to shear. There were many hobby farms in the area and it wasn't long before neighbours and people further afield were seeking my services. I was of course very slow and could never have made a living out of it, but I did for several years shear small flocks of sheep in the local area and at places like Sunbury, Woodend and East Trentham. The most I ever did in one day was sixty-six at Riddells Creek, a long way short of what the professionals could do.

One day when the farrier came to shoe Danny's horse he pointed out that the shoes had little wear, suggesting that most of the riding was done on dirt tracks or grass. He said we were wasting our money shoeing the horse and that when these shoes were worn he thought I could remove them myself, then trim and rasp the feet. I bought a searcher, cutters and a rasp and commenced doing them myself. It wasn't long before Danny's friends started bringing their ponies here for hoof trimming. We were almost living off the land as by now I had a few fruit trees coming on and Carmel used to make jam and preserve some fruit. I had a very large vegetable garden and we used to get one steer killed at the abattoirs about once a year for the freezer. Later on we decided when cattle prices rose that it was better to sell the steer and buy the cuts of beef that we liked best rather than clutter the freezer up with every type of cut, some of which we less favoured.

Carmel feeding calves and enjoying the country life. Mt Macedon in the background.

Carmel in her garden

ST. ANDREWS UNITING CHURCH
Sunbury Annual Flower Day
1989

First Prize

CLASS E SECTION 14
WON BY Mrs. C. Barden
FOR Sweet Scones

ST. ANDREWS UNITING CHURCH
Sunbury Annual Flower Day

First Prize

CLASS H   SECTION 4
WON BY Mrs. C. Barden
FOR Hand-made Rug
7-11-87

Certificate from Sunbury Flower Day for Carmel's handmade rugs.

Kyneton Agricultural Society Inc.
SPRING SHOW
SATURDAY, NOVEMBER 21, 1987

SECOND

Section 9   Class No. 3
Floor Rug   Any Technique
AWARDED TO Carmel Barden
Steward's Signature L. Thiem
Miss G. Beaurepaire, Sec.

Certificate from Kyneton Agriculture Society for Carmel's handmade rugs.

42

Possible Re-employment

I HAD BEEN RETIRED from the railways three months before my fifty-first birthday. The rules at the time were that if you were under fifty-five years of age you were subject to a medical review annually to establish if your health had improved sufficiently to offer you re-employment.

I had therefore often wondered why in my case I had not been summoned even though I had been retired for in excess of three years.

However, out of the blue one day a letter arrived informing me that I was due for review and asking relevant questions such as the number of times I had visited the doctor in the last year and seeking authority for them to contact my doctor if necessary.

I signed the necessary authority and answered their questions including the fact that I had not visited the doctor during the last year.

I was quite excited as I thought I would be a certainty to be recalled even though I was enjoying life as it was.

Carmel was not sure that it could work and she quite rightly said that the railways I loved no longer existed.

A few days later I received notification that the review had been completed and it had been decided that in my circumstances (whatever they were), no further reviews would be conducted.

I guess, but don't know of course, that my papers must have been endorsed, "never again to be employed".

43

The Fast Rail Project

THIS PROJECT WAS ANNOUNCED by the Government of the day midst great hyperbole and distortion of facts. I had been out of the railways for several years but took great interest in it when it was announced that the beautiful bluestone bridge, 1860 circa, a few metres from our home, would be destroyed allegedly because of insufficient clearance for the proposed new high speed trains. The same fate was predicted for the bluestone overline bridge at Sunbury. It was repeatedly claimed that this was the biggest upgrade of county railways in one hundred and twenty years. I could not accept this statement so far as the Bendigo line was concerned as they were ripping up one track of the double line between Kyneton and Bendigo, only upgrading to 160km an hour the old 'down' track and leaving the old 'up" track now only from Kyneton, at 130km per hour, and ripping the arches out of some bridges claiming they were too tight at the shoulders. I welcomed the upgrading of the signalling but strongly refuted the claim, often made, that it was a major factor in late running of trains on this line. The major problem was the sharing of tracks in the metropolitan area with stopping suburban trains in the morning and evening peaks when an upset to the suburban trains was not uncommon and would "snowball" to the country services. They did not propose any action at that time to remedy this. I thought the money should have been spent in the suburban area to segregate suburban and country trains, thus improving timekeeping on both systems. I had many years ago learned what the customer priorities were through frequent travel on trains, and interviewing them when complaints were made. Obviously the politicians pushing this "vote getter" had no idea. The top priority was safety in train operations but this was mostly taken for granted. Next came reliability (on time running), then frequency of services. (They did not like long delays when they missed a train). Then followed matters like speed of service, comfort and cleanliness.

I TOOK an active interest in the Bendigo line project as I honestly did not see it as value for money overall. They gave little publicity to the fact that they were single lining the track beyond Kyneton and that the old 'up' track would not have an increase in the speed allowed thus restricting the new trains to the existing speed when operating on that track and necessitating a change of direction each day after the morning peak to ensure maximum utilization of the fast track, giving priority to 'up' trains in the morning peak and 'down' trains in the evening.

I attended all advertised information sessions at Gisborne and Woodend but was unable to "sell them my ideas". I also attended a couple of meetings of a group of rail activists at Castlemaine whose main worries were the lack of proposed crossing loops on the single line between Kyneton and Bendigo and the use of non-convertible concrete sleepers. Given the much longer life of concrete sleepers, any future decision to standardise the gauge as has happened elsewhere in the State would obviously be facilitated by simply moving the rail to its new position without the need to replace the sleepers. They eventually won the day with the crossing loops but not the sleepers.

MY MAJOR CONCERNS were the bluestone overline bridges and the fact that they had not addressed the problem of shared tracks in the suburban area which meant that time saved in running in the country area would often be lost in the suburban area following slow, stopping all stations, suburban trains and getting into and out of the platforms at Spencer Street Station. I put it to them that a simple way to overcome the perceived problem was to place a speed board bringing trains back to the existing 130km per hour, each side of the bridges, similar to curve boards in use where it was necessary to reduce speed, but they would not agree, saying that anything that extended the journey in terms of time was not acceptable. I pointed out I was talking about seconds, not minutes. I then put it to them that since there had only been the one prototype train constructed at that time, could they not modify the design to slightly reduce the width of carriages at the shoulder - but again they said no. I then asked them to consider lowering the track slightly to achieve the required shoulder clearance which gave me the first bit of hope. They said they would look at this but would not consider it if blasting was involved. I then went to the 'Gisborne and Mount Macedon District Historical Society' who gave me great support on the bridges issue by writing letters and arranging meetings. I believe that due to their efforts, we eventually won the day. They agreed to lower the tracks so the bridges were saved.

I THEN PUT it to them that they could segregate the country and suburban traffic relatively cheaply and save about the same amount of time in running by constructing a third track between Sydenham and Albion and restoring and upgrading the track between Albion and Sunshine which used to service the flour mill. A flyover would be required at the 'up' end of Sunshine to retain segregation while connecting with the old 'down' independent goods line which now had very little use. The upgraded track would then go through the Bunbury Street tunnel and Dynon Yard to two new platforms to be constructed on the western side of existing platforms at Spencer Street. Trains from Ballarat would be routed via this track from Sunshine thus also avoiding the suburban traffic. There would then be no need to lower tracks at bridges or to rip up the second track between Kyneton and Bendigo. All that would have been needed was the rehabilitation of the existing tracks to Bendigo at the existing speed of 130km per hour, thus saving millions of dollars on bringing one track only up to the standard for 160km per hour operation. The big advantage of this scheme was that all passengers using the service would save the maximum travel time, not just the ones from the more distant locations of Bendigo and Ballarat. Needless to say they were not interested in this proposal, and a politician whom I had known for years told me I was wasting my time and effort as politically, they had to be seen to be spending the money in the country area, not the suburban area as this alternative would involve more than benefitting country trains. The segregation of the traffic has now occurred between Sunshine and Spencer Street Station (Southern Cross), with the new Regional Rail Project incorporating the new platforms suggested. Having been completed, although a lot more costly, it is a better arrangement as it avoids the tunnel. However, Bendigo line trains are still being delayed from time to time in both directions between Sunbury and Sunshine. These delays would be hidden in the statistics as unlike in my day, when trains up to two minutes late were considered on time, I understand that nowadays trains up to six minutes late are considered statistically "on time".

44

Current Projects

I SEEM to be always in disagreement with what the government is doing to upgrade the rail system and I must say that on the suburban side, I am unsure about the current project to tunnel under Swanston Street. My belief is that an upgrade of the signalling system on the City Loop to perhaps halve the headway (double the capacity) might have been a better option. I have ridden on several underground railways throughout the world and believe the superior one was in Moscow. They seemed to have a headway of little more than a minute but I admit I was just a tourist and yesterday's man so far as rail expertise goes. Another current project I am unsure about is the longer trains they are building. I always found that trains generally fill up from the middle (most entrances to platforms) and often they are full and standing in the middle carriages but there are spare seats in the end carriages. People do not like walking long distances. I would have preferred double deckers, the down side of which is the stairs and the fact that they take a few seconds longer to load or discharge. I acknowledge there are clearance problems on our suburban system but they could be introduced progressively, one line at a time coming into the City, around the Loop and out again on the same line or vice versa. Our Loop was designed to take double deckers but we have not availed ourselves of it to increase passenger shifting capacity as yet.

45

Travel and Overseas Holidays

CARMEL and I had always taken advantage of the travel passes available to us when on annual leave and in this way we saw a lot of Australia. When we were younger we took the kids with us and had holidays in Sydney a couple of times, staying at a guest house in Bondi but doing train trips to the Blue Mountains including Katoomba, the Zig Zag Railway and other locations. We also ventured to the Gold Coast, to Adelaide and to Tasmania where we travelled on the *Tasman Limited* between Launceston (Western Junction) and Hobart before the service was discontinued. Later, when our girls had grown older and we only had Danny we took much longer trips. We went to Perth, hiring a car on arrival and drove up the coast to Monkey Mia and then south to Bunbury, Margaret River and Albany. Another time we went by train to Alice Springs then hired a car and after visiting Uluru drove to Darwin, leaving the car there and flying to Mount Isa, then caught the *Inlander* to Townsville, thence *The Sunlander* to Cairns. After hiring a car for a few days, we returned home on *The Sunlander*, the *Brisbane Limited* and the *Southern Aurora*. Since then Carmel and I have had many trips, one highlight being taking our car on the Motorail to Perth, then taking nearly two weeks to drive up the west coast to Darwin then home on *The Ghan* and *The Overland*. Another trip which we enjoyed very much, this time by car only, was through outback New South Wales and Queensland as far as Winton and then home via Roma, St. George and Lightning Ridge. In retirement we did a fourteen-day Pacific cruise and later went to New Zealand, touring both islands in rental cars.

In 2006 we were away for nine weeks touring England, Wales, Scotland and Ireland in rental cars. We visited the counties of some of our ancestors, Carmel's in Cornwall and mine in Yorkshire, before going as far north as Inverness. We similarly walked in our ancestors' footsteps in Ireland, those of Carmel's in Cork and mine in Wicklow. We visited most of the tourist attractions including the Ring of Kerry and Dingle Bay. The rugged coastline of the Atlantic Ocean and the scenic views were outstanding. We then travelled by ferry from Rosslare to Cherbourg in France before activating our pre-purchased Eurail Passes. We then train toured many European countries with suitable breaks for sightseeing in Paris, Amsterdam, Berlin, Prague, Vienna, Zurich, Luzern, Venice, Florence, Pisa, Rome, Naples, Pompei and the Isle of Capri.

I have always had an interest in Russian history and to a lesser extent architecture, so in 2014 we did an organised tour of northern and eastern Europe. Most of the travel was by bus but there were some sections where trains or ferries were used. We had stopovers in Berlin, Copenhagen, Stockholm, Helsinki, St. Petersburg, Moscow, Minsk, Vilnius, Warsaw, Krakow (Auschwitz death camp) and Budapest. This was a great holiday but unfortunately, I became ill in the last few days so we were glad to get home again. The visit to Auschwitz was the most sobering experience that I have ever had, seeing the evidence of the horrific atrocities committed by one group of human beings on another. It really made me feel privileged to have been born and lived my life in a country like Australia.

46

Community Work

I DECIDED that overall life had been pretty good to me and my family and since I was no longer in full time employment, I should take on some community work helping out people who were less fortunate than us. I had already been a blood donor for about thirty years. Although the population of the old Gisborne Shire could be described as generally or reasonably affluent, it was surprising the amount of public housing which was scattered throughout where the occupants were often not so well off. There was a number of old Housing Commission houses in Gisborne and odd ones had been purchased in new estates. In addition to this the Council had several houses let out at subsidised rentals. These stocks had been boosted after the disastrous 1983 bushfires which all but destroyed the township of Macedon, when the Tasmanian Government donated a number of two bedroom timber cottages which the council erected on vacant lots in the Shire. Incidentally, our youngest daughter and her family were burnt out in this fire and lost everything but the clothes they stood up in and the motor vehicles they used to evacuate to our place. Sharon had a one-year-old son at the time and the three of them survived the next eighteen months or so in a caravan provided by the St Vincent de Paul Society, parked on their then vacant block. I opted to join this charity group and remained with them in an active capacity for about twenty-four years. During this time I served one term as President of the local conference but I much preferred in the field work helping people in their homes. Just like back in the railways, I was sometimes criticised by conference members for doing things differently or in their opinion overstepping the mark, but I usually won out on the basis that if our help prevented one kid from going wrong it was all worthwhile. I was perhaps a little extravagant at times but it was all in a good cause and with two opportunity shops in the region providing funds, no worthy or genuine person should be denied. With the closure of the Woodend and later Kyneton conferences, our area of operation increased considerably. However, other charities have become active in the area and it is to me a little sad that St Vincent de Paul has since closed operations from Gisborne. I have always had a great interest in history and also joined the Gisborne and Mount Macedon Districts Historical Society. I served on the committee for some years. They were a great group of people and I really enjoyed working and socialising with them. I have always had an attitude that if you are part of an organisation you must put in one hundred percent and if for some reason you cannot, you should move out. Unfortunately health problems caused me to leave both the Historical Society and St Vincent de Paul society.

47

My Brother Max

I USED TO THINK MAX, two and a half years younger than me, was obviously smarter than me. After all he never ever learnt how to milk a cow, cut wood, feed poddy calves or do many other chores when we were kids at home. Max was a reasonably capable student when he applied himself but he also left school without a secondary education. At fifteen he became a Lad Porter in the railways at Toora, further down the south eastern line. He did quite well there for a year or so becoming competent at telegraphy and other duties around the station and yard. However, as Max was prone to do a lot of his life, he tired of the work, became unsettled and resigned. After a time he re-joined the railways and worked as a junior in the telegraph office in Spencer Street Head Office. Again he tired of the job and transferred to the Melbourne Yard as a Number Taker but after a year or so, he resigned. He was very keen on boxing and unfortunately joined a boxing troupe which toured country towns in Victoria, NSW and Queensland. When he returned he was a different person. Family members always believed that this was the greatest mistake of his life.

HE EVENTUALLY BECAME a builders labourer and remained one for the rest of his working life. He was very proud of some of the sites he had worked on including the Collins Place Project. Max never married. He was often aloof from the family. There was a lot that we didn't know about him. We knew he almost idolised Norm Gallagher, the boss of the Builder's Labourers Federation (BLF) but we were not aware at the time that he became a kind of personal assistant to Gallagher. When Max died of a heart attack at age sixty-five, it became my task to organise his funeral. Being a single man we did not expect a large attendance other than the family members, but we were pleasantly surprised. The funeral parlour almost filled with people we had never seen or met. We had placed on the coffin things that we knew were dear to Max during his life. A pair of boxing gloves, a Carlton beanie, a can of beer, a horse racing form guide and a photo of him with a beer in his hand taken at Mum's eightieth birthday party held at our place several years earlier. I had arranged with the Funeral Director to have a flag of the Southern Cross available (symbol of the BLF) to place on the coffin but it did not eventuate. I was to deliver the eulogy and after welcoming those present and thanking them for their attendance, I pointed out the articles on the coffin represented things that were important to Max in his life and stated that I had also requested the flag of the Southern Cross to be on the coffin but regretfully, it had not been provided. A fellow immediately stood up and said, "If you will excuse me for a moment, I will get one out of my car boot." He brought a flag in and draped it over the coffin. I later realised he was John Cummins who had become the boss of the builders labourers after Norm Gallagher departed. I delivered my story of Max's life as I knew it, admitting there were some gaps and I thought it appropriate to ask if anyone present would like to come forward and speak. John Cummins came up and spoke at some length about Max's work as a builders labourer and his involvement with the BLF. He also made an apology for Jim Bacon, at that time the Premier of

Tasmania, who had been an organiser of the union on many of the building projects Max had worked on. He said Bacon had sent him an email the day before apologising for his inability to attend. Two other men came up who had been union organisers and spoke about Max. The funeral director was not pleased as we were almost half an hour late arriving at the cemetery. I later reflected on the day's proceedings and although I understand that people can "gild the lily" a little on occasions such as funerals, there was no doubt Max had made his mark in his chosen job. This was of great comfort to mum and family members as many of us thought at the time, that Max had wasted much of his life. I also pondered over a comment made many years earlier at a meeting by an official of the ARU who later became the Federal President of his union, which had no relevance at the time other than to embarrass me, when he stated to all and sundry, "I can't believe this intransigent person is the brother of Max from the BLF. How could they have been brought up in the same house?" I completely ignored the barb and said nothing, but it did shock me a bit at the time.

48

Finale

I OBVIOUSLY HAVE some regrets concerning my truncated railway career but still have my "what you see is what you get" personality. It was accepted for what it was by most people in the old railway but not by the majority of the new management team. I shall go to my grave believing my demise was politically motivated because of my stand against the tactics and policies of the ARU, an organisation which in the early years of the new government had far too much influence with the then Transport Minister. Had I still been there when he was replaced shortly after I retired, it may well have been a different story with a happier ending.

I was the first Chief Operations Manager in the old VicRail and as it turned out, the last. Freight was the more profitable traffic and had potential for growth provided we put our "house in order". It was something that we could have done if we were able to reform and the key issues as I have stated previously, were the rationalisation of country depots and restrictive work practices in the Melbourne Yard. I worked day, night and weekends striving to achieve the necessary reforms but with only limited success and I felt very lonely at times because I was not getting the support I was entitled to from the rest of the organisation. I believe that if the state government had not changed in April 1982, I would have been successful. Ironically, I need not have bothered as the wind down process started on intrastate freight soon after the change of government and culminated in the cessation of freight services in Victoria save for a handful of block trains, eg: Maryvale paper products, Kilmore East quarry products and a greatly reduced grain shift. The result is highrise buildings all over the old Melbourne Yard including a sports stadium and rusting or rotten rail facilities throughout regional Victoria except of course the trunk routes where passenger traffic has survived and is growing rapidly, perhaps proving a point.

I BELIEVE with proper management it could have been the same with freight but with far less expenditure required. Instead we have heavy trucks polluting the atmosphere and breaking up country roads at an alarming rate and cost. I cannot understand how politicians who claim to be concerned about the environment have let this happen and are letting it continue. As more and more big trucks go on the road, safety also becomes a bigger issue.

It would be remiss of me to close this story off without making mention of the many workmates and bosses who helped and influenced me during my railway career, to whom I shall forever be grateful. It would be impossible to name them all here but I shall never forget any of them. The major ones were my first two Stationmasters, Mr Davis at Essendon, and Mr Bregazzi at Graham (North Port). Next comes Mr Kenny my Chief Train Controller, Mr McInnes my Metropolitan Superintendent when I was a Traffic Inspector and Mr Crute, Chief Traffic Manager to whom I was a personal assistant and "Ray of all trades". I must make special mention of Mr Kenny who was probably the greatest gentlemen I ever met. He had the biggest influence on my life of anyone other than my parents and my wife. He was a great railway man, mentor and visionary. He predicted I could become a Head of Branch and also, twenty-five years ahead, the import of outside business people to senior positions in the railway. I kept in touch with Arthur Kenny on a regular basis after he retired, until he died at age ninety-seven.

49

Holiday photos

RAY BARDEN

On holiday in Yorkshire, England. Ray standing under a sign giving direction to the hamlet of Barden.

A Man of Principle

Ray at Blarney Castle, Ireland, kissing the Blarney Stone.

Carmel kissing the Blarney Stone

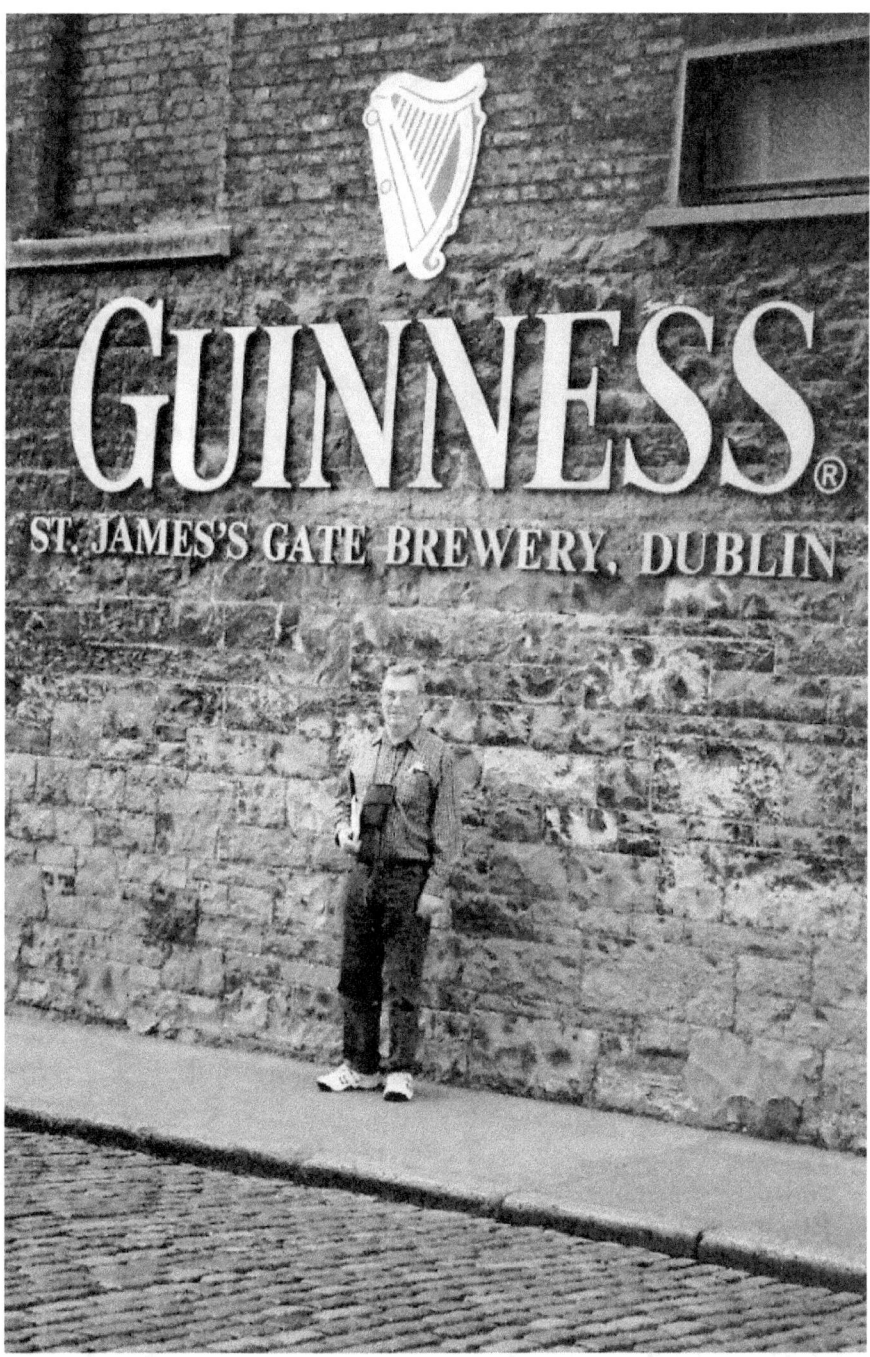

Ray outside the Guinness brewery in Dublin, Ireland

50

Glossary

AREA CONTROLLER

A signalman with responsibilities over a wide area rather than at a single location.

Ash Pit

A pit between the rails to receive ash discharged from a steam locomotive's firebox.

Annett Lock

A method of ensuring the security of points by locking with a special key.

Automatic & Track Control (ATC)

A power signalling system for single lines of railway incorporating unattended crossing loops remotely controlled from an adjacent attended location and installed on the Geelong line in 1928

Ballast The stone bed which supports and drains the track.

Block & Signal Inspector

A field supervisor and examiner of signalling apparatus and personnel.

Block Phone

A dedicated telephone connection between adjacent Signal Boxes.

Block Train
A freight train usually conveying one type of loading for one destination.
Broad Gauge
A rail gauge (distance between rails) of 5 feet 3 inches (1600mm).
Centralised Traffic Control (CTC)
A power signalling system for single lines of railway in which the points and signals at all locations are remotely controlled from a central location. First used on the Glen Waverley line in 1958. introduced to the new standard gauge line between West Footscray and Wodonga in the 1960s. Other use in Victoria included Ararat to Wolseley in the 1980s
Coal Stage
An elevated platform from which coal is loaded onto a steam locomotive
Contact Wire
The overhead wire by which power is delivered to an electric train
Down
In a direction away from Melbourne
Fireman
Originally attended a steam locomotive's fire, later the Driver's assistant or a trainee
Frame
The levers and associated apparatus in a Signal Box
Gatekeeper
A person in charge of hand-operated level crossing gates
Group
A roster involving work at multiple locations
Guard
A train crew member formerly located at the rear of a train and considered to be in charge of it
Hanger Board
An information sign showing a train's destination and stopping conditions

Interlocked Gates
Level crossing gates operated from a Signal Box
Is Line Clear
Seeking and obtaining confirmation that it is safe for a train to proceed
Lamp Room
A place where kerosene signal lamps were maintained and inflammables stored
Number Taker
Records the numbers and other details of vehicles on arrival and departing trains at major stations
Number two track
The second in a set of tracks at a location where they are numbered sequentially
Paper Train
A train operated mainly for the carriage of newspapers
Periodical Ticket
A ticket available for multiple journeys
PL Carriage
A high capacity, light-weight passenger carriage
Point Clip
A hand operated clamp to temporarily secure points in one direction
Points
A railway track arrangement enabling trains to be diverted to another track
Porter
An employee who carried out routine station duties
Safeworking
The rules and operating procedures of the various railway signalling systems
Shunter
An employee responsible for sorting rail vehicles and assembling trains
Staff (Train or Electric)

A token carried by a Driver as the authority to occupy a single line

Standard Gauge A rail gauge (distance between rails) of 4 feet 8½ inches (1435mm)

Train Controller
Plans and directs the priorities and running of trains in real time

Train Examiner
Carries out pre-departure safety inspections of trains and does minor repairs

Traffic Inspector
A travelling supervisor of station working, special traffic and emergency working

Up
In a direction towards Melbourne

Van Goods
Parcels and smaller freight items loaded and unloaded whilst the train waits.

www.ingramcontent.com/pod-product-compliance
Lightning Source LLC
Chambersburg PA
CBHW070728020526
44107CB00077B/2084